Praise for *Just Keep* ▮

This is a passion filled story of a determined individual who took on the ultimate endurance test, rowing the Atlantic, alone. This book will keep you on the edge of your seat as you read of Katie's daily encounters with the Ocean, all 70 days. Each page is full of raw emotion and incredible honesty as Katie shares with us the lessons she learnt from the Ocean, not least to 'just keep rowing.' It does not take long to realize, that for Katie it was never just about the physical challenge of rowing the Atlantic, this book is also drenched with Katie's heart and drive to raise awareness about the global water crisis. This is a story of adventure, hope and passion, as Katie uses everything in her human strength to cross an ocean whilst telling the stories of those who struggle to find clean and safe water on a daily basis.
—Julia Immonen, author of *Row for Freedom: Crossing an Ocean in Search of Hope* and founder, Sport for Freedom

It was an uncanny experience reading Katie's book. There were so many similarities in the way we experienced the Atlantic, and the insights we gained, it was like reliving my own crossing—but reading about it is a lot more fun than doing it! Great life lessons in every chapter, which are sure to inspire and uplift you, no matter what your "ocean."
—Roz Savage, first woman to row solo across three oceans and author of *Rowing the Atlantic* and *Stop Drifting Start Rowing*

Katie's book provides life lessons and inspiration for a generation of youth that will guide them to build the world we want to live in. Her focus on water, our essence of life is timely and important.
—Patty Hall, President, H2O for Life

Just Keep Rowing

Lessons from the Atlantic Ocean by the Youngest Person to Row It Alone

Katie Spotz
Mark Bowles

Cover design: Nick Coughlin
Book design: Amy Freels
Cover image: Esther Morgan photo in conjunction with *Readers Digest*

Copyright © Katie Spotz and Mark Bowles 2015
ISBN: 978-0-692-47486-0

From Katie Spotz...

This is the book I have dreamed of sharing with the world, and so I would like to dedicate it to my readers and all those that are in need of clean, safe water.

A special thanks goes to my mom and dad for not disowning me when I decided to embark on this adventure, and to Sam for believing in me from the very start. And to the one thing that kept me going in the middle of the Atlantic, I must say, thank you, chocolate!

From Mark Bowles...

To my nephew Alexander, who lost his battle with heroin addiction. Your memory has inspired me to try to craft words that can uplift others and help them see through the darkness.

I also want to dedicate this book to my wife, Nancy, who is my true love and constant companion, and to our three daughters, Isabelle, Emma, and Sarah. I hope you will be inspired by Katie's passion and that you will take to heart the philosophies and life lessons we share in the pages that follow. And if you do not want to row alone across an ocean, I am totally okay with that.

Contents

Introduction   1

Part One: Propel Yourself

Day 1: Departing Dakar with New Eyes   9

Day 2: Tankers Can Appear at Any Moment   14

Day 3: A Long Journey Begins with a Single Step   18

Day 4: Procrastination is the Thief of Time   21

Day 5: Experience Solitude, Not Loneliness   24

Day 6: Never Pass By Yourself   27

Day 7: Chart a Course   30

Day 8: Let Caution Win Sometimes   33

Day 9: Meditate by Moving   36

Day 10: Eliminate the Drag   40

Day 11: Move Like a Shark   44

Day 12: Think Beyond Language   47

Day 13: Sometimes Good Things Fall Apart   50

Day 14: Life is a Team Sport   54

Day 15: Accept Impermanence   58

Day 16: Give Yourself 1,000 Days   63

Day 17: Create an Inspiration Team   66

Day 18: Endurance is a State of Mind   71

Day 19: If You Can't See Straight, Don't Change Direction   74

Day 20: Find a Room to Get Into the Zone   77

Day 21: The Present is Enough   82

Part Two: Russian Roulette

Day 22: Wake Up to Water   87

Day 23: Take a Leap of Faith into the Unknown   90

Day 24: Playing Russian Roulette with Water   94

Day 25: Water Changes Everything   98

Day 26: Find a "Charles" to Regain Your Faith   101

Day 27: WASH Your Hands   105

Day 28: Don't Poop Where You Eat   109

Day 29: Put Your Money Where Your Mouth Is   112

Day 30: Extend Your Hand   117

Day 31: Teach Someone to Fish   121

Day 32: Always Go to the Source   124

Day 33: Create Your Own Reality   127

Day 34: Challenge Your Routine   130

Day 35: You Are the Solution   135

Day 36: Enjoy a Day Off   138

Day 37: Never Underestimate a Small Gesture   142

Day 38: Savor Your Dinosaur Water   146

Day 39: Move to Antarctica, or Stay and Conserve   150

Day 40: Failure is an Opportunity   153

Day 41: You Can't Hold It Forever   156

Day 42: Give a Crap about Human Rights   161

Part Three: Our Bioluminescence

Day 43: Remember Those Who Have Passed   167

Day 44: Thank the Giants   171

Day 45: See How We Shine   174

Day 46: Be a Little Paranoid   178

Day 47: Take Your Ship Out of the Harbor   181

Day 48: Focus on the Present and Presence   184

Day 49: Share a Moment of Time   188

Day 50: See the Sublime   191

Day 51: Be Careful What You Touch   194

Day 52: Music Touches Our Essence   198

Day 53: Dance Like No One is Watching   201

Day 54: Step Up from Rock Bottom   203

Day 55: Take the Albatross off Your Neck   209

Day 56: Expose Yourself   211

Day 57: Make Friends with a Stranger on a Bus   214

Day 58: Look Beyond the Shell   217

Day 59: Understand Instinct   220

Day 60: Remember a Hug Forever   225

Day 61: Learn to Say, "Hello, Friend"   229

Day 62: Be a Zen Mirror   233

Day 63: See the Bioluminescence in Everyone   236

Part Four: Climbing the Ladder

Day 64: Smile When You Reach Your Lowest Point   241

Day 65: Be Open to the Ride   246

Day 66: What Does Not Kill You Makes You Stronger   249

Day 67: Float Like a Bumblebee   253

Day 68: Scale the Mental Wall   256

Day 69: See What Your Body Can Do   259

Day 70: Show Your Inner Soul   262

Welcome to Guyana!   265

Epilogue: A Half Decade Later   271

Notes   281

Acknowledgments   289

About the Authors   293

Introduction

The book you hold in your hands is my account of rowing across the Atlantic Ocean in 2010, entirely alone, over a period of 70 days. Although I am the youngest person ever to do this solo (I was 22 at the time), my oceanic transit was not just a personal endurance quest. It was an attempt to bring attention and funding to those suffering from the global water crisis. In the United States, many of us take for granted that clean water is available whenever we need it, immediately quenching our thirst, watering our lawns, or washing our cars. Water flows freely from taps and is sold in expensive designer bottles everywhere we turn. This is not the case for much of the world, and in fact, over one billion people struggle mightily each day to acquire even the minimum life-sustaining amount of potable water. And when that search fails for them, as it often does, they are left to drink water that compromises their health at best, and hastens death at worst. I offer this book not just as the greatest adventure story of my life thus far, but as a way to continue to spread awareness of this humanitarian crisis.

Why row the ocean? The power of it is both awe-inspiring and mysterious. With waves commanded by the moon through its gravitational pull, and abundant life swimming within its unfathomably deep waters, it exists almost as a living poem. As President John F. Kennedy said at an America's

Cup crew meeting, "We are tied to the ocean. And when we go back to the sea, whether it is to sail or to watch—we are going back from whence we came."[1] Through my journey I gradually understood the deep meaning of his words, though I might tell him today to include rowers in his observation.

Very few people have rowed across an ocean, and in fact more people have actually climbed Mount Everest, the tallest mountain on earth (more than 4,000 have summited Everest and just over 300 have rowed across an ocean). Some of these great rowers have written eloquently about their voyages, but what separates my book from theirs is that this is not just my story.[2] This book, like my row, is an attempt to raise awareness about the water crisis. My crossing was dedicated to those whose primary goal in life is to find enough drinkable water for themselves and their families. I raised $125,000 for the Blue Planet Network through my row and have raised nearly $275,000 in total from other adventures and campaigns.

This book is a personal conversation between me and you. During my journey I learned some vital life lessons from the Atlantic. As I found out, an ocean is a great teacher. I became its student, sometimes reluctantly but often enthusiastically, and I want to communicate those lessons because I believe they can be meaningful for everyone. From students to business executives, and to people just wanting to find new ways to live life to the fullest, I hope these lessons from the Atlantic will help you see the world from a new perspective. This viewpoint is defined by hope and beauty. If you are looking for self-empowerment, the Atlantic has much to teach, and I invite you to share in its dialog with me.

I must confess that it goes against my very nature to write a book about my life experiences thus far. I thought these types of books were best written by self-help gurus, spiritual leaders, politicians, or successful businesspersons. I am none of these, but I still humbly offer you these insights, which have been meaningful for me. I simply thank you for spending your time listening to my adventures and experiences.

I have divided the book into 70 short segments, with each representing a day of my journey. As I was connected to people from more than 170 countries who followed me on social media, I am including my Twitter posts from @KatieSpotz sent during my row. These provide a rough real-time narrative of my journey. Sometimes the tweets were mine from my boat, and other times (when signed "Sam") they originated from Sam Williams, who was my friend and main land support.

I group my days into four main parts. While the ocean rowing narrative is present in all of them, each of the parts emphasizes an essential life-changing idea. The first is to "Propel Yourself." Here I talk about believing in our human potential and having faith that we can accomplish the impossible. We all have the inherent capability to grow the confidence we need to propel ourselves towards achieving our goals. I have learned this through multiple physical challenges, including swimming the length of the Allegheny River, completing a 62-mile ultramarathon in Australia, running through the Mohave desert, biking coast-to-coast across the United States, and, of course, rowing the Atlantic. I do not claim any special power of endurance. We all have this capability inside and it is there for us to unlock.

I call part two "Russian Roulette," which is a cryptic title, I know, but it is a harsh image that symbolizes the severe global water crisis. This crisis was my incentive for rowing the Atlantic, and in this section I emphasize that awareness and action are essential. With the high prevalence of water-borne disease in developing nations, taking a sip of water becomes much more like playing Russian Roulette than simply quenching a thirst. Water is essential to all of our lives, second only to air. It is also a finite resource, and currently we are not good stewards of our water supply. This situation threatens our very existence. We see this even in the United States with concerns that California is now running out of water.[3]

In part three, "Our Bioluminescence," I recount key moments when my interaction with the Atlantic Ocean fundamentally changed me in terms of seeing the beauty of the world. Ironically, being alone at sea helped me in understanding the intrinsic worth of every human being on this planet. We are all beacons of light, shining like the sun, and as a human race we can only become stronger if we take care of each other. We risk losing the race if we fail to do so. We have the power, within each of us, to make the world a better place.

Each of these three themes represents three weeks of my life at sea. The final part, "Climbing the Ladder," covers my last week on the Atlantic. It describes the end of my journey with fire, deadly storms, broken equipment, and hundreds of extra miles of rowing before the shores of South America appeared before me. The final challenge was an unexpected ladder from my boat up to the pier. As I reached that last rung, I realized I had just become the youngest person to row alone across an ocean. From that moment on, "just keep rowing" and "climbing the ladder" became my metaphors for life and guides for success.

It is important to note that I did not write each of these lessons on my boat. I wrote them years after the voyage, when I had ample time to process my life-changing adventure. In fact, it took five years from the time I completed the journey to compose them, and assisting me in that task was my co-author Mark Bowles. In him I found someone who perfectly mirrored and illuminated my philosophical perspectives and shared a passion for empowering those who lack the most basic requirements of life, like water. For us this book is about helping others, and a portion of the proceeds will assist global water projects.

Why didn't I just write the book during the row? At sea my mind was simply in survival mode. I endured brutal periods of sleep deprivation, and I often felt like a zombie (and some days even that would have been an improvement!). The last thing I could have done was compose a coherent thought on paper. Every bit of my body, mind, and soul focused on rowing. Lack of sleep, physical exhaustion, and sheer loneliness frequently took my moods to very low points. Doubts emerged: the ocean was too big, my boat was too small, or my endurance and will were not enough. I persevered, and I later realized these feelings are a natural part of life. We all feel like giving up from time to time, whether it is in athletic competition, a school assignment, a work project, sobriety, or in a relationship. Quitting is easy. Rowing through the challenges is hard. And that is life.

For 70 days I rode the waves, navigating through them, and propelling myself with all the mental and physical strength I could summon. The waves were relentless, and as they sometimes towered thirty feet over me,

I realized they were a perfect metaphor for life. The one defining characteristic about a wave is that is has its ups and downs. If it were all up, or all down, then the ocean would just be a boring flat surface. There would be no glorious sounds on the shore or beautiful cresting white waves to watch or ride. Ironically, I was not a very good rower on my college team. One reason was that I struggled to "feather" my oars on a waveless lake (feathering means turning the oar's blade so that it is parallel to the water). In the choppiness of the ocean that technique was not needed as much. So I learned to appreciate the ups and downs of the ocean waves as they complemented my skills. This helped teach me to cope with the natural turbulence of life.

The critical lesson here is that life itself is a wave, and you are the boat riding upon it. I am not the first to suggest this "life is a wave" metaphor, as nineteenth-century physicist John Tyndall beat me to the punch.[4] However, I promise to avoid his esoteric science and focus on practical lessons on how to row through the storms when times are tough, and catch the waves and appreciate the joys of life when times are good. Everything is impermanent, so enjoy the moment, be present, and appreciate the gift of life.

I invite you to come aboard my boat, *Liv*, with me for the next 70 days. I will share with you the secrets and lessons I learned from my experience with Atlantic, tell you about some of my adventures, and, I hope, bring wider awareness of those who struggle each day to drink a drop of clean water.

Nothing in life is too big, as long as you focus on just one oar stroke at a time. That is the reason for the title of this book: *Just Keep Rowing*. It is also the message of my life.

Part One: Propel Yourself

Hi Katie,

Now about your new adventure . . . Kate first of all I think I have been there for
you, maybe in your eyes you feel differently. I do want to support you. I did look
online to research this rowing and I am sorry to say Kate I got this terrible feeling
in my stomach just thinking about it. . . . Dad said if Katie goes on that adventure
you might as well kiss her good bye . . . she won't make it. I can't stop thinking about
that. Katie I do not want anything to happen to you. Please do research on this!!!
I love you . . . mommy

(Email from Mary Spotz to her daughter Katie on April 20,
2007, written three years before the start of the row.)

Day 1: Departing Dakar with New Eyes

@KatieSpotz Tweet Log for Sunday, January 3, 2010	
6:35 AM	There she rows!!! Katie left safely about an hour ago—photos and stuff will be on the website soon. [Sam]
7:28 AM	I've just checked and, about 5 minutes ago, she was safely clearing the peninsula, which is fantastic. [Sam]
3:39 PM	Rowed past freighters, small fishing boats, & islands. Can no longer see land!

Here I am on the bench again.

This seems to be the story of my life.

I find myself on a bench unlike any I reluctantly sat upon during my middle school days while I watched my friends fully engaged on the soccer field and basketball court. Today is different. Even though I am still on the bench, and even facing backwards, I choose this bench. Here I have begun an endurance quest that no one my age has ever completed. I hope to be the first, but I have a long way and many waves ahead of me.

Maybe I should explain.

I am taking in everything today as if I am seeing life for the last time. I am savoring every second, and watching the mainland slowly disappearing in the distance. I just shoved off from the shores of Dakar, Senegal,

Moments before leaving Dakar, huddled inside my cabin.

alone, on the bench of my small rowboat, *Liv*. In these first few oar strokes I'm attempting, mentally and visually to let go of the known and welcome the unknown lying to my west with the wide open ocean. Physically I'm preparing myself for traversing an ocean with neither a motor nor a sail. Only my body, my oars, the Atlantic Ocean current, and potentially the trade winds will propel me towards my planned destination of Cayenne, French Guyana, in South America. I face backwards because that is how rowers get the maximum leverage and power from their strokes. I have also upgraded my bench to a sliding seat (to utilize power with my legs and back) covered in sheepskin. So as I start this epic journey, I feel a little like a historian looking back to where I have been, and further back in time to the great voyages that preceded me on these waters.

What are the famous ships of the Atlantic Ocean? There are many, but the most recognizable are probably the *Mayflower*, the *Niña*, the *Pinta*, and the *Santa Maria*. It makes me smile to add an unlikely name to the list: *Liv*. She may be unimpressive to some, coming in at just 19 feet in length, compared

Leaving Dakar, Senegal, in West Africa. Here is my last view of land for 70 days.

to the 100-foot-long seventeenth-century *Mayflower*. Though *Liv* is small, she is less cramped in an important way. The *Mayflower* housed more than 130 people, and in my boat it's just me. My goal is to tackle the ocean alone, along with my boat and the Wilson tennis ball with the face my friends at the Rotary Club of Chagrin Falls (Ohio) drew on it. If a Wilson volleyball worked as company for Tom Hanks in the movie *Cast Away*, maybe my tennis ball will do the same. I just hope to stay in my boat the entire time.

And so I watch as the African shore slowly fades away. Although I am looking into the past, and thinking about the future, I know that only the present matters. Being present is more than enough. The slapping of my oars into the water sounds like a beating heart, which pounds ever more heavily as I watch the massive freighters around me.

I am starting in the morning because I have a number of very hard hours of rowing to cross the peninsula of Dakar. My first challenge will be these tidal currents that push me away from where I want to go. My goal, though, is to row from shore to shore, unaided, and so my journey starts with this very difficult task. After that I must remain vigilant because I will be in a great deal of sea transport traffic.[5] Getting sunk by a tanker is to be avoided at all costs!

As I venture onto the ocean, I will have an opportunity to see something else as well—what's inside myself. I am preparing for a period of silent introspection unlike any other in my life. I feel like one of those desert monks on a meditative retreat 2,000 years ago, except I am rowing and will not see any sand for a long time. The monks found great insight through contemplation. I plan to open myself fully to the lessons the Atlantic will teach me, and I hope its messages will sink in. But please, let that be the only thing that sinks!

So many people have helped to get me to this point; it feels a bit surreal to actually be underway. I was getting advice from many seasoned ocean rowers all the way up to a few days ago. Pascal Vaudé emailed this advice to me, and I am following it as I pull away from shore: "Do not be tense on your oars at risk of having very quickly blistered hands. Pull your oars with your fingers and not the apple of your hand! Expect also a thick, soft cushion for your seat sliding to limit the risk of buttock pain. You will lose weight considerably during your trip and very soon you'll be sitting on your bones. It will be difficult to sit for 8 hours or more on a hard seat!"[6]

Hopefully, weight loss will not be a problem with 300 chocolate bars on board!

I embark on this journey with a quote from French novelist Marcel Proust to guide me. I have scrawled it in black marker on *Liv*'s inner white wall, above my map of the Atlantic. It reads, "A real voyage of discovery lies not in finding new landscapes, but in having new eyes." I may have not gotten the quote exactly right, but I've captured its truth. Whether you are traversing an ocean or performing an examination of your own life, having new eyes is the key to true discovery and fulfillment. What matters in life is not that you visit each of the fifty states, or see every ancient wonder of the world. What is significant is how each experience changes you (small and large) and the wisdom you gain from it.

I make this the first lesson of my journey because it will be with me for every one of my million-plus oar strokes. See the wonders of the world that surround you. You do not have to be standing at the base of the Great Pyramid to gaze upon a wonder. A laughing baby, a soaring bird, or the wind blowing upon your face are common wonders we often close our eyes to. This way of seeing life will help me cross the Atlantic, and it is a lesson to carry with you no matter your surroundings or challenges.

How does one begin to achieve this? It is not through forcing change for yourself. It's deeper than that, and it is a process of becoming. What you see matters less than what you become along the way. When you have the courage to let go, and watch the security disappear, that change can happen naturally.

It is from this unusual position I sit, an athlete who once struggled to get into the game, now about to live life to the fullest. It is all about the eyes. Although they are, as some have said, the windows of the soul, they are also windows to the wonderful world around us. It is with great excitement and anticipation that I leave land behind today, with eyes to see the world in a new way.

Now, I will try to get some sleep after my first hard day of rowing through the tidal currents.

Day 2: Tankers Can Appear at Any Moment

@KatieSpotz Tweet Log for Monday, January 4, 2010	
6:29 AM	Having spent a day on the Atlantic Ocean in her rowboat, Katie has covered 44 miles, with just 2,435 to go! [Sam]
8:47 PM	2am wake up from my AIS alarm. Too close for comfort with two passing freighters at the moment!

Have you ever been rudely awakened by your alarm clock in the morning?

You know the feeling, like, "I can't believe it's time to get up already." Sometimes you hit the snooze button just to put off the inevitable. But when it is two in the morning and the AIS (Alarm Indication Signal) goes off on your tiny boat, floating in a dark ocean, 44 miles from shore, all of your senses are quickly engaged and heightened by the potential danger. The AIS alarm announces something much more than the start of a new day. These emergency beeps indicate that another boat is in the vicinity, and a collision is possible.

That is the way my first morning on the Atlantic began.

It did take me a moment to regain my senses. After the fifth beep of my AIS I fully extracted myself from sleep, and returned to the new reality of my life at sea. I was in my tiny rowboat cabin and panic finally shocked my body to pure adrenaline alertness. I knew I was still so close to the shore that there were many boats nearby. Now one was too close to me. My instinct took me instantly to my VHF radio, hanging on the cabin wall.

The radio crackled and I called out loudly, "This is ocean rowboat *Liv*, do you copy?"

It was the most painful silence I ever heard in my life.

Again I called out, "This is ocean rowboat *Liv*, DO YOU READ?" Silence remained the only response.

Not having any other option I opened the door of my cabin and entered into the warm night air. There before me were the ominous and penetrating lights of a giant tanker, only a half mile away. It drowned out the stars and punctuated the darkness with its powerful and threatening light. You know the cartoon image of being in a long dark tunnel when suddenly the spotlight of a train appears ahead? I was living it. I knew that because of their incredibly large mass, tankers are very difficult to steer. They require between two to five miles and at least fifteen minutes to perform an emergency stop. From my perspective, low on the ocean's surface, I couldn't determine the tanker's course of direction, so I was unable to simply row away. There was nothing I could do but stand and watch the tanker approach. My thoughts raced to the months of preparation for this journey, and there I was helpless, standing, swaying with the waves, watching the impossibly large ship approach me in the night.

The minutes passed and I remained there, knowing I was invisibly bobbing on the ocean and inconsequential to the path of the tanker. I wondered, "Would anyone on board even know if it struck me?" Along with its blinding lights, I could see its massive size, and eventually I could hear its engines. I waited, my fate and my life in its hands. And then the moment came when I realized there would be a few hundred feet of ocean that separated the tanker from my *Liv* and my life. I am reminded of some lines from Henry Wadsworth Longfellow's *Tales of a Wayside Inn*:

Ships that pass in the night, and speak each other in passing,
Only a signal shown, and a distant voice in the darkness;
So on the ocean of life, we pass and speak one another,
Only a look and a voice, then darkness again and a silence.[7]

The freighters are MUCH larger than they appear! Here is one passing by me at a much more appropriate distance than the one last night.

I wish I could have heard some voices! The silence after the passing was very different from the radio silence I heard a few minutes earlier. What was silent terror became peaceful silence. I watched as the giant vessel passed me, disappearing into the dark horizon. With the danger gone, I began to appreciate its power and grace as it sliced through the water. Every flirtation with your own mortality brings a newfound appreciation for life. In that silence I crept back into my cabin, and I tried to find sleep again, my heart still pounding. I was just thankful that morning was approaching. I knew then I would be rowing with the rising of the sun.

I realize this situation isn't uncommon in our lives. I know we do not often play chicken with tankers in the ocean, but we often want to be in control of our destinies. While frequently we are the ones calling the shots, there are other times when we need to accept the fact that control is not ours to have: a cancer diagnosis, the loss of a loved one, an addiction, a natural disaster—the metaphorical "tankers" that can appear in our lives at a moment's notice. That's when our only option is to stand on our little ship and accept our fate bravely.

The Atlantic's lesson for me today is this: We will all confront tankers of one kind or another in our lives. For a moment we will be helpless and

This is me leaving Dakar on day one and getting a sense of how small I am next to these massive freighters.

left simply to watch and see which direction destiny will lead. After that a new course is set and we have an important choice to make. I could turn around and row back to Dakar thinking, "My boat is too small against this ocean and the tankers that live here." Recoiling in fear is not the response I choose. I am rowing forward, aware of the danger, and resolutely determined to get across the Atlantic through my own power. The message is: do not let life's tankers overwhelm you. Respect them and avoid going blindly into their paths. But do not back down from their presence. An entire ocean is yours to explore if you are able to keep rowing.

Just a note on my progress. These first two days have been better than expected. My mileage has been good, and I have not even hit the helpful trade winds. Overall I am feeling strong, and very pleased (and a bit surprised) that I do not feel seasick. I rowed ten hours yesterday, and another ten today (past still more tankers and Senegalese fishing boats), and my body is adjusting nicely . . . so far. I was a little sad (and excited) to pass by two small islands. That was my last chance to see land for a long while.

Day 3: A Long Journey Begins with a Single Step

@KatieSpotz Tweet Log for Tuesday, January 5, 2010	
5:32 AM	Katie just keeps on getting better—she's now covered 53 miles in the last 24 hours and is currently heading straight for Cayenne. [Sam]
3:36 PM	Was peering over the side of the boat to take some pics of some turquoise fish when I spotted 20 ft away—shark fin!

Three days in and I guess I am really doing it now! The land is long gone and I am feeling the isolation set in, although at the same time I am energized. Many other rowers have told me how difficult it is just getting a journey like this underway. I have taken the first step—or row—and I am looking forward to continue taking them for as long as I can. Success is not assured by any means, but my will is strong. The dangers of tankers have passed for the time being, and my biggest enemy this morning is the sun.

The highlight so far (other than the tanker missing me, which was a real bright spot) has been watching all the birds and fish. I am being followed by creatures of both the sea and air. And then there are those that think they belong in *both* the sea and the air. These flying fish are going to drive me crazy, especially ones like those that landed on my deck last night!

The sun is so very hot. Out here the sun dominates a cloudless sky in ways I have never experienced before. Even wearing my sunglasses I cannot even begin to looks towards it. Its radiance highlights the beautiful shades of blue that surround me, with the sky above and the rising and falling ocean below. My protection is a well-stocked supply of sun screen. I began the morning applying it thickly to every spot of exposed skin. I cannot imagine how terrible a sunburn would be in these conditions, rowing under a relentless sun and in the salty air. I wonder how the early ocean voyagers did it without bottles that clearly labeled the SPF protection. I have heard that natural substitutes includes olive oil, rice extracts, lupine plants, and zinc oxide paste also work well. Natural is great, but I will stick with my fool-proof synthetic version.

I am lathered up now with my sweet-smelling cream, and its scent mixes with the ocean breezes. It smells like I am getting ready to spend the day lounging on the beach, but instead I'm preparing for a hard ten-hour day of rowing. With my hat and shades on, I settle into being alone in the sun, quietly propelling myself across this unthinkably vast expanse of beautiful water. I am feeling very small right now in my tiny boat, but my determination is strong and I am confident that I planned for this as best I could. It is hard—impossible maybe—to put into perspective the incredible amount of preparation, planning, and training that has brought me to this point. However, instead of getting lost in that maze of complexity, I choose to focus on a simple message: "Just do it!" I owe the successful commencement of my voyage to this simple phrase.

Nike really nailed it with their "Just do it!" campaign because that forceful command lies at the heart of every successful venture. Of course Nike was not the first to capture this vital idea so succinctly. An ancient Chinese proverb, attributed to Lao Tzu, reminds us that "A long journey begins with a single step."[8] For me, the journey of 3,000 miles across the Atlantic began with a single row of my oars three days ago.

Preparing my body to power at least 10,000 oar-strokes every day required blood, sweat, and tears. My training demanded that every moment I would "just do it," because success is not a compromise or an event scheduled for later. Each day I spent hours with a rowing machine or out on Lake Erie's open water. Once you've begun, that first step you take (or oar stroke in my case . . . I need to forget about walking for a while) is forever behind you. As another old saying goes, "the first step is the hardest." That is true, but once I commit to the first ten minutes it becomes easier for me to continue than it does for me to stop. Momentum is a powerful force. After you generate it, ride its wave to the shore. This is a lesson that is as true for a transoceanic row as it is for any goal in life: set the goal, just do it, never compromise, and ride the wave.

Day 4: Procrastination is the Thief of Time

@KatieSpotz Tweet Log for Wednesday, January 6, 2010

| 11:13 AM | First time using the watermaker this afternoon and thankfully worked perfectly. Need lots of water rowing in +90 temps |

Yesterday, I shared my mantra for success. Maybe it is Nike's or Lao Tzu's mantra, but its origin does not really matter. The message is what counts. I invite you to make it your own because it will repay you in life. But I only shared half of the equation yesterday—the body. There is another, even more important side to consider—the mind.

First, though, let me tell you a little about my current mental state. I am doing well so far, but the funny thing is that my expectations of a visually engaging environment are not quite being met. People liked to tell me I was constantly going to see amazing new natural splendors. And while it is certainly beautiful out here, in some respects it is more like staring at a painting, as opposed to watching an action-packed movie. The past three nights I have curled up in my cabin to sleep and I have awakened to the exact same scenery in the morning. I know, I shouldn't complain. It is beautiful, epic in scope, and it leaves me breathless. Still, though, it is sameness. This is true of training or studying too. The mind always has to adapt to the reality of the moment. Sometimes you have to find beauty in the monotony.

As intense as my physical training was, there were a great many days when that was actually the easy part. I soon discovered that the mental aspect of my training was a tremendous challenge, even bigger than I imagined. Without a rightly ordered mind, the body will do nothing. If I wanted to "just do it" then my mind had to initiate the process. Eventually the mind and the body become one indistinguishable whole.

The first challenge was confronting the negative thoughts that can precede the desired action. When you're facing a six-hour workout (or a challenging school or work assignment), it's easy to fill your mind with thoughts of "too hard" or "too much" or "too far." I do sometimes have a tendency towards procrastination. Not only does procrastination take an incredible amount of time and energy, the longer you wait the more difficult it is to begin. As the eighteenth-century English poet Edward Young once said, "Procrastination is the thief of time."[9]

To tame this beast it's essential to analyze its cause. While it might start as a lazy mood, as in "I just want to lie on the couch all day," this was not my problem. For me procrastination is more about not wanting to start something until I am confident that I can do it perfectly. While striving for perfection may be admirable, the hesitation and inaction it can cause is not. Time was being stolen. The more I pushed my training aside, the easier it became to justify doing something else which didn't contribute to my goal. Procrastination can generate a momentum of its own.

How did I overcome this? What thoughts did I fill my head with before a big training day? To make my training easier I put my mind on autopilot. I scheduled training first thing in the morning before my brain had a chance to devise an exit strategy. I knew that once I was working out, I was less likely to stop. I also learned that waiting for the procrastination to pass was futile. I just had to do it, and my mental autopilot was a great strategy. In your life, if you have a meeting with your boss, you don't negotiate with yourself about whether or not you want to show up. If you have a test at school, you don't debate with your teacher about taking it. You just do it. I had a six-hour meeting with my boss every day.

The reward of "just doing it" and not procrastinating is seeing new vistas and perspectives on life.

Anything you do can become habit, and once I learned to circumvent my tendencies to procrastinate with autopilot, I gained positive mental motivation. For me, motivation rarely comes before a desired goal. I don't think I have ever been motivated to row ten hours in my life. But after one minute I am motivated to go one more. And after two minutes I am motivated to go two more. Every minute or hour I row makes it easier to keep going another minute or hour. This is the crux of today's lesson: develop positive mental habits that align with your goals and then you will learn how to "just do it." This is not easy. Like everything in life it takes practice.

Day 5: Experience Solitude, Not Loneliness

@KatieSpotz Tweet Log for Thursday, January 7, 2010	
6:15 AM	Katie has no support boat at all—she is completely alone in the Atlantic Ocean. [Sam]
11:32 AM	Heard some splashing and looked over to see about 20 flying fish emerge from the water. Very cool!

I have achieved my first small distance milestone, as I am now well past the 100-mile mark. I did a lot of training on Lake Erie and 100 miles there seemed so far. Now it is just a nice round number and a small piece of this 3,000-mile journey. Still, this has been an important point for me. Many of the ocean rowers who failed in their attempted crossings pulled out within the first 100 miles. This brings me some satisfaction, not at their failure, but that so far my plans are working out. Overall I am very pleased to be away from land, and I am looking forward to hitting the trade winds. As soon as I do, I am going to celebrate with a movie! Today the audio entertainment will be my favorite *Comedy Central Presents*.

Five days in and I have gotten a small taste of being alone with the ocean. Last night was the first time my AIS did not go off at all. I need to redefine "really alone" out here: there are plenty of living creatures around me. It's like Times Square on New Year's Eve with the schools of fish, dolphins, birds, and the uninvited sharks. I never imagined the frequency of the flying fish shooting out of the water and I found three on my deck this morning. Thankfully sharks don't fly! Of course, these creatures can't offer companionship in the way that humans can. With no support boat following me, the only human contact I have is through my email, my blog, and my phone. So I am alone with my boat *Liv* and my Wilson tennis ball.

I look at this time as a gift. How often can we be truly present with ourselves for an extended period? We spend our lives today managing interruptions. TV, internet, and cellphones constantly intrude on our abilities to experience each moment fully. Even when we encounter new and exciting things, we interrupt them trying to get a picture, or a selfie, and sometimes we forget entirely to engage our senses with what is happening around us. We have become something like Pavlov's famous dogs who he trained to salivate at the sound of a bell because they knew food was coming. When our smart phone vibrates we check it, and we give it priority over what we are currently doing at that time.

The ocean is my blank slate of uninterrupted existence. To be honest (and when you are alone with yourself for months at a time you have to be) this is something that scared me before I embarked on this journey. I wondered about what I would think about during all that time by myself and whether I would enjoy the person I found at sea. I had never spent so long without human contact. How could I be sure I wouldn't go crazy being alone? I imagined all the scary thoughts and emotions that might pop up. What if I was bored, anxious, sad, afraid, frustrated? But, most frightening of all, what if I was lonely?

I remembered that loneliness isn't necessarily defined by the number of people around. Some of the loneliest moments I have experienced came in countries where I could not speak the language. Being lonely is a state of mind, regardless of whether you're in the middle of a city or an ocean. At least that's what I told myself before I got to the ocean. Now that I am five days in, I can feel the truth in this. I am assuredly alone, but I do not feel lonely. I have my family and friends and supporters back home and our physical distance is irrelevant. They are with me in spirit every stroke of the way, and I know this will continue. So it is not loneliness I feel at this point. It is something else.

The theologian Paul Tillich wrote, "Loneliness can be conquered only by those who can bear solitude."[10] This is something I have thought about quite a lot. "Loneliness" is a word that defines the pain of being alone, while "solitude" celebrates it. In a state of loneliness you are seeking contact. In a state of solitude you thrive just by yourself. Both words describe the same physical condition, but they are complete opposites in terms of one's mental state. My goal has been to approach the ocean as a time of peaceful solitude, and not a place of anxious loneliness. The poet May Sarton expressed a similar sentiment: "Loneliness is the poverty of self; solitude is the richness of self."[11]

The lesson today is that when you are alone, strive to transform that experience away from loneliness and towards solitude. You won't be lonely when you learn to accept and enjoy the person you are alone with.

And now, onto the real challenge of the day: brushing the mess of hair on my head!

Here I am before I confront the challenge of taming my hopelessly messy hair.

Day 6: Never Pass By Yourself

@KatieSpotz Tweet Log for Friday, January 8, 2010	
3:28 PM	Time to bring out the sprouting kit. Munched my way through all my fresh fruit today
4:28 PM	You know you are tired when you wake up with food all over yourself to realize you fell asleep halfway through your meal. Oops

I talked yesterday about the privileges of solitude. I still feel privileged to be alone (especially when I spill food all over myself and no one is there to see), so it remains on my mind. The waves are something I am not quite used to yet. They certainly have not been gently rocking me to sleep. It feels more like I am in a bumper car ride at the amusement park (Cedar Point for me!) with someone else driving blindly.

I can get used to these bumps and bruises. What I was most physically concerned about before I started my row was seasickness. If you could see me, you would notice that I just touched the back of my ear to ensure that my little patch is still affixed. It is! After extensive research I accepted the advice of many that these Transderm-Scop sickness patches were the way to go. I knew I needed this because I would get "sea" sick on Lake Erie, and that was not even the ocean. Even though I never spent more than a night alone on Lake Erie, I felt sick almost as soon as I rolled over the first wave. Remarkably, this little patch is doing its job.

So, I recommend not only the proper technology and precautions when travelling, but also a proper mindset. Pay attention to yourself in the moment, and don't let the journey be about the destination. Saint Augustine articulated this mindset well:

> Men go abroad to wonder at the heights of mountains, at the huge waves of the sea, at the long courses of the rivers, at the vast compass of the ocean, at the circular motions of the stars, and they pass by themselves without wondering.[12]

I would remind him that women can certainly wonder at these things too! But his point is still important. We travel to far-off places to see new things. We long to travel so we can gaze on the oceans, smell the mountain air, taste exotic foods, and hear the sounds of different cultures. Of course these enrich us, but we so often overlook the most significant wonder of the world—OURSELVES.

As Augustine admonished, "Don't pass by yourself without wondering." Don't fill your life with so many experiences that you drown out the sounds of silence and the meaning of life residing within your own heart. I actually started on my quest to know myself in this way before my row began. Meditation played a huge role in my mental preparations.

I was instantly intrigued when a friend told me he had participated in a ten-day silent meditation retreat. It consisted of twelve hours of meditation in a lotus position while observing "noble silence" for the entire ten days. This is a fast from external stimulation with no reading, writing, talking, or eye contact with another human. While sitting in stillness for those 120 hours, I learned that you are doing a lot more than nothing when you are meditating. You are opening your eyes, ears, and heart to a deeper reality. As the Persian poet Rumi wrote, "Close both eyes to see with the other eye."[13] That unseen "third eye" is the one in all of us that best connects us to our insight and intuition.

While there are many ways to meditate, I liked to keep it as simple as possible. My focus was breathing naturally and normally. On the first exhalation, I counted "one" in my head. Then I inhaled slowly (can't forget that), and counted "two" as I exhaled that breath. I went all the way to "ten" and started again. I focused on my breath as it entered, filled and left my body. And if my attention wandered, I gently brought it back to the present and began counting again. As simple as it was, that experience gave me the tools to better understand my mind and it prepared me to handle the roller coaster of emotions I have already experienced at sea.

I smile when I think that my rowing seat is like a hyperactive lotus position. Actually, though, in sitting meditation you learn to practice that same awareness no matter what you are doing, whether you are still on a cushion or struggling to row your boat. This training helped me replace that cushion with my sheepskin rowing seat, while still immersing myself in the solitude that lets me really examine who I am. The Atlantic Ocean becomes something like a mirror for my soul, stripping away all of my daily chores, conversations, and responsibilities.

Not everyone has the opportunity or the desire to lose themselves in the middle of the ocean or sit for ten days at a meditation retreat. That is okay! The lesson for today is to find your own ocean or sanctuary. It might be a walk in the woods, a quiet corner of a library, or a peaceful room in your house. Enable it to be a space where you do not "pass by yourself." Make an appointment and meet yourself there. Make *"you time"* matter by giving it the same priority as you do with "family time" or "work time." Silence the outside world (especially your phone!) and become aware of the moment you are experiencing. Concentrate on your breath: make it deep and deliberate from the diaphragm, and try to not direct your mind, even though it will drift. You may not like everything you find. No one is perfect. But the opportunity to be honest with yourself and truly experience who you are can be life changing in a positive way.

Day 7: Chart a Course

@KatieSpotz Tweet Log for Saturday, January 9, 2010	
5:41 AM	Have been at sea for a week now. A good face scrub and deep conditioner for the hair to celebrate! Yay
8:01 PM	In her first week, Katie has averaged just under 1.8mph—ocean rowing is not high speed! for her route so far. [Sam]

Apparently I could walk across the Atlantic faster than I am rowing. I have just received an email from Rick, my weather support. He said, "Expect higher winds" and these are in the forecast for the next two or three days. Right now they are northeasterly winds, and the ocean current has turned more favorably from the east at .25 to .5 knots.[14]

I have reached the one-week point now and I discovered that a little time for personal cleanliness really helps buoy the spirits. It is amazing how "dirty" you can become even when there is no dirt in sight. With that small success, what should my next milestone be? It is impossible for me to make a target 3,000 miles away my next goal. I always need to set smaller goals so that I can feel a sense of progress and achievement.

Everything is a challenge out here. If cooking a meal is merely a delicate balancing act, managing to get a few hours of sleep is a monumental achievement. You might say that everything takes three times as long to complete, but even that is sometimes an understatement! I am learning to take this in stride, and I try to simply accept how frustratingly slow each small activity is. So, my next milestone? Maybe just to make it through today.

I am also trying to get used to being in the middle of nowhere. As I reflected at the start of this journey, life is much like the waves that surround me here on the ocean. There are lots of ups and downs (and more side-to-sides at night than I care for), and my boat and also my emotions ride them as best as we can. These words are rolling around in my head: "Life is a wave upon the sea of chaos in a world where land is nowhere in sight."[15] That is certainly me right now. I am tossing about on this chaotic sea. My goal is Cayenne, French Guyana, South America, and it is nowhere in sight. This can be overwhelming.

It brings to mind what we all must do when pursuing distant goals, as they require a much different strategy than short-term objectives. For example, if the task is writing a paper for school, it's fairly easy to map out the necessary steps: go to the library, do some research, develop an outline, write a draft, revise, and submit. Yes, this is certainly challenging, but the "land," the destination, is always in plain sight.

What happens, though, to the same student's more distant goal, where the "land" is unseen, a goal such as preparing a plan in high school that will open the doors to college admission? This is much more complex, and the finish line more distant, especially if one starts early. This achievement map is difficult to draw, and becoming overwhelmed at some point is probably a given.

Of course the challenges of long-term planning significantly affect adults as well. For example, how do you get a promotion at work? There are multiple short-term steps that add up—one hopes!—to realizing that goal. This includes the simple things like getting to work on time, demonstrating a positive attitude, being reliable in completing assignments efficiently and on schedule, and looking for ways to improve the environment for the people around you. Whatever the situation, defining the short-term goals, and attaining them, is the key to long-term success. That, and hard work—which is always present each and every step of the way.

How do you measure progress and success when you are pursuing such a distant goal that the land (the destination) is out of sight for a great deal of time? How do you know your direction is true? Imagine if I had no compass or GPS on *Liv*, nor an understanding of where the sun rises and sets each day. If that were the case I might see land after 70 days of rowing, but that shore could be Africa, where I started. In other words, it's easy to get turned around in the middle of pursuing a long-term goal.

So when the destination remains hidden, it is essential to develop a system to chart your progress, and stick to it. I have real-time feedback with my GPS, but I still note the position of the sun during the day and of the stars at night. I also chart my coordinates daily in a logbook with waterproof pages (you can never be too careful!). This means that even though the land—and my destination—will be invisible for nearly all of my voyage, I have multiple techniques by which to ensure my direction is true and my progress on track.

That is the lesson for today. Consider for a moment your long-term goals when the destination is distant and out of sight. This might be saving for retirement, getting a promotion at work, or achieving a goal in an athletic competition. Whatever your objective is, take an inventory of the techniques you are using to gauge your speed and direction. In the world of fitness, elite athletes will also chart their progress in several ways, like testing their VO_2 max (which is the maximum rate of oxygen consumption), body composition, mile repeats, race times, and so on.

These multiple techniques keep us on track and primed for success. I cannot say for sure exactly how many days land is away from me at this point. But I am confident in my course. Even though I row through a sea of chaos right now and the land is nowhere in sight, I know that every oar stroke gets me closer to my destination, even if I'm being blown off course—and sometimes backwards.

Despite my slow forward progression right now, I keep reminding myself that no matter how small a contribution each pull on my oars makes, I need only ensure my course, and then stay determined to complete that next oar stroke . . . and the one after that. This is the secret of long-term success when pursuing distant goals. As Mother Teresa once said, "We ourselves feel that what we are doing is just a drop in the ocean. But the ocean would be less because of that missing drop."[16]

I like to ask myself this question: If I did what I did today every day, where would I be in one year, five years, or ten years? Divide your long-term goals into segments, keep making that next oar stroke, and one day your horizon will appear.

Day 8: Let Caution Win Sometimes

Have you ever seen the movie *Groundhog Day*? Bill Murray is doomed to relive the same day over and over again until he slowly improves as a human being. That sounds familiar right about now. Every day so far has been exactly the same. Except for some punctuated moments of fear and amusement from waves, tankers, birds, and fish, it has been row, eat, attempt to sleep, and repeat. And I have many more weeks ahead of me just like this. I remind myself: "Just keep rowing, Katie!"

The last few days have been hot with little wind. Recently, I have also been noticing hundreds of fish swimming quickly and tightly westward, perhaps as part of some sort of migration. Now that I'm adjusted to sea life, I have been doing more night rowing, which has been a real treat. The stars are amazing! It's just so humbling to be such a tiny speck in the blue. The moon is a much more pleasant rowing companion than the sun. I like the heat, but I do realize that you can have too much of a good thing.

My living conditions on the rowboat are, for lack of better words, unusual. Maybe it's a little like living in a New York apartment where every space serves multiple functions. My bedroom, living room, dining room, kitchen, and office exist within 36 square feet. With its nine-foot by four-foot dimensions, my cabin is more like a coffin with just enough room for my waterproof foam mattress. I have my supplies packed tightly in every little corner, and I have tried to make this space as cozy as possible. However, there is one aspect of my living space that I cannot get used to—what lives under my bed.

There are 6,000 feet of open water between me and the sea floor. In that space are fish, sea turtles, dolphins, eels, jellyfish, whales, and, yes, sharks. And for that reason I have not been in any hurry to jump into the ocean to cool off. I still need the protective confines of my boat. I saw the movie *Jaws* when I was a kid, and I have also seen real sharks out here in the ocean. I do not want those two images to meet with my feet and body dangling slowly in the water, taunting a shark looking for an easy meal.

Today, however, I really wanted to take the plunge. Rowboats require very little maintenance. Aside from cleaning out the filter for my water maker and charging my electronic devices from my solar panels, I have little else to do but row—except for one critical task. I need to keep the hull of my boat clean. I wish I could row through a "boat wash" with giant, automatic scrubbers like a car wash, but, clearly that is not going to happen. You would think that being hammered with waves would keep *Liv* clean, but that is not the case. Barnacles grow on the sides of my boat, and they impede my progress. This morning I finally told myself that every day I avoided cleaning the sides and bottom was another day for more barnacles to grow. They were making my hard-earned miles even more difficult. I also realized that avoiding the monsters under your bed (which in my case was literally true) does not make them go away.

I had another incentive this morning to get me past my fear. It was so very hot that a dip in the ocean seemed like a wonderful treat. That is what I focused on—the cool water, and not the dangers of the unknown and the creatures that inhabited it. Making me even more uneasy was that my oar bumped into something unknown. I hope it was just a really big fish.

Finally I could procrastinate no longer, so I grabbed my snorkel, mask, and scrubber and looked into the water. When nothing peered back at me I dangled my toes. Spider-Man talks about his "Spidey sense" when he feels danger. Sometimes you rush up the basement steps at night feeling a presence behind you. I do not know what it was that roused my senses, but I looked cautiously into the water again. This time I saw such an unusual creature, bigger than a fish but smaller than a shark, and it had large green spikes! It did not look friendly, and I was not about to find out if its bark was worse than its bite! I lost my nerve, climbed back into *Liv*, and told myself simply to stick to my mantra, *Just keep rowing*. I tried to put the barnacles out of my mind, and forget that spiky green fish.

My excitement was not over for the day. As night was falling, while I was still rowing, I heard and felt a loud, jarring thud. My entire boat shook. I cautiously peered over the edge and this time what I saw were eight large tuna swimmingly wildly and closely to my boat. For two hours they kept me company, circling and banging into *Liv*.

It is easy to tell yourself to simply confront the monsters under your bed. We all know that avoiding your fears does not make them go away. Facing them is the fastest way of getting where you want to be. As President Franklin D. Roosevelt famously said, "We have nothing to fear but fear itself." That is all well and good in theory, but sometimes fear overtakes reality. Sometimes the fear wins and you back away from the edge and don't jump. It is important to know that we cannot live every day like a daredevil. Some days you just have to hide your head under the covers. You are not letting fear win. You are simply telling it that you want to fight it another day. I will take the plunge, but just not today. It is foolish to ignore fear and much wiser to take the appropriate time to learn to master it.

Day 9: Meditate by Moving

I am nearing another of my mini-goals—the trade winds. I am still a few days away but they should provide some positive momentum for me. The winds' assistance will not just be physical, but also mental. They are a gentle helping hand from Mother Nature, pushing me in the right direction, and I am rowing with the flow. These trade winds take the form of moving air near the equator. I am in the North Equatorial Current and they are blowing from Africa to South America. But they are pushing me a little south too, and that is why I am aiming for French Guyana. The trade winds are like interstate highways for all sailors. Historically they have helped everyone from emperors attempting to expand their nations to voyagers seeking to discover new lands. Now they just have to help me and my little boat. As good as this sounds, though, I am not simply riding a swift current and catching favorable winds out here. If not for my rowing, my estimated 70-day journey would take years to complete, and who knows where I would wind up?

That is the good news. The bad news is that these trade winds are also the lane for the emergence of tropical storms. If one develops I will be right in the center of it. Such is life, I suppose, and we always have to take the good with the bad. The hurricane season starts in June, so I hope to be safe by that time. For now I will continue to endure this brutal sun, and grumble about it a bit. But I know full well that the searing sun is much easier to deal with than surviving a tropical storm in a rowboat.

This is not the first time I have propelled myself along with the gentle aid of a current. In fact the first time I did this in an endurance setting, I broke a world record, and more importantly gave myself the confidence that I had the mind and muscle power to row the Atlantic. My goal was to swim the length of a river . . . any river. The Allegheny just happened to be the closest, and as it turned out, no one had done this before. Rivers have lessons to teach us too. Grab a chair and I will tell you the story. Or better yet, grab an oar and help with this rowing!

My quest started on July 22, 2008, in Raymond, Pennsylvania, where I hiked 27 miles, tracking the Allegheny from a small stream to a point where I could actually get in and swim. It was a demanding nine-hour trek through farmland and into deep forests. Some of the terrain was challenging. I crawled through thick brush and scrambled over rocks. I also climbed over a beaver dam, under an electric fence, and managed to avoid some angry cows and a bull, but not before ripping my pants on a barbed-wire fence. All this and my swim was yet to begin. There was not a simple trail! Eventually, at Coudersport, Pennsylvania, the river became deep enough to swim, though early on I was alternating between swimming and trudging through thick mud. I persisted, eventually swimming all day long, and one month later I became the first person to swim the river's entire 352-mile length.

Unlike my current solitary situation on the Atlantic, on the river I had James Hendershott, my friend and safety kayaker along with me. He carried supplies in his kayak, and was also my downstream eyes, ensuring I did not swim into an oncoming boat. My body did not have the AIS alarm on it that *Liv* carries with her.

During the way we encountered wonderful wildlife, including bald eagles, muskrats, snapping turtles, white-tailed deer, water snakes, weasels, great blue herons, bats, mussels, clams, and frogs. There were also some surprises. Swimming into a deer skeleton was not fun, nor was crashing into tree branches hidden in the water. But I continued on, despite the obstacles, with my fins, wet suit, snorkel, and mask.

Each night we found a place to camp near the river, searching for as flat a location as possible. Our meals were not extravagant, but we got quite good at making oatmeal and pancakes over an open fire every morning. By day, our fuel came in the form of trail mix, and at night we celebrated with pasta and canned meat. I missed my fresh fruits and vegetables! Ironically, at the same time that I was swimming slowly, Michael Phelps was winning gold medals at the Summer Olympics in China with world record speeds. I might have envied his pace, but my beautiful solitude in the depths of nature more than made up for it.

For that month I averaged 12 to 15 miles per day as I swam westward, and then eventually turned north towards New York, where the river empties into the Allegheny Reservoir and its 27-mile lake. It was actually at that point that I met my biggest challenge. James and I found ourselves without fresh water. I wound up swimming eight hours that day without taking a sip of water, which is something I do not recommend. It also felt like I was swimming in glue because of all the waves from boaters and jet-skiers. The irony of swimming all day and being so thirsty is amusing now, but not so much then. At the end of the day we boiled water and dissolved emergency water tablets. Thankfully we did not get sick and I was able to continue to swim through the reservoir.[17] To make that night even more challenging I could not sleep because I had a burning, itching rash all over my body. That was fun!

The river got much more populated when we approached Pittsburgh, and that certainly disrupted my ability to get in a swimming zone. On the positive side though, we met a lot of nice people who let us sleep on their yachts along the way. The beds felt amazing! The swim came to an end at Point State Park, where the Allegheny and the Monongahela rivers come together to form the Ohio River. I actually wanted to keep going because I loved it so much, but James needed to return to school. My parents, aunt, cousins, and a few friends met me at that end, along with the media and people I did not even know who were reading my blog posts.

One week before the swim, on July 17, 2007, I answered the following question in my blog: *Why Swim*? I said that I was drawn to many aspects of this challenge. One was external: to raise funds for Blue Planet Run

Swimming behind James on the Allegheny River.

Foundation. But I also wrote, "I get into this zone when participating in endurance events and it becomes a form of meditation for me."[18] This swim taught me a vital lesson about life: moving is meditation. You do not have to sit like a silent, still monk in order to explore the mysteries of your mind. In fact the repetitive motion of swimming, biking, walking, or running can become a vital catalyst for self-realization. That made all the difference in my mental preparations for this row. I knew if I could swim 10 hours a day, I was ready to row 10 to 12 hours a day on the ocean.

Moving is not just meditation for me. It is an essential part of life, and humans were made to move! Finding time every day to do nothing but physically propel yourself forward will do more to create a positive mindset than you ever might imagine. You do not have to swim the length of an entire river. Just walking around the block is an important start. Any activity will do, but it is essential to keep your mind focused solely on what you are experiencing. Try to eliminate distractions and be mindful of the moment. Over time if you keep doing it, and practicing, your body will relax into the motion and enable your mind to enjoy the ride.

Day 10: Eliminate the Drag

@KatieSpotz Tweet Log for Tuesday, January 12, 2010	
4:50 AM	Have no self control when it comes to turkey jerky. Must have more turkey jerky!
7:51 AM	Turns out that rowing on 4 hours of sleep is fairly challenging after all

Two days ago the monsters under my bed at night got the best of me when I was afraid to jump in the water and swim. Yesterday, reflecting on my Allegheny River swim has put me even more in the mood for treading water in the ocean. Today I am convinced I am ready to confront my fears, and take that leap of faith into the deep blue below me. Caution will not win this time. I am ready to jump in the ocean. As I was sleep-deprived last night, and because the sun was so unbearably hot (with the temperature hitting triple digits), I realized it would do me good to take advantage of the infinite cool water surrounding me.

Still the fears resurfaced. *Liv* was keeping me alive. She protected me from the unknowns of the ocean, and my practical side told me to stay in the boat. That was my survival instinct talking. It is not unlike parachuting out of an airplane. When I did that I heard the same voices in my head telling me I was crazy to jump out of safety and into a free fall. I survived that jump, and so it is time to attempt this one. Not only will it cool me off, but it will give me the opportunity to clean *Liv*, which will in turn increase my speed and efficiency. Every day now I have been leaning over the side of *Liv* and letting my hands trail along in the water. Even that was refreshing, so imagining my whole body in the water is enough incentive. Why in the world would I not do this? Oh right, the sharks.

I began my preparations, telling myself that jumping out of a boat is not as scary as jumping from an airplane. "But there are no flying sharks, Katie," responded a cautious voice inside. I ignored it, reached into the hold and got out one of my security straps, attaching one end around my waist with a carabiner, and the other to *Liv*. This would be my tether, like an astronaut uses in space, and my lifeline in the ocean. If this one cord broke, or I became disconnected from it, I would likely drift away from *Liv*, and toward a slow death by drowning. I tried to put that out of my mind as I slipped on my mask and snorkel, and grabbed the barnacle-scrubbing brush. That was all it took to get ready, and I was set to go.

With my straps again checked and rechecked I looked over the edge of the boat, scanning the water for creatures that might do me harm. I saw nothing this time to raise my level of fear, so I knew I just had to take the plunge. Upon hitting the surface of the water I was rewarded with the most amazing sensation of water engulfing my entire body, bringing instant relaxation. Submersing immediately drowned out the world above and my ears were filled with the muffled and bubbly sounds of the ocean. It felt like I was in an isolation tank. For a moment I did not even care to look around under the water to see if I was alone. It was an extraordinary feeling and I savored it.

I was instantly out of the sunshine and under the water with my hair floating around me. I felt weightless, a little like a mermaid, drifting in the watery universe. Slowly I let myself bob to the surface, and with my arms outstretched, feet slowly peddling, I pushed my head above water. I took a few minutes just to relax, and then I began to look about. Nothing dangerous lurked, and so I decided to get down to business, which meant swimming under *Liv*. Snorkeling gear in place, I somersaulted down, kicking my feet up, and under the boat I went.

I finally overcame my fears and met my neighbors under my boat.

I was amazed by what I saw. It was like an entire ecological system existed under *Liv*. There were so many different fish swimming close to the hull, and they were very small—only a few were bigger than my clenched fist. They seemed to take refuge in the protective area under my boat, which with all the algae and barnacles also provided them food. The fish were not frightened by my presence. Clearly they had not seen *Finding Nemo*!

The fish were welcome to stay around as long as they liked, but the barnacles had to go because I needed to eliminate anything that caused drag. So I began scrubbing, and about 30 minutes later *Liv* was back to her sleek self, ready to slip through the waves. I called my first swim a success.

I realized while I was under water the lesson the Atlantic was teaching me today. Because of their drag, the barnacles on my boat are a perfect metaphor for life. In scientific terms, drag occurs when forces act opposite to the relative motion of an object. This causes friction, and prevents the object from moving as efficiently as it could towards its destination. It is not just boats in the ocean that encounter drag. Humans do too as they travel through life. Clearly we are not walking around with barnacles on our bodies (at least I hope not!). But there are so many negative forces in our lives that slow our progress, prevent us from achieving our goals, or at worst, harm us.

As I got back into *Liv* I started assessing my life. What were some of my attitudes and actions that caused me drag? Who were people who had a negative influence? This list is different for everyone, of course. You might have a friend pressuring you to do something counterproductive to your health, your grades, or your career. Or it might not be anything external at all, but rather internally generated drag. Perhaps you have a personal fear that prevents you from taking a risk. I have certainly experienced this feeling many times in life. In fact just two days ago I was afraid to jump off *Liv*. This risk was worth taking, and eliminating the drag is a necessary part of everyone's life. But the first step is being honest with yourself about where drag exists. It takes courage to identify and eliminate it, but once you do, you will move more freely though life.

Day 11: Move Like a Shark

@KatieSpotz Tweet Log for Wednesday, January 13, 2010	
6:29 PM	Katie hasn't been feeling on top form the last day or so, but isn't slowing up at all. At this rate, she has just (!) 50 days to go! [Sam]

I have already made the point about the importance of progress, and that each oar stroke gets me closer to my destination. However, the reality on the ocean, as in life, is that the pursuit of a goal is rarely, if ever, a tale of consistent progress. We all go through periods when our enthusiasm wanes, obstacles appear in our paths, injuries or sickness limit our activities, or we perceive it is too hard to continue. At that point we have two choices: we can give up, or we can embrace the challenges and continue forward.

I am going through some difficulty at this stage. I did not sleep well last night, I am feeling a bit ill, and rowing forward is extremely difficult. I am experiencing both the physical and the mental challenges of my row. On top of all of this, I realize that my oar strokes are not propelling me as I expect towards my destination. The swirling winds are strong and in some cases I am actually losing ground, or, in this case, water. I am feeling a little like a machine, if machines could feel fatigue. I row eight to ten hours, and then eat a meal (snacking in between, of course). The rowing is monotonous, and the food is too. The sky is beautiful but it is the same each day. The ocean is wondrous, but other than the size of the waves and the occasional clouds, and it also remains the same as it was the day before. My only notion of progress is an electronic blip on my GPS screen. I could be on a stationary rowboat in a gym somewhere. The sensation would be the same, except for the waves. Always the waves.

The pursuit of every goal has its own unique challenges. One I underestimated back on land was what my reaction would be when expectations and reality diverged. I carefully planned my route from Africa to South America. My weather advisor charted a route that took advantage of the prevailing winds and currents, while also minimizing the risk of storms. He now gives me my daily weather reports at sea. With his help I have access to information that predicts where the wind might take me.

This creates expectations. If the weather report says strong winds from the northwest, I expect them to be that way. If the weather report says weak winds from the southeast, I form a different expectation. The quickest way to disappointment is when there is a clash between anticipated reality and the actual reality. And we all know the weatherman can be wrong. It is like going to a baseball game, expecting a sunny day, and sitting instead through a soggy rain delay. Today is one of those days, and I feel myself and my boat drifting backwards.

My mind is repeating counterproductive mantras: *I should be going faster* or *the wind should be picking up by now.* Even worse is *the wind shouldn't be pushing me back towards Africa!* When the sea is as endless as it always appears to me, it is hard to stay motivated. Disappointment over drifting backwards can be enough to shatter my confidence, and I feel like I am losing grasp of the last strand of hope that keeps me going.

Today's lesson is one I am learning minute by minute. The Atlantic is teaching me that sometimes you drift backwards, even when you are doing everything you can to move forward.

I knew when I first started thinking about rowing the ocean I had two options.

> Option one: *Row the Atlantic.*
> Option two: *Regret not rowing the Atlantic.*

A lifetime of regret seemed more difficult than spending a few months rowing across the Atlantic. So my decision was to take the easier route of the two, and to start rowing.

I am now trying to maintain this logic on the ocean. On days like today, when I am struggling to push forward, experiencing fatigue, and feeling myself slipping down towards despair at my lack of progress (or even being blown further away from my goal), I present two options for myself.

Option one: *Keep rowing.*

Option two: *Stop and forever live in regret.*

When I put it this way to myself, I find that rowing is easier.

Easier yes. Easy no. If I just keep rowing, everything else will take care of itself. I think this conclusion puts me in good company. Sharks, for one, drown if they stop moving. For them, movement is life itself. By keeping their bodies in constant motion their gills are able to extract oxygen from the water. I am going to follow the example of the shark and keep moving. Also, consider the words of Confucius: "It does not matter how slowly you go as long as you do not stop."[19] I am in agreement with him. I am going slowly, but I am not about to stop. Instead I will relax my expectations, allow myself to drift backwards, and simply keep moving, breathing, and rowing.

Day 12: Think Beyond Language

When I struggle here on the ocean, one thing I do is reward myself with a treat to lighten my mood. Or better yet, I *plan* to give myself a sweet-tasting reward once I have attained a new distance goal. This delayed gratification is a great motivational technique. Today my hard work earned me edamame covered in dark chocolate. Yum!

The longer I am out here the more I appreciate my mental preparations. Sure, I am glad I focused on strengthening my core by holding planks, practicing on the stationary rowing machine, and taking *Liv* out onto Lake Erie. Preparing my body was important. However, even though it is early in my row, I believe that my mental training is what will be most valuable in sustaining me on the ocean, and keeping me sane (for the most part).

Ocean rowing is different from most other sports because it is such a solitary endeavor. Between my start and my finish I will spend over two months isolated from all other physical human contact, which means that the will to propel myself must come entirely from within. Football teams like to say that the crowd is the twelfth man on the field because its energy and cheers so inspire the players. I have none of that, and this is why mental training is so vital.

Zen was one aspect of these preparations.

What is Zen? It is nothing, and it is everything, at the same time.

Religious scholar Huston Smith describes it like this: "Entering Zen is like stepping into Alice's looking glass. One finds oneself in a topsy-turvy wonderland where everything seems quite mad—charmingly mad for the most part, but mad all the same. It is a world of bewildering dialogues, obscure conundrums, stunning paradoxes, flagrant contradictions, and abrupt non sequiturs, all carried off in the most urbane, cheerful, and innocent style imaginable."[20] He related three stories of what a Zen master did when asked to describe the meaning of Zen. One raised a single finger. A second kicked a ball. A third slapped the inquirer across the face. Zen is not violent. This was intended as a slap to awaken the questioner from static mental thoughts.

Zen is weird! Maybe that is why I like it. Weird is always more interesting than the usual.

Aside from the "topsy-turvy wonderland" (which is a great way to describe my time here on the ocean), how does this crazy Zen prepare my mind to row? It breaks down the language barrier. Language is terrific for communicating our basic thoughts, but it still requires that every idea, image, desire, and emotion become objectified into discrete words placed one after another in formal sentences. Are words really up to the challenge of describing the way a sunset looks and feels when you are all alone in the middle of the ocean? I might try, but I would fail. Can words adequately describe what true love feels like, or do you actually have to experience it? If you have ever been in love you know the answer to that.

Zen is the mystical process of triggering enlightenment through meditation and in exploring the spaces between our words. That is kind of like reading between the lines but at a very complex, and yet simple, level.

It is a practice that is all about "Seeing into one's own nature."[21] Monks often describe this enlightenment with elusive "koans," signposts that point the general direction toward the path to enlightenment. Koans are parables that share frustrating secrets whose meaning is veiled and obscured from easy comprehension. They are passed from generation to generation and given to students to meditate upon, often for years. Each contains a truth about life that is abstract, hidden, and eternal. Koans enable us to think beyond the structure of language.

Consider this koan, called "No Water, No Moon," in which a student nun named Chiyono struggled for years to attain the Zen mind. One night there was a full moon, and she was carrying water in her very old and worn bamboo pail. All of a sudden the bamboo snapped, the bottom fell out of the pail, and the water spilled to the ground. At that moment she attained enlightenment and wrote this poem:

> In this way and that I tried to save the old pail
> Since the bamboo strip was weakening and about to break
> Until at last the bottom fell out.
> No more water in the pail!
> No more moon in the water![22]

You can see why Smith called Zen "charmingly mad" with "bewildering dialogues, obscure conundrums." And yet, meditating for hours at a time upon stories like Chiyono's brings one closer to understanding a secret about existence. It enables the practitioner to see life in a new way, with mindfulness. This new "seeing" is the key to it all.

"No Water, No Moon" is actually my lesson for today because it moves us beyond language. Like a Zen teacher, I am not going to tell you what this lesson means (not that I could). Meditate upon it yourself. Think about how meanings move beyond language. Come back to it tomorrow or the next day. Don't try to solve it, but instead, experience it. And perhaps it might become a signpost to a truth about life for you. You may find that you will also begin to become more connected to your experiences. Hearing the wind rustling leaves, sitting on a rock in the forest, or feeling a wave crash over you—these are best experienced in the realm beyond words.

Day 13: Sometimes Good Things Fall Apart

@KatieSpotz Tweet Log for Friday, January 15, 2010	
6:09 AM	It's my boat so I make all the rules. There will be singing, dancing, & lots of chocolate every day. And rowing, of course!

I like the rules of my boat. It's not unlike that feeling when you first get your own apartment. Being alone and organizing and controlling your own space gives you a sense of freedom and independence. It is a little more difficult to invite friends out here on the ocean like I might in an apartment! But there will still be lots of singing, dancing, and chocolate.

What is compromising my dancing, though, are the larger waves at this time. I talked a few days back about the trade winds assisting my forward momentum. They are doing that now, but they also seem to summon the waves to greater heights. Yesterday I estimated them to be about 20 feet tall. That may not sound like much, but from the surface of the water, they are towering over me! For now at least, these are not constant, but more random. They take me by surprise. I keep rowing through and over them but I am always on alert, and it is a never-ending mini-roller-coaster ride. Sometimes I feel like I am in the midst of a Hollywood disaster movie with waves crashing over me. There is no one calling "Cut!" though, and I do my best to remain upright. At any moment a wave coming from the proper angle could capsize me. My two cabins are airtight, so I can withstand what the ocean throws my way. My heart is certainly beating much faster, adrenaline is flowing, and several times I asked myself, "What am I doing out here?"

What did bring me out here? Several things. One was the attempt to challenge the limits of my endurance. That decision to row across the Atlantic Ocean brought about a thousand more questions and problems to be solved. The most important decision of them all, though, was what boat to row. That tiny space would become my trusty companion and new home. I had to pack everything and anything I would need to survive efficiently. Since transoceanic rowing is not what you would call a popular sport, I knew there were not many boats out there that were even capable of the journey. So I asked myself, "Where would I find such a rowboat?" I love to find a good deal on eBay, but I was pretty sure these types of craft were not to be found there. Cost was also very much a factor. I was a college student on a limited budget, saving everything I could from my summer jobs of babysitting and lifeguarding.

After several months of searching an informational website for ocean rowers, I finally found an ocean-worthy rowboat for sale within my budget, which was $8,000. If price were no object I could have located some pretty amazing boats, built with the latest and lightest carbon fibers—some as much as $100,000. Instead, I felt a little bit like Charlie Brown picking out a Christmas tree. Eventually I found the perfect boat. Well, she was perfect for me. However, the one that fit my personality and checkbook had problems. First, she was wooden, so she was much heavier to row. Second, she required a long list of alterations, since she was built for two rowers instead of one. Third, she had already weathered some very extreme storms, including four cyclones and two hurricanes. That cannot be good, right? Finally, the most challenging hurdle was that she needed to be delivered from Central America to the United States.

I learned that she was docked at a port in Costa Rica after a previous ocean crossing. The good thing was that the boat apparently could withstand the rigors of the deep ocean, including some pretty powerful storms. But obstacle after obstacle arose because of the red tape associated with releasing it from the country. It didn't make things any easier when the portmaster shared with me that someone might be living in it!

In my mind this boat was "the one" that would make my dreams happen. I couldn't imagine rowing in any other boat, despite the problems, and probably also because I knew that a composite model was beyond my means. In other words, my heart was set on "my" bulky, wooden boat in Costa Rica. Fast forward several months later: the only thing I was achieving was mounting debt as I tried to negotiate the bureaucracy. The final straw was when I finally learned that the owner couldn't transfer the title to me because the seller didn't legally have authority to make that transaction in Costa Rica. If I had only known that months sooner!

The boat was not going to be mine. Furthermore, I was losing faith in the community of ocean rowers I was planning to rely on to provide me information about crossing the Atlantic. My good boat deal became nothing but a good-sized debt. My piggy bank was empty, so I couldn't even begin to look for another boat. Back I went to square one.

I had two things going for me. First, I had time and second, I still had this unquenchable desire to row across the ocean. Words of inspiration also came from an unusual source. Charles Kettering, who headed research at General Motors from 1920 to 1947, once said, "Keep on going, and the chances are that you will stumble on something, perhaps when you are least expecting it. I never heard of anyone ever stumbling on something sitting down."[23]

Well said, Mr. Kettering! This became one of the first lessons that the Atlantic taught me, and it was before I even came close to her waters. *Sometimes good things fall apart so better things can fall together.* So with my desire intact, time on my side, and my willingness to stumble forward, I began to look for sponsors. What I found was indeed a situation much better than I had ever imagined, because I discovered companies that believed in my idea as much as I did. It wasn't easy, but the funding came with time and another boat became available just when I needed it. Everything fell into place even though it wasn't the way I had imagined it.

The boat I am making my rules on today was not my first choice. I think I will save the story of *Liv* until later, and I am sure glad I have her. Just do not tell *Liv* she was my second choice! She and my Wilson tennis ball make for excellent traveling companions, and they never judge my dancing or singing . . . or even my chocolate consumption.

Mini Wilson 1 wanting a turn to row. Thanks to the Chagrin Valley Rotary Club for making this companion for me, and for keeping Mini Wilson 2 safe back home.

Day 14: Life is a Team Sport

Two weeks at sea now and with my suntan, blisters, calluses, sore muscles, bruises, and salt-crusted hair, I'm finally beginning to feel like an ocean rowing gal! I've quickly learned how to cook a meal while being hit by waves, how to wash my hair with 10 ounces of fresh water and, more importantly, how to fit 5,000 calories into my body on a daily basis (and it turns out the latter has proved to be the most difficult).

The waves are calmer today. That means the trade winds have died down a bit, so I am getting less rowing assistance, but this is a give-and-take I am eager to accept right now. In my cabin I felt a little bit like I was inside a big dryer at the laundromat, being tumbled endlessly. This does make passing the time when I'm not rowing very difficult. The constant motion prevents me from enjoying a book (I didn't bring any other than audio books), writing, or even getting some sleep. I am able to jot notes on waterproof paper, type, blog, and tweet, though!

There was something new to concern me. Last night I was sleeping (or shall I say attempting to sleep) when I heard a loud banging on my boat. You know how you get startled when a branch hits your windowpane during a nighttime rainstorm? It was kind of like that, only a little scarier. It made for a tense and sleepless night, as the sound and the vibrations never stopped. My first hope was that it was not something broken. At best, that would be time-consuming to fix, and, at worst, potentially journey-ending.

Some of the beautiful creatures inhabiting the waters below me.

Once morning came I exited my cabin and peered into the water. There I quickly saw the problem. It was a giant sea turtle! So beautiful and wild, and he returned my gaze with his wise eyes. I stared in amazement, taking in his detailed shell of brown and green jigsaw-like pieces. His flippers and tail moved so slowly, effortlessly, and efficiently, but his eyes soon left me and returned to searching for small, tasty fish swimming around my boat. The turtle seemed to want to be my companion for a while as he swam alongside me. Certainly he had no fear of humans, probably because he had never seen one, and he had nothing to worry from me. I like the company, and if he could push me a little it would be even better!

I wanted to make my turtle a Twitter star today, but I am unable to tweet because my satellite phone cannot get a connection. I am sure that this silence is a lot harder on my family and friends back home than it is on me. Sometimes watching and waiting are much harder to endure than the person slogging, or rowing, through a challenge. It is now the start of my second week of rowing, and I really think my job is easier than worrying about a loved one alone on the ocean. And I am not really alone! I have lots of living

The friendly faces on my photo strips and a bird taking a rest.

creatures around me, as well as reminders of home. This includes two rows of photostrip stickers of important people in my life, which stare at me as I row.

Since I cannot tweet with the outside world, maybe this is a good time to get back to my boat story. Yesterday I shared how things fell apart when I attempted to get my first boat. It was not a story of loss, though, but actually of gain, because it was through those hard times that I gained *Liv*. The process taught me that I needed the support of some great people and companies who made this voyage possible. Rowing solo is a team sport!

My journey toward getting this boat began when I contacted Paul Ridley, who was preparing to embark on a row from the Canary Islands to Antigua. He was on the east coast, and I happened to be biking from Cleveland to Boston, so we arranged for a time to meet. I immediately fell in love with his boat, but had no idea how I could afford it. That began a lot of hard work building relationships with people and organizations who shared my vision. At first I was lucky just to receive messages like, "No Katie, we cannot help you but good luck with your goal." Most of the time my sponsorship requests were ignored. To keep my spirits positive I told myself that each "no" brought me closer to a "yes." I was fortunate. After a great deal of patience and persistence, I attracted a great outpouring of support for my cause. Paul Ridley's boat cost $40,000, and it included gear. The total budget for this trip ballooned to $100,000, and my team made these funds possible. (About $50,000 was cash sponsorships, and the rest came from in-kind sponsors).

Who are they? My Title Sponsor is Spire (formerly known as GaREAT), located in Geneva, Ohio. With 170,000 square feet of activity space, it is the largest indoor sporting complex in the United States. My first Gold Sponsor includes Pentair Water, which serves clean water globally to commercial, industrial, municipal, and residential markets. World Shipping Inc., my second Gold Sponsor, has been shipping on all the major deep-sea trade lanes for more than 50 years. My Silver Sponsors include Kinetico, Guardian Technologies, Moen, and weatherguy.com. Bronze Sponsors include Sattrans USA, Aetomic Web + Print Marketing, Tecmark, Trail Foods, WaterRower, and Clear Choice. I also have many great official suppliers for my trip.[24] There were individual people on my team who brought important specialties. This included weather support, public relations, sports psychology, web design, and yachting clubs.[25] So you can see, rowing alone across an ocean is by no means a solo sport.

So my lesson today is this: not only is rowing solo a team sport, but really every successful venture in life depends upon quality people surrounding you. We've all heard the famous African proverb which says, "It takes a village to raise a child." It also takes a village to enable someone to row across the Atlantic! It is not just me out here, as the spirit and support of so many others transformed my dream to a reality.

And when you think deeply about it, very few activities in life are truly solo. As humans we depend upon the connections we make with other people. They elevate, inspire, and enable us to achieve our dreams. People who will truly support you in your aspirations can be hard to come by. It takes a special person to encourage you to pursue something they might personally think is dangerous or a little crazy. My parents fell into this category, but their support, despite their reservations, means so much to me. So value these people in your lives and let them know the contributions they make are real and directly make a difference. It is not only rowing solo that is a team sport. Life itself is the greatest team sport of all.

Day 15: Accept Impermanence

@KatieSpotz Tweet Log for Sunday, January 17, 2010	
11:44 AM	Fun fact—9 of every 10 living things lives in the ocean. Makes you wonder what's happening below the surface
11:48 AM	Distracted yet again by my fishy followers. Just took a dip with 30 fish under the boat

I have quite a few audiobooks for my iPods but the only ones I have listened to so far are by a Zen teacher, Cheri Huber, who gave me more than 30 of her audiobooks for my trip. Her teachings have definitely helped me to accept and embrace my endurance challenges. A few days ago I talked about Zen as one component of my mental preparation. Today I want to talk about a second, which is Vipassana. This requires a story, and I have plenty of time to tell it.

One summer break during college I volunteered for two weeks in Thailand. During that time I had the opportunity to teach English to schoolchildren there, help in the rice fields, and build a home for a villager. After my volunteer duties were over, I decided to stay a little longer to explore the country and also attend a Vipassana retreat. Though different from the Zen tradition, Vipassana is a meditation practice from India, dating back more than 2,500 years to the Buddha. The word Vipassana itself means to "see things as they really are," and the practice helped me to do just that. Mindfulness about one's own breathing and attention to one's thoughts are used to gain insight into the nature of reality. The emphasis is to become truly present and to transcend our tendency to hide from uncomfortable experiences.

I was excited, yet apprehensive, to get to the meditation facility. But before the retreat began, I signed up for an excursion to visit the hill-tribe villages. This involved a hike of several days up to Chaing Rai Province. There was only one problem. I started feeling weak and a little strange, and during that first night in the woods I began shivering and then sweating from a fever. I knew something was seriously wrong because I was sweating more than I ever had, even in an endurance challenge. That morning I was dizzy, disoriented, and barely able to talk, let alone walk any further. One of the other hikers mentioned having similar symptoms when she had malaria. A guide thankfully was able to get me out of the deep wilderness and back to a town. I took a bus to a hospital in Bangkok, and believe me I had no problem in getting a seat all to myself. No one wanted to be near me.

In my daze, and given my almost complete inability to speak the Thai language, it was a struggle to understand what was happening to me, but I knew I was in for a battle. I have very little recollection of what happened during the next few days. I assume I had malaria, but whatever it was, it erased my memory of the worst of it. I was discharged before I regained my health because they needed the bed for another patient. I eventually recovered, but I had to put my meditation retreat on hold.

Flash forward a few months to the winter of that year. My dad was driving me to central Michigan where there was a very similar meditation retreat held in the middle of nowhere at an old military base. After my dad dropped me off I went to a barracks dorm room where I would be living for the next 10 days. I unpacked my few belongings, and there were very few because they had a strict do-not-bring list that even included scented deodorant. I walked to a huge hall lined with giant windows and very cold floors. Remember, this was in the middle of winter.

I took a seat on my mat and our meditation guide came to address us on our focus for the days that followed. He said: "Through an investiga-

A picture of "Happy Katie" before getting sick in Thailand.

tion of the mind and body, we can increase our ability to be fully present in this moment. We become more aware of, and more comfortable with, our thoughts, emotions and physical sensations, and lessen our identification with these aspects of our being as self."

I see now that this experience prepared me, like nothing else could, for blocks of 12 hours of rowing in which I confront time, boredom, and strain in ways I thought unimaginable. If life is a team sport, Vipassana is the complete opposite. Yes, there were other people at the retreat, but we were segregated by gender, and were not permitted to talk, or even look others in the eye.

I was completely silent for 10 days, just paying attention to breath, body, and mind. No cellphones, no books, no pencils or paper. It was on this retreat that I truly discovered how to embrace being alone. It is hard trying to define it with words. Imagine describing to someone how to ride a bike. You say, "Ok, then you just sort of balance and off you go." Meditation is like that. It is the practice and not the theory. Internally I felt like layers were melting away and I was closer to truth and a deeper understanding about life. I practiced how to live in the present and to engage fully in that moment. I began to appreciate techniques to combat my impulses and overcome my desire to seek comfort. I sat, meditated, and learned to just be.

Oddly, this is as simple as focusing on breath. I was aware of the voices of discomfort that came and went with each rise and fall of an emotion. I learned how to watch them as I inhaled and exhaled each breath. And they faded away, or I transcended above. I never knew which. Whatever happened, I was witnessing impermanence.

There is one Vipassana teaching that especially helped prepare my mind for the Atlantic. One of the three marks of existence in Buddhism is impermanence. This means that all existence on earth is in a state of change. Its official name is "Anicca" and it is the lesson for the day. I think I will let the Buddha's Samyutta Nikaya (Buddhist "Connected Discourses") explain: "All is impermanent. And what is the all that is impermanent? The eye is impermanent, visible objects . . . visual consciousness . . . whatever is experienced as pleasant or neither unpleasant nor pleasant, born of eye-contact, is impermanent."

Everything in nature changes: trees, clouds, flowers, grass, oceans, you name it. Humans too are in constant flux as youth inexorably moves into old age. "All that is solid melts into air," wrote Marshall Berman, echoing the writings of Karl Marx.[26]

I think of this in times of struggle, pain, worry, and suffering out here on the ocean. I also reflect on this in moments when I am elated. The acceptance of impermanence helps me to experience these emotions fully, and enables me to let go of the expectation that those moments will last forever. The highs and lows will not last because these sensations are fluid, like a wave. It is because I have accepted this impermanence that surrendering my body to 10 to 12 hours of rowing a day is not as difficult a challenge as I expected. The first week was certainly immensely hard, but now at the end of the day I feel ready for another. I am even anxious to push a little harder, but I know I am still at an early stage and I do not want to risk injury. I say this not to boast in any way at all. I believe anyone could physically manage rowing all day long. I do not believe that I have superpowers. All humans have an innate capacity to endure the challenges that come their way, even the ones we manufacture for ourselves to test our limits. The first step is accepting impermanence and welcoming suffering, because it is just a momentary experience.

Day 16: Give Yourself 1,000 Days

@KatieSpotz Tweet Log for Monday, January 18, 2010	
3:29 PM	Cotton candy skies for the last few days or low level stratus type clouds as my weatherguy would say
3:29 PM	Mini-Wilson 1 says hello to Mini-Wilson 2 back in Ohio!

Warning—a contradiction alert! Yesterday I was talking about how you should accept impermanence. I need to qualify that because there are some things about our lives and our passions that require a permanent mindset. Dreams of attaining anything important do not happen in an instant, or overnight, or even in a week. They take time—sometimes 1,000 days. Let me explain what I mean.

It took me exactly 990 days to go from having a dream about rowing across the ocean (I mark the start from when I first emailed my mom about the row), to launching *Liv* from the shores of Dakar. In between I went from being a teenager to a 22-year-old, and from someone who knew nothing about rowing an ocean to a well-prepared person starting to row across one all alone.

I still have that original email to my mom telling her of my plan:

On Thursday, April 19, 2007 5:57 AM, Katie Spotz wrote:

Mom-

I have this weird calling that's telling me to follow my heart. I can't stop thinking about it, I will regret not doing it and this worries me because this is huge! I would have to raise $100,000 and I want to. I want to devote my life to these adventures. I need to go for it mom. Mom, it IS possible. I believe. I don't know why I want to do this exactly but I just know I do. And I know that when I want to do something—I should follow the "beat to my drum." I am serious about this mom.

This is life changing. Defining my life. Enriching my life.

I need to mom. I just have to. I want to follow my dreams. I know this is crazy but what did you expect!? Mom, I am determined. I am not afraid of the obstacles—more afraid of passing up an opportunity. It would mean so much to me to have your support. This can happen mom.

Katie

My point in sharing this is that you can see how far away I was when I started this adventure. There were so many unknowns. It required determination, perseverance, and time.

I was determined to fulfill my quest to row the Atlantic. I persevered through many serious obstacles. And I gave myself time—which turned out to be about 1,000 days. And notice that does not guarantee success. It just got me to the starting point on a path that I believe will enrich my life.

I think this thousand day idea is a good one. Consider what else could be done in the same amount of time. Historian Arthur Schlesinger wrote a classic on the John Kennedy presidential administration and called it *A Thousand Days: JFK in the White House*.[27] Robert Reid wrote a book on the architects of the World Wide Web and subtitled it *1,000 Days That Built the Future of Business*.[28] If you have no plans of becoming president or inventing something as transformative as the internet, there are still millions of personal passions to seize. You can get a law degree or an MBA in 1,000 days. You could get a GED or complete a community college program. On a global scale, the United Nations has a World Food Program called "The First 1,000 Days." This attempts to provide nutrition from the mother's pregnancy to the child's second birthday.[29]

The lesson for today is that 1,000 days can change your life dramatically. It is a length of time that can propel you into new directions and places you never thought you could go. What might happen if you gave yourself 1,000 days to attain something that seems out of reach? Or you could start smaller, promising yourself to commit to a new passion. Try 10 days as a step in the right direction, and then 100. Where would you be in one year if you continued to do over and over again what you started on day 1? This is a great way to break large problems or goals into smaller ones. For example, I am not looking at my row as one 3,000-mile trip. Instead I consider it to be 3,000, one mile increments.

Consider Malcolm Gladwell's book *Outliers: The Story of Success*.[30] In it he describes his 10,000 hour rule, which is that successful people have devoted that many hours to practicing and perfecting one specific task. And guess what . . . I spent about 10 hours a day for 3 years to prepare for my row. That almost exactly equals Gladwell's 10,000 hours. It is good to know I have put in the time to give myself a chance at success!

What are your dreams? What could you do with 10,000 hours, 1,000 days, or another set period of time, provided you guaranteed the determination and perseverance? Take the time and propel yourself towards them.

Day 17: Create an Inspiration Team

It has been kind of a tough day today—tough enough that I even conveyed some of this emotion to my mom in an email. I typically shield her from my hardships, but I sent her this message earlier today:

Ok, so I have a "tough girl" image to maintain here so no need to go blabbing. :-)

This afternoon, I started to feel a bit down. Nothing serious, don't worry. I am rowing all day every day so it is to be expected, as I go through these same kinds of emotions on land, I can handle it.

Anyway, so I was feeling down and crawled into my cabin to rest and try to refresh. I heard some noise and realized it was static on the VHF radio. I said hello a few times to see what boat it was. Nothing. Then I looked at my gps to see if there were any boats in the area. None. So then I realized it was a sign from Pal. She wants you to know she is watching over me.[31]

Now, you are probably asking, "Who is Pal?" Give me a moment, and I will tell you.

Each day out here on the ocean is broken down into about 10,000 segments or pulls of my oars through the water. Once I get into the rhythm of it, the action can be almost like breathing. Unless you are breathing mindfully in yoga, for example, you spend most of your day unaware of your

At the finish of my first marathon. This was a huge moment for me because I remembered so clearly struggling to run a single mile less than a year from the race. Endurance is a state of mind.

breath. The autonomic system in your body takes over and frees your mind to focus on other tasks. Rowing can be like that at times and then I feel like I am cruising on autopilot. And I can experience just the opposite when my body is tired and in pain. I feel every muscle. Each stroke is a challenge. I am aware of each struggling breath, kind of like breathing if you have a lung problem. These comparisons bring to mind my grandmothers, and my bike across the United States. Let me share with you how this all fits together.

The story begins in October 2005 when I was a college freshman and completed my first marathon in Columbus, Ohio. While I was training for this I did a lot of bike riding, and shortly after the run I heard about the Big Ride Across America. How big was it? All the way across the United States, coast to coast, from Seattle to Washington, D.C.! What attracted me to it? First was the scale of the challenge, over 3,300 miles. Second was the opportunity to see the United States from a different perspective. And finally I wanted to do this to honor my two grandmothers, Mary Mullee and Joy Spotz, who passed away from lung disease. As soon as I saw that the American Lung Association was the charity beneficiary of the Big Ride I knew I had to do it. Lots of people seem to have nicknames for their grandmothers, and we called Mary, "Pal" because she used to say to my oldest brother, "Where's my little pal?" He then started calling her "Pal," and eventually we all did. Pal died of pulmonary fibrosis and my Grandma Spotz succumbed to emphysema. Pal had actually given up smoking as a present to me on the day I was born. The ride became my way to celebrate their memories and help others at the same time, because there are over 33 million people who suffer from chronic lung disease.

I had almost a year to prepare; we planned to leave from Seattle in June 2006. I was working on my nutrition/exercise physiology degree and my training was limited. So I ran three times during the week, swam, and trained with weights. The only time I could do long bikes rides was when I covered between 100 and 150 miles over the weekend. Actually the ride from my home in Mentor, Ohio, to Kent State University was about 100 miles, and that was a perfect distance (except for lugging books with me). The other thing about the Big Ride was that I just barely met the 18-year minimum age requirement. I turned 19 in April 2006, and just two months later I started the journey.

At the beginning of summer 2006, 45 riders from across the country met up in Seattle and we set out. Keeping roughly together we averaged about 83 miles per day (riding with someone passes the time much more quickly than alone . . . I guess I forgot about that on this row!). We started each day at about 7 a.m. and then by late afternoon stopped to pitch our tents, eat, take care of our bodies, and prepare to do it all over again the next day. Every six days we took 24 hours off to rest and see the sights in the town we happened to be in. It was the first time in my life that my body became so entwined with a self-powered transportation device and my Giant OCR 2 bike served me well. My row boat is huge and heavy by comparison!

Stopping for a picture with my riding buddies in the Badlands of South Dakota during the Big Ride Across America.

Every rider raised at least $5,500 for the American Lung Association (altogether more than $250,000), so I felt like my grandmas were smiling over me throughout the journey, especially during the challenging parts. Overall we ascended 96,000 feet. But the nice thing is that, to paraphrase Newton's Law of Gravity, what goes up must come down. Gravity is such a reward when you are balanced upon two wheels and the descending road is smooth!

The ride took 48 days, and my grandmothers were a constant motivation. They endured so much suffering and pain as their diseases progressed in their lungs that even the most challenging day on the bike ride paled by comparison. If they could endure all of that, I knew I could keep propelling myself forward.

The lesson I learned on that ride, and that I carry with me here on the Atlantic, is that it is really important to find a person (or people) that inspires you. If you choose wisely, and let that person into your heart, you will find they provide you with power, energy, and confidence when you need it the most. My grandmas were excellent motivators for me, because they were valiant fighters for their lives until the very end.

If you let someone inspire you this way, you find incentives and will be able to do things you might not expect. Remember, I had only done a single complete marathon prior to this Big Ride. I had no idea whether I had what it took to bike across the entire United States. At 19, I was the youngest woman there, and almost everyone else was experienced riders in their thirties, forties, fifties, and even one rider in his seventies. But my "Inspiration Team" gave me the strength to not just take on the challenge, but also succeed.

This also was the first event where I raised money for a charity. In the end I was able to contribute more than $6,000 to the American Lung Association, and I learned an important personal lesson. I found that I could combine two of my passions in life—endurance and charity work.

Who is your inspiration? If there is more than one, then create an "Inspiration Team." Consciously think about them before engaging in a life challenge. Their support will keep pushing you forward, even in moments when you do not think you have the strength to carry on by yourself. As Cheri Huber, my favorite Zen teacher, says, "You will do for the love of others what you would never be willing to do for yourself."[32]

Day 18: Endurance is a State of Mind

@KatieSpotz Tweet Log for Wednesday, January 20, 2010	
6:25 PM	Katie's flying today. Over 40 miles nearer to Cayenne in the last 24 hours! [Sam]

I remember a lesson I brought with me to the Atlantic: endurance is a state of mind. Being of sound body certainly helps in long, endurance challenges. What is even more important, though, is the right frame of mind. I learned this back in 2007 when I decided it would be a fun idea to run a 100 kilometer ultramarathon (62 miles) in Melbourne, Australia. This was an event to raise money for Oxfam, an international grouping of 17 organizations working in 94 countries to find solutions to poverty and injustice. It was certainly a worthy cause.

I thought my body could handle it without falling apart, and I had a "just finish" mentality. I had already run a standard 26-mile marathon, had completed a half-ironman, and biked across the entire United States. Even with those experiences behind me, I underestimated the challenges of the ultramarathon.

The day started nicely, but as luck would have it, Australia decided to have its hottest day in March in 70 years. As the temperature climbed over 100 degrees, my team and I started experiencing heat rashes over our legs. The

One of the restful moments that were few and far between during the 62 mile ultramarathon in Australia. Here we are taking a break to eat.

energy was sucked right out of me and I had not even hit the halfway point. When I finally did reach that milestone my feet were soaking wet. I stopped to check on them because they were wet beyond mere sweat. I found more blisters than I had ever seen in my life. They were popping as I ran and this is where most the wetness came from. Only 31 miles of rugged terrain left!

This is where strength of mind took over for a failing body. I attained a runners high and those endorphins let me make 12 additional miles while feeling pretty good. My feet were numb, and so I just ran, taking advantage of this moment. There were lots of walkers by that point, and they thought I was a little insane. And yes, they were probably right. What I found was that walking tensed my muscles severely and the running loosened me up. I was numb, running was shortening my time out there, and so I went all in.

Keep in mind this was a trail event, and not on paved roads. The final 13 miles (about a half-marathon in length) was beyond brutal. Ultra-endurance events are different from traditional races because you begin to hurt in unusual areas, like your neck and lower back. My body started reminding me of the pain I was in, and by nightfall it began to rain, changing the trail to mud that pooled over my badly blistered feet. At this point I felt like I was watching my own dreams and I started pinching myself to wake up. I became a little concerned when I could no longer even feel this because I knew my nerves were losing sensation. At the final rest stop I saw that many people were experiencing bodily shutdown. This was really frightening, as they were moaning, screaming, and throwing up uncontrollably. Endurance athletes really know how to have a good time!

How did the trail end? It would have been nice if it was a well-paved downward slope. But no, instead it was just the opposite—a steep climb. Thick fog settled in and I couldn't see more than 10 feet in front of me. That didn't matter so much because I was only focusing on one step at a time. I inched my way up, and every step felt like it took the endurance necessary for an entire marathon. The one bright spot was that the race organizers gave us a rope to hold on. This also gives you some idea of how steep it was too. I finally saw the finish line and I decided to cross it in style. Though I was delirious, nauseous, and covered in rashes and blisters, I cartwheeled over the line and into collapsed exhaustion.

I sent my mom an email when I was recovering and said this "was by far one of the most, if not the most, difficult challenge I have ever experienced. I was in so much pain that I felt like crying but did not have the energy! Words cannot describe how much pain I was in, it was unbearable." I really thought I needed one of those mechanical lifts to get me up and down stairs!

I hope the money we raised for Oxfam made a difference. I do know that the experience made a difference for me in what I learned about myself. I explained this to my mom afterwards in more positive terms than my previous email, "Fears and doubts can not stop me! Endurance events make me feel alive to know that my mind can take my body past what is thought possible."

I am reminding myself of this right now as I row. I am in pain, but these feelings will not stop me. They are impermanent. Endurance is a state of mind, and it will take over if my body cannot. I ended my email to my mom with this question: "Just ask yourself this: 'What would you do if you knew you could not fail? It doesn't have to be sporting events but any aspiration you hold.' You may just surprise yourself."

Day 19: If You Can't See Straight, Don't Change Direction

@KatieSpotz Tweet Log for Thursday, January 21, 2010	
9:33 PM	Another solid day for Katie as she steadily makes her way across the Atlantic. Can anything stop her?! [Sam]

What better way to end a long day of rowing than with an extended period of pure terror! At first I thought eight sharks were circling around my boat. The ferocity in which they were banging against it was remarkable. Upon closer inspection, though, these were actually large tuna. Who knew they were so big and powerful! Why must they keep banging into my boat? These, I promise you, would not fit in those Chicken of the Sea cans!

Other than this noise, my main problem is that I am expending more energy during the day than I am getting back at night. I put the blame for this squarely on the human body and its need for sleep. Mozart wrote, "When traveling in a carriage . . . or during the night when I cannot sleep; it is on such occasions that ideas flow best and most abundantly."[33] I should have brought Mozart on this ocean voyage with me. He would have had a lifetime of ideas out here, because no one is sleeping.

This question of why we sleep is not just something half-crazed ocean rowers dwell upon. Scientists do also, and they have still not pinpointed the exact reason that all humans need some form of daily hibernation. They have narrowed it down to several important theories. One is the inactivity theory which suggests that humans learned to sleep at night to keep them safe from other predators. The stiller one was, the greater chance of survival. Thus the sleepers were the safest, and able to procreate and pass on this sound sleeping trait.

A second theory is as a method of energy conservation. Our metabolism decreases significantly during sleep (as much as 10 percent) and therefore in societies where there is a competition for food, sleeping becomes a successful survival strategy.

A third theory is that sleep is restorative. Many studies point out that the body has a remarkable way of taking care of itself while asleep. That includes improving cognitive functions, tissue repair, muscle growth, protein synthesis, and the release of growth hormone.

Finally scientists have suggested a brain plasticity theory, meaning that the brain goes through developmental stages while asleep. Infants sleep between 13 and 14 hours a day, because their brains are going through such significant changes.[34]

When I read studies like this I hear myself saying, "Okay, I get it. I need to sleep. I want to sleep. And I can't sleep." An ocean rowboat is excellent for rowing but it fails at everything else. It is lousy as a kitchen, bathroom, bedroom, and living room. Aside from eating, the one thing on my mind after rowing 12 hours is sleep. I have mentioned this before, but it is the challenge that is not going away, and it looms larger each day (or night) that I fail to enter deep REM sleep.

After almost three weeks out here, I have not slept longer than three hours at a stretch, and I am lucky to get two hours. The interruptions are many: a bigger-than-average wave crashing over me, a flying fish thudding loudly on deck, the struggle to find a moderately comfortable position, the discomfort of sleeping in a hot, stuffy coffin like cabin, or the ringing of my traffic alarm. Why is it so hot? I cannot risk sleeping with the cabin door open because *Liv* would not right herself if she capsized. So when I need air, I have to wake up to get some.

The result is a constant state of exhaustion. I feel like I have crossed some unusual threshold where I am too tired to sleep. It is like my body is rejecting all my wise ancestors who programmed sleep into my body after millennia of natural selection. Now that I have completely obliterated my natural sleep cycle, and have passed through the realm of extreme sleep deprivation, I am in a state of intense insomnia.

Not only do my muscles and body suffer, so too does my mind. I have suggested that endurance is a state of mind. I am starting to wonder if insomnia is the mind's Achilles heel, or the critical chink in my mental armor. I am irritable. I am impatient. Overall my emotions are on a constant roller coaster. I am finding that small things that should be met with a shrug of my shoulders are enough to push me close to a complete breakdown.

Case in point: water in my continuously leaking hatch ruined a package with a bag of chocolates in them. My reaction? It was an instant explosion of tears and crying. In the back of my head a tiny voice said, "Katie, it was chocolate, not the death of a close friend. You still have a Twix." But the tears continued.

I did not think I was ever going to ever say this: "I feel like I want to quit." I cannot see the sunsets anymore. I cannot appreciate the wildlife. I sense that I have slipped off the edge of self-confidence into a pit of weakness, tiredness, and insecurity. There is my emergency beacon, the EPIRB. It seems to be tempting me to turn it on. Then I could just stop and be transported to a place where I could sleep.

This has been my thought for the past several hours. And then somewhere the voice of the Atlantic comes to me with its advice and lesson for today. The worst time to make a decision is when you are low. The time when you are most desperate is the time when you should avoid decision making the most. In times like these, close your eyes (sleep if you can) and stay the course. Desperation, depression, and exhaustion cloud my eyes like a thick impenetrable fog. I'll make decisions only when the big picture of life returns to my line of sight.

Day 20: Find a Room to Get Into the Zone

It was a tough day yesterday. I survived by not making a decision. And now I have hit a milestone that has really lifted my spirits—in fact, I have now reached 26W, or the quarter point. For the past couple weeks I have been focusing on 26W, about a fourth of the way to Cayenne. A fourth is not as significant as half, but most ocean rowers find this first leg to be the most difficult and thus worthy of a small celebration. Once I reach this milestone I want to do something like have an extra chocolate bar or two (or three), perhaps call home on the satellite phone, or maybe have a dance party. Can you have a party of one?

Remarkably, I had something of a welcoming party. I was rowing along, and less than a mile away from 26W, I spotted not one or two, but ten to fifteen dolphins! I dropped my oars, peered around the boat and was almost in disbelief, seeing so many dolphins surrounding me. For 20 minutes they swam around my boat, under my boat, and even jumped out of the water a few times doing flips and tricks—nothing short of amazing. And when they swam away, I began rowing, hoping they might stop by once again. Ten minutes later they did just that!

Despite this excitement, there is so much rowing still ahead of me. And as I look out at this infinite sea of blue, oddly, do you know what it reminds me of? The complete opposite of water—the desert.

Let me first start with a story about Thor Heyerdahl. He was the Norwegian who in 1947 sailed across the Pacific Ocean in his hand-built raft,

Kon-Tiki. He left from South America (the place where I am rowing to, though the opposite coast) and sailed west to the Tuamotu Islands. He wanted to prove that ancient peoples were capable of long sea voyages, and that their cultures mingled, so he made his dangerous 5,000-mile journey to do so. I am thinking about him today not because we share a passion for crossing oceans, but instead because of his appreciation for the beauty of the desert. "It is rarer," he wrote, "to find happiness in a man surrounded by the miracles of technology than among people living in the desert of the jungle and who by the standards set by our society would be considered destitute and out of touch."[35] In my opinion there is nothing wrong with modern technology itself (it is all in how it is used), but the desert is a place where I have experienced a unique perspective on life.

Let me tell you how I made this discovery.

Two months after I completed my Allegheny swim I felt compelled to go running. This did not mean a jog around the neighborhood or even a marathon. I wanted to go someplace barren and empty, so I selected the Colorado and Mojave deserts. In November 2008 I gathered some essential items, including a runner's three-wheeled baby stroller for my gear, and found a ride out to Yuma, Arizona. I charted a course that led me through the Sonoran Desert and into the Mojave Desert. I simply started running, all alone. For the next 10 days I averaged about 20 miles per day, but I never really knew for sure how far I ran because I only had maps, not a GPS tracking system. The extreme heat subsided as I gained elevation into the Mojave, and it got colder and colder at night. Once there was snow and frost, I ended it. I wanted to keep going but became concerned about hypothermia. Or maybe it was just a hatred of the cold. I went to the desert for heat, and certainly not snow! Either way, I packed up and returned home. Who knew that snow, and not heat, would end my desert run?

The journey was tremendous. As I ran I looked out into the nothingness and felt very much at home. I realize now that my attraction to the ocean is similar to what drew me to the desert. Obviously the ocean and desert are not barren places. Much life exists. Nevertheless the landscapes and waterscapes have an almost infinite sameness to them to the human eye. A bleak and barren landscape helps me to get into "the zone."

What does "the zone" mean for me? You hear athletes talking about this place when they reach a level of performance that seems directed by a sixth sense. Basketball players get into the zone when the basket feels so big to them that they cannot miss, no matter where they are shooting from, or who is guarding them. For me the zone is different. It is a meditative space in my mind with heightened focus and awareness. Deserts and oceans, enable me to attain this perspective easier than any other place on earth. Why? I am not exactly sure, but I think it is because there are no distractions, and it is a blank canvas for my thoughts.

I suppose I am in good company. I think of the Desert Fathers and Mothers, monks and nuns who escaped Egyptian civilization in the third century AD to live as hermits. They meditated alone in the desert for years at a time (though they had visitors), and while I think that is pretty remarkable, a lifetime in the desert is a bit much for me. I only needed ten days. I am an impermanent hermit.

What an experience it was sleeping under the stars at night (awesome), listening to wolves in the distance (terrifying), and feeling alone and strangely connected to the world (peaceful). But I was not alone the entire time. At one point I met a guy biking through the desert who showed me how to cook a raw cactus and eat it. It was not bad. Certainly not as good as a watermelon, but if you are hungry it does quite well. (Just remove the needles first!) I also ran into a man and wife who lived in a trailer. They took me in and we spent an evening together. I talked about my run and endurance adventures, and they discussed their spiritual views on life. They shared an idea that was very new to me at the time; the soul chooses the body it lives. If this is true, then I guess if I have a complaint with my parents I have no one to blame but myself, since I chose them!

What is the lesson that landscapes like the desert and ocean teach? Consider Virginia Woolf's book-length essay, A Room of One's Own. In 1929 she wrote about the need for women to find their own spaces from which to figure out their places in the world. Since she was a writer, she said she needed a "room of her own if she is to write fiction."[36] But the "room" is really more of a metaphor than a housing requirement. We all need a place

Me and my baby stroller, filled with camping gear and supplies, alone in the desert.

where we can find ourselves. In fact, if we do not find such a place, it can become very difficult to discover who we are. The room gives us the freedom to try, experience, fail, and succeed, all without the fear of judgment. We all need a room of our own to propel ourselves into the zone.

This is what drives some people to climb mountains, drive fast cars, surf gigantic waves, or skydive. Our rooms do not have to involve only extreme activities. A walk in the woods, a workout at the gym, a session on a yoga mat, a canoe down a stream, a run around the neighborhood, a coffee in a quiet café, or a book while lost in the library stacks all qualify too. There is no one right way to enter the zone. Take the scholar out of the library and stick her on a mountaintop and she might be too terrified to come close to a deeper sense of awareness. Or put a mountaineer into a library and she might feel nothing but boredom with the imposed silence. The point is, there is no one right room. The beauty of life is that there are an infinite number of rooms, but it becomes very difficult to propel yourself if you cannot find that space that satisfies your soul. When you find that room, it is a beautiful place to be.

Take some time to explore the various rooms of life, even ones you don't think you will like. There is always an exit, so you won't be trapped, and I think you will find the journey to be life changing in many unexpected ways. Once you find a room that resonates with you, you will find access to your own zone.

Think about the "rooms" you have explored in your life. Where were places you felt more energy, unexpected calmness, or elevated awareness? Maybe these were places you just passed through and never gave yourself time to experience fully. Perhaps they are places you have always wanted to explore. Either way, you might find that opening an old door or walking through a new one will propel you into a zone you never thought you could reach.

Day 21: The Present is Enough

I just finished a 10-hour row, and unlike a long day at the office, there is no going home at the end of my day. There is no going anywhere, and this can be frustrating because I am *not* rowing for 14 hours. While there are some chores and housekeeping to do here on *Liv*, I do have a lot of time to fill, especially because it is still so hard to sleep. Often my mind slips into an empty space, blankness, nothingness, particularly as night overtakes the ocean. I felt like a meditating zombie, if there is such a creature.

I am sitting here right now, bobbing on the dark waters, listening to the same sounds someone would hear if they were lost at sea. There is the ambient noise of the waves caressing the boat and collapsing in on themselves nearby. The wind exerts a gentle touch on my body. Fish unexpectedly fly out of the water, and three weeks into my journey they still startle me. And here I am, done with my rowing, finished eating and cleaning, looking at the stars and the moon, rocking in my boat, unable to sleep, and thinking.

I am thinking about the past, my endurance challenges, and the importance of propelling myself in life, against all odds. In particular I am thinking about the ninth day of my Allegheny swim, because it was on that day that I had an unusual moment of insight, where I understood with perfect clarity my place in life. I realized two things: "The present is enough" and "What you become is more important than what you achieve." In my blog, I wrote about it like this:[37]

> *I am loving this challenge. I enjoy feeling against all odds. The swimming requires much focus and is mentally intense. I'm constantly adjusting myself to stay on course with the winding river. The water is cloudy so I have no sort of distraction. No scenery to view or people to chat with to make it mentally easier while swimming.*
>
> *Favorite moment of the day was feeling that the present is enough. More than enough. There is so much richness in our present moment. I have a habit of investing so much energy into the future that I miss out on now. But today I felt at peace with now, not constantly seeking more, more, more. That is one aspect that draws me to endurance. I also enjoy endurance events because I feel I gain a better understanding of change. Or acceptance of change. With endurance, your body and mind are going through rapid change. Almost every day I am reaching a strong high point and strong low point. But I learn it is easier for me to accept those changes instead of fight them. By learning to accept change in endurance events I feel I learn to carry that attitude throughout my life.*
>
> *What I become is more important than what I achieve.*

Sitting here now, alone on my boat, I could be worried about the future, or long to change something in my past. But I am not doing that. The present is enough for me. It has to be. We cannot change the past, no matter how much we sometimes live in it. The future is eternally out of our reach. The only thing we have is the present moment, and therefore it must always be enough. All we need to do is come to this realization, wake up to it, and remind ourselves it is true.

This reminds me of an ancient Zen story about two monks walking in silence from one village to another. They reached a river that was higher and swifter than usual and next to it was a beautiful young woman who was unable to cross on her own. She politely asked if one of them could help her. The younger monk said, "Absolutely not. I have taken a vow not to touch a woman." Then, with compassion in his heart, the older monk said, "Come. Climb upon my back, and I will take you across." On the other side, he placed her on the ground, she thanked him, and the two monks went on their way. With each step the younger monk continued to dwell upon what happened and he became angrier and angrier. Many hours later the two monks arrived at the monastery, and the younger one could hold his silence no longer. He shouted: "How could you touch that woman?" The older monk smiled and said, "She needed my help. I set her down hours ago. You are the one still carrying her."

> Don't let yesterday use up too much of today.
> Don't let today be focused solely on tomorrow.
> *The present is enough.*

That brings me to my second insight. I understand now the central purpose for my life, and it is not to achieve things. This, I know, sounds very counterintuitive in the context of a successful life. Nevertheless, it is still quite true. My purpose is not to swim a river, bike across a country, run through a desert, or even row across the ocean. My purpose is not to *achieve*, but to *become*. I want to *become* someone who makes a difference in the lives of others in the world. I want to *become* someone I am proud to be. The achievements will have occurred as a by-product of that becoming. If you focus only on the achievements, you might not like the person you become along the way.

Trappist monk Thomas Merton wrote, "Do not depend on the hope of results. . . . Concentrate not on the results but on the value, the rightness, the truth of the work itself."[38] And to continue his thoughts from my perspective, when you orient your life towards valuable and true work, then you begin to reach your human potential, and become someone who you will want to be.

To call these mere "lessons" does not do them justice for me. They are the foundation stones upon which I am now building my life. I am living in the present as fully as I can. This does not mean that I ignore planning for the future. But I do so with the goal of *becoming* and not achieving.

Part Two: Russian Roulette

For me it was very difficult to be supportive of Katie at first. I guess I was being selfish by wanting her safe first and foremost. I have later realized it is not my place to dictate Katie's life . . . I have my own for that.

My only job for now is to pray that the angels watch over her.

(Email from Mary Spotz, Katie's mom, to Kit Williams, on the second day of her row.)

Day 22: Wake Up to Water

I feel as if I am starting a new leg of my voyage now. I have completed three weeks on the ocean, and I am not sure what the future holds. As I said yesterday, I am living in the now. It seems as if, up to this point in the row, my thoughts were all focused upon myself. Introspection is important; it serves as a foundation as we propel ourselves through life. However, we cannot dwell on ourselves too long. I am an ongoing work in progress (hopefully it had progress!). I doubt I am in any danger of becoming Narcissus, who stared at his own reflection in water so intently that he drowned (I have seen a lot of water lately, though). But now I am ready to look outside myself and at the world.

In preparation I am going to whisper softly the nursery rhyme whose words we have heard so often we tend to ignore and dismiss them as childish:

> Row, row, row your boat,
> Gently down the stream.
> Merrily, merrily, merrily, merrily,
> Life is but a dream.

That last line was always the part that perplexed me most when I was a kid: "Life is but a dream." What does that mean? If it is, then how can we awaken from the dream, and enter into reality?

There is a classic film called *Joe Versus the Volcano*. In it Tom Hanks and Meg Ryan find themselves in many odd situations, one of which is being stranded in the middle of the ocean (and you wonder why it's on my mind). Early in the film, Meg Ryan's character makes this observation: "My father says that almost the whole world is asleep. Everybody you know. Everybody you see. Everybody you talk to. He says that only a few people are awake and they live in a state of constant total amazement."

It's time to wake up. Looking around me on the ocean tonight, under the stars that are twinkling bright, and below at the moon glistening white off the surface of the dark Atlantic, I am in total amazement. I certainly make no claims that I am truly awake, but I am in amazement.

From the vastness of the ocean to the singularity of a water drop . . .

I am thinking about a Zen koan, "A Drop of Water." Let me paraphrase it like this. Gisan, a Zen master was enjoying a very hot bath. He called to his young student and told him he needed a pail of cool water to mix in with the hot. The student did as asked, and after filling the tub to the brim, he had some water left in the pail. Without thinking he dumped the remaining water onto the ground. This greatly angered Master Gisan and he said: "Why didn't you give the rest of the water to the plants? What right have you to waste even a drop of water in this temple?"[39] It was at that moment that the young student understood something essential about nature and his relationship to it. He instantly changed his name to Tekisui, which literally means a "drop of water."

Remember the Proust quote I wrote on the inside of *Liv* before I left Dakar? "A real voyage of discovery lies not in finding new landscapes, but in having new eyes." It *is* all about seeing, and that simplistic homonym is everywhere I look these days: *The sea enables me to see.* The ocean is providing me with a book of life lessons. My vision is far from perfect, but what is apparent to me now is something Tekisui realized so profoundly that he changed his name. A drop of water changes everything, and given a change, it can awaken you. This drop of water is the lesson for today. It is something so small, and yet so profound. It is a finite resource and nearly a billion people do not have easy access to a single, disease-free drop. It has the power to change the world. That must be my focus now, though I think I will keep my name.

You can see the Proust quote written on my cabin wall, above my map.

Day 23: Take a Leap of Faith into the Unknown

@KatieSpotz Tweet Log for Monday, January 25, 2010	
4:52 AM	Note to self—check rowing shoes before slipping my feet in. Surprised by a dead fish!
2:39 PM	No swimming for me today. Saw a shark fin four times. Must have liked my music.
8:11 PM	Can anyone explain what these glowing specks in the water are? Every night I see them and have no clue what they are!

An email from Rick, my weather support, said I should expect isolated rain showers and increasing wind speed and wave heights. They are two to four feet now but should be swelling to seven feet soon.[40] A little rain sounds good actually, and it will be a nice opportunity to de-salt my body.

As I slowly row further and further away from civilization, I am feeling a little smaller each day than the day before. Today I am feeling more isolated than usual for some reason. Thankfully I am not "lost" and can contact others in an emergency situation. But I am a needle in a haystack—or maybe I should change that saying to a "rowboat in the middle of the ocean." I am not sure which one would actually be harder to find!

Despite the isolation, I feel a calm sense of security and even coziness here on *Liv*. I know I have all the essentials I need to survive out here for a long time. I have plenty of food (and chocolate), and really an infinite supply of water, as long as my solar panels and desalinator keep working.[41] I know my boat can withstand dangerous storms, and I'm starting to trust that I am physically and mentally prepared for them as well. That frees my mind to think about what I am here for—water.

Everything starts with water. Without it, there is no beginning to life on earth nor any continuation for the creatures currently inhabiting our planet. A lack of water means extinction. This seems obvious, but I had to travel halfway around the world to make the life-changing realization that much of the world's population struggles to get access to clean water. How did the world's water crisis did became a central part of my life? The story has quite an ironic twist.

I was born near Cleveland, Ohio, and people there (perhaps a little envious of the warmer seaboard climates) refer to their location on Lake Erie as the "North Coast." The big difference, other than the weather, is that the eastern and western coasts border saltwater oceans, and Lake Erie, minus the concerns about pollution, contains fresh water. It is one of the five interconnected Great Lakes, which account for 20 percent of all the fresh water in the entire world. The Great Lakes—Huron, Ontario, Michigan, Erie, and Superior (there's a useful acronym HOMES to remember)—represent the largest surface system of fresh water on Earth. They are second only to the polar ice caps (which are a challenge to drink). And yet the significance of fresh water, and the crisis for so many who lack it, did not dawn on me until I went to Australia.

Time for another Australia story!

Perhaps I was blinded to these problems by the sheer abundance of fresh water while growing up. There was always a giant lake, so big I could not see the other side, just around the corner or over the hill. Travel north a few miles from wherever I was growing up, and there was Lake Erie.

So I was 19 in Ohio, and I was not finding college as intellectually satisfying as I had hoped. I wanted to pursue something in the area of environmental science but I had trouble relating what I was learning in the classroom to a potential career after graduation. At 16 I started a two-year college program at Lakeland Community College, and then I went to Kent State University for a year. I wanted my third year to be outside Ohio, and my first semester exchange was at California State University. For my second semester exchange, Germany and Australia beckoned.

I could not make up my mind which country I wanted to study in. I could earn the necessary qualifications to teach English as a foreign language in Germany, and I thought it would be a passport to travel the world. Australia, however, called to me on a more personal level. Yes, it had great educational opportunities too, but more than that I had always just wanted to visit this "land down under." Ever since I had an Australian pen pal as a child, I had dreamed of living there. I would rip her letters open with feverish excitement when they arrived, dying to see the pictures of koalas and kangaroos she sent. I loved how she called her mom "mum."

For several weeks I debated about these two destinations, and as often happens in my life, an external clue opened my eyes. In this case though, it was my ears. It was the day my forms needed to be submitted, and if I didn't decide then, I would have to wait another year to travel outside the country. That morning I woke up and turned on the radio. This wasn't something I would typically do. I think I did it hoping to fill my head with anything but the voices of panic because I hadn't yet made a decision. The first song on the radio for the day? "Land Down Under" by Men at Work. The song made the decision for me.

Fast forward to my arrival in Melbourne, Australia, where I went to begin the environmental science program at Deakin University.

There are words in the English language that define an extreme and sudden moment of clarity and insight. Inventors call it the "eureka moment." Artists and philosophers might have "an epiphany." Sometimes I just say "aha," but perhaps a more appropriate term is a "sea change." I had one of those moments at Deakin University while I was sitting in a seminar. The professor made the startling claim, "The wars of the future will be fought over water."[42] In fact, she said, "In some countries this is already happening." This shocked me.

She was not talking about fighting *on* water, as pirates and navies have been doing for centuries. This professor was talking about wars fought *over* access to fresh water. The idea struck me like a lightning bolt. The survival of the human race depended upon access to water, something I had always assumed was a given. But what if it was not? I soon learned about the world water crisis, and as the days went on, I knew my future would be deeply entwined with this issue.

Although this was an immediate shock that resonated with me, I did not know quite how to respond at first. I relate it to Elisabeth Kübler-Ross' "stages of death." First I was in denial. Then this changed into anger, an emotion that stayed with me for a while. I skipped over bargaining and depression and jumped right into acceptance. For me, acceptance meant action.

What could I contribute though? I certainly did not have the wealth to be a philanthropist. I was not an engineer who could build wells or drill holes. I realized what I had was the ability to raise awareness. One in eight people on Earth lacks clean drinking water. Sadly their voices are not being heard. I was going to amplify them and share their struggles, and if I could raise awareness and money to bring them relief, then I knew I would begin to fulfill one of my purposes on this planet.

My lesson today is this—rarely can you plan the future in its entirety. Sometimes you have to take a leap of faith into the unknown. One of my beliefs is that there is a plan in place for us, and we get to discover it a little bit at a time. At that point in my life the veil over my future parted a bit. I didn't know how I was going to raise awareness. I thought at times that the problem was too big for me to make much of a difference. I had doubts that I could successfully give speeches that would rouse people to action. While there were all of these "no" reasons facing me, I knew I simply needed to tune them out, and tune in to that hazy idea that I had to do something. I was going to take a leap of faith, hoping the haze would fade into clarity. Sometimes in life you just have to jump in. The unknown awaited me, and I was eager to meet it.

I just had no idea at the time what I was jumping in to. I could not have imagined it was going to be the middle of the Atlantic Ocean! But here I am, and the leap of faith has made me a more committed believer in this cause.

Day 24: Playing Russian Roulette with Water

@KatieSpotz Tweet Log for Tuesday, January 26, 2010	
11:10 AM	You know you are getting a bit spoiled when anything below 80 degrees starts to feel cold. Today is one of the few cool and overcast days.
6:53 PM	Reached a third of the way across. Looks shockingly like yesterday and the day before. No surprises there!

Prepare for a sobering discussion today. As they say in television, "Parental discretion advised." I know this contrasts sharply with the beautiful skies above and the blue ocean around me right now. Forgive me for a moment, but I need to be blunter than I usually am about the water crisis we are facing. Sometimes we need to stare a problem right between the eyes, or even directly down the barrel of the gun. Though chilling, that is what I want to do right now.

Water is a conduit for life, but it is also a devastating and efficient gateway for death and disease. This is an extremely troubling contradiction of human existence and we so often overlook it in the developed world. It is a given that every day we need to consume a great quantity of water. Basic estimates are that we need 2.4 liters of it to regulate our temperatures, protect our nervous systems, cushion our joints, and eliminate waste from our bodies.[43] Have you ever had an extended time in your life when you had to consciously think and plan about how you would get water? I know I have not.

We need a lot of water, and yet in many communities throughout the world, taking a drink of water is literally like playing Russian Roulette. This is by no means a Las Vegas wheel of chance. Instead Russian Roulette is a lethal game (which should never, EVER be played) that involves taking an empty revolver, placing one round in a chamber, spinning it, closing it, putting the barrel in your mouth, and pulling the trigger. If the revolver holds eight chambers, then you have a one in eight chance of dying.

This is a horrific idea that I shudder even to consider. However, imagine playing this game every day, every time you took a drink of water. This is the reality for millions of people because the water they struggle to find is not life-giving, but it is, on the contrary, as lethal as a loaded gun pointed to the head. This is not hyperbole.

Consider these facts. Eighty percent of all disease in this world is caused by unsafe water and poor sanitation. In other words, dirty water kills more people each year than guns, knives, and automobiles combined. You can take this even further. Add up all forms of violence that kill people, and these still do not equal the death tolls caused by unsafe water.[44] Contaminated water is so dangerous because it transmits a variety of diseases, including cholera, dysentery, hepatitis A, typhoid, polio, and diarrhea. Remarkably, the World Health Organization (WHO) estimates every year 360,000 children *under the age of five* could be spared from horribly painful deaths due to diarrhea if we began to address key risk factors.[45] This is preventable. As you can see, the comparison between drinking water and playing Russian Roulette is not so farfetched. In some communities, children would have better odds playing the game than drinking the water. In fact, in some cultures, parents resist naming their children before the age of five because so many of them die.

Here are more devastating facts:[46]

- 1.8 billion people use a daily water source that is contaminated with feces.

- 840,000 deaths occur each year due to unsafe water and poor sanitation.
- Each year waterborne diseases and improper sanitation claim **MORE** deaths than wars.
- 41 children under the age of five die *every hour* from diarrhea contracted from contaminated water.[47]
- 90 percent of the 30,000 deaths that occur every week from unsafe water and unhygienic living conditions are children under five years old.

I know the facts well and they still astound and confound me. I mean, how do you visualize 840,000 people? Think about a giant football stadium, on the night of a big game, with standing room only. The Ohio State Buckeyes' stadium holds almost 105,000 people and they fill it for every one of their home games each year, which is typically seven games. That means more people die from water and improper sanitation each year than attend these games. It is a horrific tragedy on a very large scale.

Or imagine this. Approximately 50 kids can sit in a standard school bus. Line up about 7,000 school buses and pack them with children. That is how many under the age 5 die each year from water. Those buses would stretch, end to end, about 66 miles. Consider how much media attention occurs when a single bus crashes in the United States. How much media attention is now given to 66 miles of buses of children dying from water? Not nearly enough.

Infrastructure problems further complicate this situation. For example, 50 percent of all schools in the world do not have access to clean water. Something as simple as regular hand washing could eliminate 35 percent of diarrheal cases. But, hand washing requires water. If I were born in certain places in India, Kenya, or Malawi, I would have to walk four miles from my home just to get water. And I would have to be prepared to wait a long time once I got there because the lines are often up to eight hours in length. Would you use that precious water for drinking or washing your hands?

The problem is not just one of time, it is also one of incredible energy expenditure. Walking four miles to get water is just one problem. Return-

Here are some of the students I met in Kenya. Though the water jug is close at hand, will the contents make them sick?

ing home with that water means carrying containers that can easily weigh 40 pounds. And keep in mind that this water is not guaranteed to be safe. The water is visibly dirty at best, and invisibly disease-carrying at worst. People willingly play Russian Roulette with this water they have spent so much time and energy to obtain, because the alternative is death. Imagine giving your child a drink of water that you know has a real chance of killing him or her. And imagine having no other choice.

I said at the start to prepare for a sobering discussion today. That is what I have tried to offer. And there is no lesson associated with this, because the idea of one "teachable moment" seems unnecessary, given this devastating situation. Despite—or maybe because of—the horrors I have described, this grim situation inspires me to take action. The deaths haunt me. The reality is frightening. To equate a child taking a sip of water with him or her playing Russian Roulette is horrifying. And yet that is just part of an average day in the lives of far, far too many children and adults in our world today.

Day 25: Water Changes Everything

@KatieSpotz Tweet Log for Wednesday, January 27, 2010	
9:20 AM	Just learned I am losing my ability to stand the hard way! Too much rowing and not enough walking for my leg muscles these days

I thought I would share a little secret with you today that only I and about a million sea creatures know. I have been rowing entirely naked. Certainly I have never done that before, but I have read that other ocean rowers shed clothes not because they are exhibitionists, but for purely practical purposes. And that practical reason is salt. It is not just the water that is everywhere. The salt is too. Just a few days into the row my comfortable clothing became stiff and cardboard-like from salt saturation. This made the constant and repetitious rowing seriously irritate my skin. Therefore, it was a no-brainer. Off came the clothes.

This is something I avoided entirely while training on the fresh water of Lake Erie. Now I feel like I am like a peanut in some ways, being roasted under the sun and salted. The salt clings to me everywhere, even my eyebrows, and my hair has been transformed into some type of frightening crystalized creature with a will of its own. What is worse is that salt stings when it gets into cuts and abrasions, and I have so many of these "war wounds"—or shall I call them "row wounds?" The salt is not the friend of these cuts because it ensures that they stay raw and susceptible to water reopening them.

These are my water issues for today. They are comparatively minor. On an infinitely more serious level, I think about how others around the world struggle to find clean drinking water. They experience something far worse than salt irritations on the skin or stiffened clothing. When your existence is defined by the constant search to find clean water, each day is a struggle for survival.

It may go without saying, but water is the foundation of life. Consider Maslow's famous hierarchy of needs. This is the triangle of needs arranged in order of importance for survival. At the bottom are the physiological needs, which includes water. At the top of the triangle is "self-actualization." How many of us have the luxury to pursue goals for the purpose of self-fulfillment? Perhaps we take classes to further our educations. Or maybe we plan a vacation. These activities are terrific and so vital to enjoying life. But many people are struggling, on a daily basis, just to secure their basic survival needs. This makes me ask, "What can I do to help move them up in the triangle?"

The proximity to water also relates to the second rung from the bottom on Maslow's triangle—safety. Women and children in Africa spend many hours each day walking to retrieve water, and their personal safety is often in jeopardy along the way. Therefore, the secondary threats presented by the lack of water are significant and often hidden from outside onlookers. When you add fear to a struggle for water, life can quickly become unbearable from a physical and mental perspective.

The lesson for today is simply this: "Water changes everything."[48] It is not only a daily necessity for individual survival. Water is the bedrock of community itself. According to Scott Harrison, the founder of charity:water, "Clean water gives children the opportunity to attend school and get an education. With education, communities are able to raise up strong leaders, making it possible to break the cycle of poverty and allowing future generations to improve their quality of life."[49]

So when I get a little down on myself, I reflect on this world crisis. It can be depressing, certainly, but spun in a positive way, it inspires me to act! Knowledge of the crisis helps me to keep my life and my struggles in perspective, and provides me incentive to just keep rowing.

Day 26: Find a "Charles" to Regain Your Faith

@KatieSpotz Tweet Log for Thursday, January 28, 2010

| 6:23 AM | Today my patience is making up for my lack of having "big guns". Steady as we go… |

It has been one of those days where my entire focus has been rowing. I have not even seen a ship in several days. However, I do have some companions. Remarkably there have been birds flying overhead for almost my entire journey. It took me a little while to figure out the reason that they liked to circle me (thankfully they are not vultures awaiting my demise!). At first I thought they were attracted to the bright yellow *Liv*. But no, they follow not for aesthetics but because they are hungry. I have so many fish that take shelter under my hull that these schools are sitting ducks, and the easy meal has attracted the birds. They patiently circle around me and when one fish gets too close to the surface, the bird dive-bombs and snatches it. I do not mind the birds thinning them out a bit, especially the flying fish, because I typically have several lying dead in the cockpit after I attempt to sleep through the night.

The more I reflect on these groups of fish, I realize their schools are communities of protection for them. If a fish swimming alone encountered a predator, he would become its next meal, no questions asked. If a fish encountered a predator when he was with a thousand of his schoolmates he has much better odds of survival.

Ironically, the more I look at the ocean, the more clearly I see the lives of people and the needs of communities at home. I have talked about my main reason for being out here, rowing for water, to gain awareness of the water crisis, and to raise funds for it. It was really important for me to see exactly the communities my efforts were to benefit. So I took a month-long trip to Kenya. Now chances are, you've heard a little bit about Kenya. You might have seen pictures of its stunning wildlife or watched the amazing world-class Kenyan runners. Of course, I saw all that. I met a man who ran a marathon every day. He was wearing flip flops. And I saw lions and zebra so close that I could hear them inhale and exhale. It was amazing.

To be honest, for most of my month in Kenya, I was completely overwhelmed. I felt smaller then than I do now out here alone in the ocean. I saw sicknesses that wouldn't go away, mountains of trash that were so "normal" that kids played in them, and homes with mud floors that were unsafe even to breathe in. I felt like there was nothing I could possibly do to help. In Kenya I lost confidence that I could make a significant impact. I wanted to see it all change—every stomach full, every hospital bed empty, and every drop of water clean. I knew the need was there but I felt like it was just too big, and I was too small and insignificant.

One boy named Charles changed all that and gave me a glimmer of hope. Late one day I was heading home from the fields in Kenya, wallowing a bit in my hopelessness. Remarkably, I heard some laughter. I couldn't imagine what would make someone who faced such struggles of daily living so happy and excited. I was so intrigued by these sounds of joy that I rushed over to see what was going on. I then saw Charles, and the objects that elicited his delight were rusted nails, bottle caps, and a few wires. To most, trash. To him, treasure.

Charles and all his friends had turned these seemingly useless materials into their very own toys. Charles had created a truck, and pride and joy radiated from his eyes. With this one moment, I regained my faith.

Here is a beautifully smiling Charles, and the imaginative toys that he and his friends constructed from trash.

My eyes opened and hope returned. When these kids didn't have soccer balls, they made them from plastic bags. Girls constructed necklaces and dolls from strings and other "useless" trash. Although they possessed nothing of material value, their spirits and imaginations transformed their reality into, for a moment, the excitement of an American child on Christmas morning.

These kids found strength in being together and in inspiring each other to make something from nothing. Imagine what they could do if they had real toys, homes, books, schools, and clean water. "Everything you can imagine is real," Pablo Picasso said.[50] Charles and his friends imagined real toys, and created real laughter in a place that would bring most people to helpless tears. Charles has helped me imagine a way to do something to help. Charles' face is a beacon of hope that reminds me that even if I can assist just one child with my row, a gift of immeasurable worth will be given, and received.

And so today I row surrounded by these schools of fish, symbolizing Charles and his "school" and the community among the trash piles. The lesson is that we all lose faith in our beliefs, dreams, and causes from time to time in life. It is natural to experience periods of desolation. Therefore, we all need a "Charles" who will be that inspiration and helping hand; a person who can recalibrate our minds, and refocus our bodies towards the direction of the greater good. A "Charles" is the consolation in the dark night of desolation.

Day 27: WASH Your Hands

@KatieSpotz Tweet Log for Friday, January 29, 2010

| 2:36 PM | Awkward, but it works. First time using the solar shower and enjoying one of the few moments of being squeaky clean. |

Salt is everywhere, and though it is a constant nuisance, living with it these past weeks has made my solar shower today feel so nice. It is such an unusual sensation not to have my body and hair encrusted in salt. Being squeaky clean is a feeling I forgot several weeks ago. Even though my boat rocked as the weak stream of water flowed down over me, I imagined I was in a comfortable hotel somewhere recuperating after a long run. I have a pretty good imagination, but this was a stretch even for me. When it was done though, I had a moment of relaxation like I have not felt in many days.

I know that even though I call this shower system "awkward," in reality it is far more efficient and simple to get myself cleaned off here than it is for many people in the world. When we think about the global water crisis we sometimes only see it as a problem of clean drinking water. However, water is essential for helping to wash bacteria off our hands. When drinking water is scarce, it is even rarer to have the luxury of washing your hands after going to the bathroom or before a meal. I certainly saw this firsthand in Kenya, and the health impact of the sanitation crisis is devastating.

Students in Ethiopia stand behind a H2O for Life banner after the completion of a water, sanitation, and hygiene project that will make their lives much safer and healthier.

The Centers for Disease Control and Prevention (CDC), as well as other clean water organizations, often lump together water projects under the acronym WASH. This stands for <u>WA</u>ter, <u>S</u>anitation, and <u>H</u>ygiene. They use some very strong words when equating hygiene and sanitation with access to water, saying it is a "human right, not a privilege."

The good news is that the numbers of people lacking the right to water are decreasing in some parts of the world. That said, 780 million people still lack access to a source of "improved water," which is a piped household water connection, a public standpipe, a borehole, a protected dug well, a protected spring, or rainwater collection. These 780 million people are forced to drink from unprotected wells which are often contaminated with fecal matter and other waste runoff, or they have to rely on surface water from rivers, lakes, ponds, or streams, which typically have high bacteria contents.

This is not just a drinking issue, but also sanitation problem. The World Health Organization and UNICEF found that only 63 percent of the world has improved sanitation facilities. These are defined as a flush toilet/ latrine, a composting toilet, or a pit latrine with a slab. In Africa only 30 percent of the population has access to these improved facilities. In total, 2.5 billion worldwide people do not have improved sanitation, which means they have to use a hanging or bucket latrine, or their only option is simply, as the CDC describes it, "open defecation in fields, forests, bushes, bodies of water, or other open spaces."[51]

As I said yesterday, everyone needs to find a "Charles" to elevate their faith. Despite these very depressing statistics there is hope out there. Sanitation alone can reduce water-related deaths by 37.5 percent.[52] Simple hand washing can reduce water-related deaths by 35 percent.[53] There are organizations in the United States that partner with schools in water-deprived areas to develop the infrastructure required to dramatically improve the sanitation facilities.

The remarkable thing is that the cost to do this is not extravagant. Here is an example. For less than $2,500, H2O for Life can make a significant improvement at a specific school that needs help. This organization makes a point of covering all three of the WASH areas, supporting projects that benefit water, sanitation, and hygiene. The list of open school projects changes all the time. For example, currently the Mzomtsha School has 200 children (100 boys and 100 girls) attending a facility with significant water and hygiene deficiencies. What will $2,500 do for this school? It will provide the following:

- Construction of additional water tanks, including stands and taps.
- Construction of splash pads to existing tanks and soakaways at all tap positions.
- Supply of water to existing toilet facilities.
- Rehabilitation of existing toilet facilities.
- Reduction of danger to learners through signage and the backfilling, compacting and concrete casting of unused pit holes.
- Training on health, hygiene operations, and maintenance.

When I told this to Mark, my co-author, he said, "Wow, I spend that much money on a vacation to Disney with my family. What is more important in life, yet another trip to see Mickey Mouse for my three kids, or sharing that money with 200 students in Africa to provide them with safe water facilities, and undoubtedly saving lives?" He is still going to take his family on trips, but he (and his social justice group, Just Faith) adopted the Mzomtsha School through H2O for Life. They surpassed their fundraising

Here I am giving charity rowboat rides at the Just Faith Walk for Water which raised funds for the Mzomtsha School in South Africa. Thanks to my co-author, Mark Bowles (standing in the water), for maneuvering me to the dock and the helpful shove-offs.

goals for WASH projects at this school by holding a community lecture and sponsoring a walk for water.

The lesson for today is this. We so often hear the phrase "Wash your hands before a meal" here in the United States. We constantly tell our kids, "Wash your hands after using the bathroom." There is a sign in most every restaurant bathroom for employees to wash their hands before returning to work. The reminders are necessary because we often consider this task an "inconvenience." And yet there is always an improved sanitation facility right around the corner or in the next room.

Take a moment and imagine not having *one* of these facilities in your *entire* city or town. What would that mean for your health and your family's well-being? When you do, the simple act of washing your hands will never be the same again. I am not suggesting that you never go to Disney, or that you feel guilty if you do. Appreciate the amazing standard of living that we have become accustomed to in the United States, and look for ways to raise awareness (or funding) to those who are literally unable to wash their hands.

Day 28: Don't Poop Where You Eat

I have heard that one of the most frequently asked questions of astronauts is how they go to the bathroom in space.[54] I can believe it because before I left I was often asked how I planned to relieve myself on my ocean row. Let me tell you, it is quite glamorous. I will not share pictures of this, but I assure you I do not have a fancy lavatory with deodorizing disks, automatic flushers, hot and cold running water, antibacterial soap, fresh towels, and a smartly-dressed attendant. On the contrary. I am simply using a bucket. That alone is a challenge, but remember that the bucket is a moving target. Yes, that is as fun, and challenging, as it seems. And I assume you sense my dark sarcasm here!

This is not merely an inconvenient aspect of rowing for months on a tiny boat. It is actually a health hazard. Human feces contains bacteria, and so I must be constantly vigilant to disinfect any waste that spills when an errant wave catches me unaware. Getting this bacteria into my food or water supply could be deadly. I learned very quickly to always check the direction of the wind before dumping my bucket overboard. That is a mistake you only make once! This is one of the challenges I will have to endure for roughly 70 days. For many people throughout the world, this is a way of life. And for far too many, poor sanitation is their cause of death.

Sanitation has been an ongoing public health concern throughout history, as John Duffy eloquently wrote in his book *The Sanitarians: A History of American Public Health*.[55] Take for example the Civil War, fought in the United States between 1861 and 1865. To date, more Americans died in this war than in any other conflict. On average, more than 500 soldiers died per day, and by the war's end 620,000 lay dead. Most people think these soldiers died on the battlefield, but in reality two out of every three deaths occurred from disease, typically from poor sanitation.[56]

Though poor sanitation is a historical topic for the United States, it is still the reality for much of the world today. I want to repeat something I have said before because it is important enough to discuss again. Roughly 2.5 billion people do not have improved sanitation sources, and without a latrine, people have no choice but to defecate in open water, fields, or forests.

This sounds horrible, but do you know what? It tastes even worse.

And that is exactly what happens. People are tasting it, especially in Africa. Latrines are important because they prevent human excrement from flowing into the sources of drinking water. No invention has saved more lives than the toilet. This is not the most exciting history to talk about but, it is quite true.

The flush toilet is a relatively recent component of modern life, and it is now indispensable for those who have it. Though invented in 1596 it did not become widespread until the mid-nineteenth-century.[57] Prior to this people relieved themselves in outhouses, chamber pots, holes, or directly on the ground. I saw a lot of this in Kenya, though not too many people had fancy chamber pots. Rolls of toilet paper did not become popular until 1902 (imagine living without it!). And as many people like to joke, Thomas Crapper played an important role in this history. Although he did not invent the toilet, he was a prominent London plumber in the late nineteenth-century who installed them in royal palaces.[58] Of course his name became synonymous with them.

Though we often do not appreciate how lucky we are to have these conveniences, the World Toilet Organization does attempt to raise awareness about the many people who do not have this luxury. In 2013 the United

Nations General Assembly established World Toilet Day, recognized every November 19, to bring attention to this problem.[59] Though I applaud them for this, I personally think this is more than a one-day-a-year issue.

Why is this a *crisis* now and not a mere *inconvenience*? Of the 2.5 billion people without improved sanitation sources, 1 billion of them defecate in the open. This is not only demoralizing in terms of human dignity, but also a danger to human safety. Women and girls in these situations often refuse to relieve themselves during the day because there is no privacy. Many of them stop going to school as soon as they start menstruating. The sanitation issue effects both men and women. More than 80% of sewage in developing countries is untreated and channeled to rivers, lakes, and coastal areas. These are the same places that people go to gather their drinking water.

My lesson title today is to simply not poop where you eat. While this is good advice, and something that we in the United States do without thinking, my point is, one billion people on Earth have no choice. Where they go to the bathroom is where there also go to eat and drink. The result is a loss of dignity and the increase of disease and death.

I could have called my adventure on the Atlantic, *Row for Sanitation*, instead of *Row for Water*. Both are intrinsically intertwined. But rowing for sanitation and hygiene is simply not as pleasant to talk about as rowing for water. The bottom line is that sanitation projects are vital and we need to fund them throughout the world. Poor sanitation kills children and adults every day in the twenty-first century—just as it did our own Civil War soldiers in the nineteenth century. It is within our power to end this public health catastrophe.

Day 29: Put Your Money Where Your Mouth Is

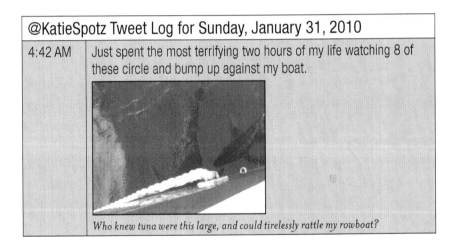

Who knew tuna were this large, and could tirelessly rattle my rowboat?

I need to do something to take my mind off of the horrifying sound of these fish that seem to have a personal vendetta against my boat. Whenever I hear something bump against my boat, my mind jumps to "shark!" This is always the case, whether it is flying fish, a sea turtle, or these giant tuna. What I would like to do is get some revenge by eating them! Fresh fish over a fire sounds delicious. But I have something even better than tuna . . . chocolate!

Hmmm . . . maybe that's why the tuna are banging against my boat so persistently. They want my chocolate. Well, it is all mine! Here is another crazy thought about those darn tuna. Maybe they think I am a giant piñata because if they cracked *Liv* open, A LOT of chocolate would spill out.

I had enough foresight to take as much chocolate as I possibly could to energize myself physically and mentally. Every day I set a target and I reward myself with a chocolate bar when I reach that goal. Psychologists call this "delayed gratification," while cartoonists depict it as a carrot on a stick. Whatever, though! It works as incentive and as fuel and it's my way of giving myself a pat on the back or a high five. As the Zen koan asks, "What is the sound of one hand clapping?" I guess it's the same as one hand high-fiving when I'm alone on the ocean. Although it kind of sounds to me like a chocolate bar being unwrapped too.

There are some benefits to this treat. Chocolate not only tastes oh-so-delicious but the dark kind has the ability to boost your mood and keep your heart healthy. I posted a partial inventory of some of this food on my blog the other day while I took a break from rowing. After I did I got this email:

> *Dear Ms. Spotz,*
>
> *I was truly inspired by your journey but I have one question. Why did you take so many chocolate bars? You could have taken more healthy stuff.*
>
> *From, Brandon*

Here is the list that made Brandon so incredulous!

> *300 Clif bars (lots of different flavors)*
> *210 dehydrated lunches/dinners*
> *98 dehydrated breakfast meals*
> *90 Snickers bars*
> *80 Bumble bars*
> *70 trail mix bags (small)*
> *50 Twix, Butterfinger, and Hershey's bars*
> *42 dehydrated desserts (cheesecake or chocolate pudding)*
> *40 salmon or tuna packs*
> *18 bags dried mango (plain and spicy)*
> *12 bags of beef or turkey jerky*

7 bags of dried plantains

8 bags almonds

12 bags cashews

5 bags dried cherries

6 bags wasabi peas

8 hard bread packs with almond butter

12 bags of crackers

10 bags dried pears

10 bags of Mission and Calimyrna figs

8 bags of dried peas

7 boxes of biscotti

30 sunflower packs (small)

200 GU Energy gels

100 GU Blocks

7 bags dried blueberries

40 bags of gummies

50 fruit leathers

6 bags of flattened banana

4 bags of mangosteen

12 packs of chocolate covered ginger

4 bags of tangy almonds

3 bags of whey protein

2 packs of Fig Newtons

6 bags of sesame crepes

2 bags of chocolate cookies

Nuun electrolyte replacement tablets

1 sprouting kit with lots of seeds!

So there it is. I am convinced that there can never be too much chocolate.

But here is the thing. Chocolate has a dark side. I have been talking about the horrible water and sanitation issues in places like Africa. There is something else we should be aware of too. Chocolate comes to us at a very high price.

In her book *Bitter Chocolate*, Carol Off explains that the West African nation Côte d'Ivoire (Ivory Coast) is responsible for almost half of the world's cocoa production. Poor farmers are beholden to the cocoa cartel, which continuously demands more beans for less money. Their response has been to use the cheapest of all labor sources—indentured servitude by adults and thousands of children who have never even tasted chocolate.[60]

Water is central to this story as well. The reality, according to The International Cocoa Initiative is that "Children in cocoa growing areas face the realities of rural poverty" and this includes a lack of "access to potable water." Poverty induces adults to use children to survive and reduce labor costs on farms. Estimates are that between 10 to 20 percent of all children on cocoa communities on the Ivory Coast and Ghana are involved in child labor.[61]

What are options for consumers who want to eat chocolate but do not want to support and fund slave labor? One option is to look for chocolate certified as "Fair Trade." If you visit Fair Trade USA you can find products from clothing to food that comes with the guarantee that the farmers are paid fair prices and ensures they do not use children or slaves in the production of their goods.[62] In the world of chocolate, Fair Trade also means cocoa beans that are grown in ways that do not harm the environment. The beans are organic and shade-grown under the rainforest, as opposed to on land depopulated of rainforest trees.

The lesson for today is that we all need to consider becoming socially responsible consumers. Imagine if you lived in New York in the 1850s and you went to purchase clothes. If you saw shirts made of cotton grown on southern slave plantations in the United States, would you buy it knowing what you know now about the horrors of American slavery? And by the way, there is a water cost to everything we purchase. For example, 700 gallons of water are required to make a single cotton shirt, while 2,600 gallons are needed to make a pair of jeans. Our dollars are like votes that support certain practices. You can encourage the kind of world you want to live in simply by being aware of how you spend your money. One blueprint for how to do this is Ellis Jones' *The Better World Shopping Guide* (or betterworldshopper. org). Jones grades more than 2,000 companies on a scale of A to F in terms of environmental sustainability, human rights, community involvement, social justice, and animal protection.

I know I am not perfect here and have a lot more to learn with my own buying habits. But if I purchase a product (chocolate or any other) made by child or slave labor, then I have to accept responsibility for the fact that I must indeed support, or am silently complicit, in these practices.

I also know that loving the people in places like Kenya and helping them establish clean water projects is not enough. They also need to earn a living wage in non-slavery conditions.[63] People in Africa need to have clean water and sanitation, and they must also have the opportunity to earn a fair wage.

Cast your votes wisely.

Day 30: Extend Your Hand

Such a beautiful sky tonight! The stars punctuate the darkness and the moon lights my way like a comforting spotlight that seems to shine just for me. What is even more reassuring is knowing my family and friends are looking up at a similar sky, or at least they will be when darkness falls in their time zone. We are never really alone in the world; we are connected through the land under our feet and the sight of the cosmos above. We all share one home, which is our precious Earth.

I have talked about the importance of teams before, but really our team is the human race. If you played sports I am sure you remember the bonds you formed with your teammates. I never really experienced this in middle school because my position on the team was mostly on the bench! I first felt it with my riding buddies in the Big Ride Across America.

I wish we would sometimes look at all of humanity with that same team spirit. On the basketball court, when someone falls down there are always multiple hands extended immediately to help her or him up. The reality is that there are a lot of people "down" on our Earth right now through no fault of their own. They were simply born into conditions of poverty where water, hygiene, and sanitation are rare luxuries. We can all offer hands to help them up, because they are valuable members of our human team.

Tackling a problem alone is not usually the best way to proceed. That's one reason I am so thankful for Rotary clubs around the world. With 1.2 million members and 30,000 clubs, they personify the power strength in numbers offers for creating positive change both locally and globally.[64] The anthropologist Margaret Mead wrote, "Never doubt that a small group of thoughtful, committed citizens can change the world; indeed, it's the only thing that ever has."[65] Imagine if those committed citizens numbered 1.2 million? Well, you don't have to. Just look at Rotary's track record and you will see.

The Chagrin Valley Rotary Club in Ohio has been a tremendously positive influence on my row. Even before I left they raised more than $15,000 for safe water projects to support my goal, and they tell me they are planning another fundraiser when I get home. They follow my daily progress too, and each week someone holds their Mini-Wilson twin ball (apparently they call it "The Deuce") and give a "Where's Katie" report. In fact I see their comments on my blog all the time. Here's a post from Mark Besand:

> I'll be tuned in like I'm sure many of your other followers will be to hear how you're doing as you close in on the finish. Keep up the great work! I can't tell you how proud all of us in the Chagrin Valley Rotary Club are of your remarkable accomplishments. Also, we have another $200 coming in from the November fundraiser which will be donated through the website.... All those people drinking clean, safe water ... what a wonderful thing. You're making quite a difference. Take care. Row strong, and see you soon!!! Mini-Wilson 2 (the deuce) says hi too.

The Chagrin Valley Rotary Club also arranged an extended stay for me at the home of a family from the Dakar Rotary Club before my departure. I spent more than a week meeting their members, seeing the city, and exploring its markets. The majority of the people who watched me embark were Dakar Rotarians. I am sure that no matter where I land in South America, the Rotarians will be there in full force too.

Rotary clubs all over the world inspire me with their commitment to promote peace, fight disease, save mothers and children, support education, and provide clean water. They have been doing this for more than a century, starting with Paul P. Harris, who founded the Rotary Club of Chicago in February 1905. It was one of the first service organizations in the world. The name came from rotating the meetings through the homes of its earliest members; soon the gatherings were rotating to places throughout the world. Just 16 years after Harris founded Rotary, there were clubs on six continents.

When I think about the water crisis being too big to solve, Rotary is there, not just with its worldwide reach, but also with its inspiring successes. Consider this: in 1979, Rotary started a global fight against polio with the goal of immunizing 6 million children in the Philippines. Today only three countries worldwide are polio-endemic. There were 125 in 1988.[66] If we can almost eradicate polio, then we have the power to provide clean water to all people.

This is the lesson for today: good things can happen when you extend a hand and join others who are reaching to help as well. Two people working together are stronger than two people working separately. The result is that real change can take place. Remember Margaret Mead's message about committed citizens changing the world. We really do have the power to make the earth a better place. It certainly can seem like a never ending battle, but I suggest overcoming that perspective with a little tunnel vision.

Extend a hand to help someone up.

The two of you can help two more people.

The four of you can then help another four.

Repeat.

The law of exponential growth is powerful because if the trend is repeated just 22 times, with each person helping just one other, more than 1.6 million people could receive a hand. This is how change happens. Imagine a tiny snowball at the top of a hill. As it rolls and gains momentum it gets larger and larger until it's an avalanche. Our small efforts can result in an avalanche of change. All it takes is extending your hand, helping others in need, and enjoying the personal fulfillment that service can bring.

This does not mean you have to travel to Africa or India or any other place to find poverty. It can be in your home town too. Mother Teresa famously said to people who wanted to leave their homes and join her in Calcutta: "Find your own Calcutta." In other words, we can "think global, but act local." Sometimes it is not about going far out of your way, but just finding a small, everyday way to help others. All we have to do is extend a hand.

Day 31: Teach Someone to Fish

I am not sure why I tempt myself thinking about ice cream and lemonade. And even if there really was a floating lemonade stand out here I don't have any money with me to pay for a drink! Perhaps I could barter with some trail mix or chocolate. Now, see, I am getting just a little silly. Then again, what's wrong with that? At least it puts a smile on my face. Ahhh, but it would be a pucker if I only had lemonade.

Back to a little reality and something else I said in my tweet about a lucrative business. If you really wanted to develop a profitable lemonade stand, buying lemons from the store would not be the best option. A better approach would be to learn how to grow and cultivate lemon trees. Then you could develop your product inexpensively and sustain your business for the future. It's like that well-known proverb: "Give a man a fish and you feed him for a day. Teach a man to fish and you feed him for a lifetime."[67] Or in my example, give a girl a lemon and she can make a glass of lemonade. Teach a girl to grow a lemon tree and she can make lemonade for life!

This really is a powerful idea and it is at the heart of missions to help people in poverty-stricken areas of the world. One example is Aqua

I took this picture in Kenya when the Aqua Clara international team was teaching the locals how a biosand filter works. These filters remove water pathogens like bacteria, protozoa, and viruses.

Clara International, which is the charity I visited in Kenya. Some of the funds raised by my row will support water projects there. Aqua Clara's main technology is a biosand filter which produces clean water that meets World Health Organization standards for developing countries. They achieve this through both technology and teaching strategies. Their mission is to transfer "technological know-how to local community leaders who will then be empowered to meet the needs of their communities."[68]

As a result, they are a living embodiment of that proverb. Aqua Clara does not import water to these communities because that would be like giving them a single fish. Instead they teach people how to develop their own sources of clean drinking water where they live. Why is this alternative so effective? First, the technology allows communities to purify water from streams, ponds, wells, and even municipal water systems. Second, all materials are sourced locally. Third, the Aqua Clara strategy is not just about technology because it also changes behaviors. The organization works with local community leaders and trains them to use the technology. This leader adopts and promotes its use among the village. When this person spreads that knowledge to others, it eliminates the need for someone from the outside to spend weeks or months developing the trust of an entire village. Finally, this works because it is sustainable for the long term because it relies on the village itself to self-perpetuate the practice.

Aqua Clara also provides entrepreneurial opportunities through locally owned affiliates which support a larger community or network of villages. The affiliates are taught how to construct the filters, install and maintain them, as well as how to run the business. This empowers a community, teaching its members how to "fish."

I saw this firsthand in Kenya and was so impressed not just with the technology and how it purified water, but also in how the African people *felt* about themselves. Charity is not about just giving something to someone. It is also about elevating spirits and empowering self-sufficiency. I remember talking to one woman who became an Aqua Clara entrepreneur. She was so enthusiastic about the opportunity it provided. I will never forget what she said to Claire, the woman who taught her how to become a CDE (community development entrepreneur): "You made me someone." How powerful is that simple phrase! Aqua Clara taught her to fish, and provided her the knowledge to share that with her community.

This is a good lesson for how we can best help those in need. Are you providing a single fish for someone to eat, or are you helping to teach them how to fish for themselves? Both ways of giving are important and admirable, but we need to be aware of how to increase the efficiency of our efforts. Empowering someone to help themselves in the future is ultimately the way toward long-term solutions.

Day 32: Always Go to the Source

Remember playing with a jack-in-a-box as a kid and the scary excitement when that puppet popped out? The anticipation was half the fun. I never realized I would have that same experience rowing an ocean. First of all, who knew fish jumped out of the water so frequently? I mean, what are they doing? Do they think they're dolphins? They never fail to get a scream out of me, even though I should be used to it by now. Serves them right for getting their own shock when they land on my boat and flop around. They still get the last laugh because I have to scoop them up and throw them back into the water. Oh, Katie . . . laughing fish?

Speaking of fish, the lesson yesterday was how important it is to design charity work that metaphorically teaches people how to fish, instead of devising ways just to give them the fish. This is a really critical point and brings to mind a modern Parable of Good Works. It goes something like this.

Long ago there was a village located near a river (I always like a good water parable!)[69] Its people were happy, had shelter, and plenty to eat and drink. Then one day a villager noticed something very alarming. At first he could not believe his eyes, but then he confirmed that there was a baby floating down the middle of the river. Without thinking twice he jumped in and saved the baby from drowning. The man had done a good deed!

The next day that same villager was again walking along the river, and this time he saw two babies floating downstream. Just like he had the day before, he jumped in and rescued both of them. He still thought this was an isolated event, but the next day he changed his mind as now four babies were floating down the swift waters. This time he could not save them by himself and cried out for help. On the fourth day there were eight babies and at that point the village elders called a meeting. They devised an extensive plan to save all future babies in the water. This included training teams of swimmers, erecting watchtowers for early warnings, staffing round-the-clock patrols, setting up care centers to treat the babies, and instructing villagers in the art of resuscitation. While babies were saved, more and more came each day, and eventually the villagers could no longer save them all. Over time the village learned to live with the fact that though they saved many babies, many more were dying. There was nothing they could do.

One day though someone asked a radical, but logical question: "Who is throwing the babies in the water in the first place? If we stopped the source then we could solve the tragedy." The village elders voted down his plan. They said that the manpower and resources required to mount a team to venture upstream into the unknown would compromise their ability to save the babies they saw every day.

This parable asks a question we confront today as we embark on charitable missions to improve conditions throughout the world. Are our efforts concentrated on plucking individual babies from the river, or are we working towards actually changing the system so that no more babies are put at risk in the first place? This is a difficult question. It is easier to save a single baby: the reward is immediate, and we are confident that we are doing good works. On the other hand, going upstream could take years, result in numerous unforeseen frustrations and failures, and in the meantime more babies would float by, out of reach.

This is exactly the situation we confront with the water crisis. You could raise $2,000 and buy bottled water and send it to Africa. Certainly it would be welcome there and directly reduce the thirst of many people for a short period of time. But this contributes absolutely nothing to solving the problem of Africans dying of thirst from a lack of water, and contracting diseases from contaminated water. Bottled water is a Band-Aid. What we need is a physician to cure the cancer, and that means long term, systemic change.

If you are sending water to Africa, that's great and we thank you. I invite you to join our team venturing up river. We have a very difficult task ahead and stopping the misery, suffering, and death at its source. Our journey is a long one and it is sometimes challenging to measure progress. Ultimately, we need to teach the world to fish.

That is the lesson for today. Consider the Parable of Good Works and apply it to the social action in which you participate, or would like to participate—any charitable endeavor. What role are you playing? Are you stationed along the banks of the river pulling a select few babies to safety? Or are you trudging upstream, ready, willing, and able to stop whatever force is depositing babies in the river in the first place?

Now if I could only figure out the source of all these flying fish and the reason they are landing on my boat!

Day 33: Create Your Own Reality

@KatieSpotz Tweet Log for Thursday, February 4, 2010

| 8:45 PM | Katie's rapidly closing down on the half-way mark. She's now rowed over 1,000 nautical miles. [Sam] |

The halfway point is an important moment. Imagine a great, long, dark tunnel. You are walking *into* the tunnel until you hit the midpoint, at which time you are suddenly walking *out* of the tunnel. Perhaps this is common sense, but the mental boost this moment represents cannot be overstated. It's a sudden transition between being closer to the finish than the start. I am getting very close to the important moment when I row past the halfway mark on my journey. This means a great deal to me.

As you can see, it's a mental game I am playing with myself, and it is critical because success in an endurance challenge is more mental than physical. Also, the difference between traditional sports and ocean rowing is huge. Out here on the ocean there is endless sky and water and little else. The motivation to continue is all internal because there are no screaming fans out here. I am not expecting any boats at the halfway point, honking their horns and waving "Go Katie Go" banners.

Instead I am existing without external motivation, and also without the frills of my normal life. I do not have the luxury of a shower, bathroom, kitchen, or even space to walk. Every night I fall asleep (or try to fall asleep) in a wet bed. The only strawberries and fresh fruit I eat are those I dream about. I long for a fresh salad, or really anything that is "fresh." Even something cold would be amazing because I have no way to cool my water. As you can guess, that means no ice cream! At least I can keep my chocolate below the waterline so it does not become a melted mess in this heat (not that this would stop me from eating it!).

Today is also extremely hot. I should just copy that and paste it on top of my report every day. But I'm really feeling the sauna today, with the constant sun, and no hope of shade in my future. Except my hat. That is all the Ocean Rowing Society allows because a canopy could be refashioned as a sail to catch wind to propel myself. What I would give to row under a big leafy oak tree and rest for a few minutes. A mirage in the desert is water. I wonder if a mirage in the ocean is an apple tree!

To add to all of this, it is impossible to stay clean. You might think that wouldn't be the case because there is water all around, but being hot and sweaty all day long, day after day, results in bed, clothes, hair, and everything else being grimy and smelly. No wonder no one wants to meet me at this halfway point.

I don't blame them!

The only way out of this is through my mind. I choose not to be held hostage by negative thoughts. I should say *I try* to do this. I am certainly not always successful and the battle against detrimental thoughts is a daily one.

Yes, I am a tired, dirty, smelly mess and I would love something fresh to eat. If I focus only on this, though, it has a way of magnifying my discomfort. The reality is, I am far better off right now than many millions of people on Earth.

I choose to see with positive eyes and that changes my situation dramatically. I know where my next drink of water is coming from, and I know I can pretty much drink as much as I want. I have some semblance of shelter, and even though it is hot, I know I will be relatively secure, even in hurricane-force winds. I also know where my next meal is coming from. I might be bored with trail food, but I'm not hungry. No matter how bad it gets out here, it's luxurious compared to what many people endure on a daily basis.

Hope is the ultimate luxury. This sort of reminds me of the "feast of imaginations" of the Lost Boys in the movie *Hook*, which is a retelling of the Peter Pan story. Hope and imagination are powerful forces in life, and they can help to create a new reality.

I have hope that I can complete this row because I have now crossed an imaginary line, the halfway point. I have manufactured hope in symbolic carrots on sticks which I have packed for myself in terms of lots and lots of chocolate bar rewards (though an actual carrot sounds good too!). And I have the most important hopeful reassurance knowing that this journey is temporary. Rowing a boat will not be the rest of my life. It is transitory until I reach family, friends, food, and a comfortable bed. This perspective transforms what I could easily see as hellish misery, but in reality it's something that can feel like home.

I think we sometimes look at our lives from unhealthy perspectives. For some reason we are too often *wishful* instead of *thankful*. I certainly suffer from this too! I might wish I had a dry bed, cold water, or fresh food out here. I'm trying to turn that around and instead affirm that I'm *thankful* that I have a bed, water, and food. One of my favorite spiritual writers is Louise L. Hay. In her book *Life!: Reflections on Your Journey*, she writes, "I say 'Out' to every negative thought that comes to my mind. No person, place, or thing has any power over me, for I am the only thinker in my mind. I create my own reality. . . ."[70]

What an awesome message for a journey like the one I am on! I have adopted it as my mantra as I cross the halfway point, and it is also my lesson for today. I am going to create my own reality! I am traveling the seas in luxury, the captain of my boat *Liv*, and also the captain of my life. I know a positive attitude cannot magically clean dirty water, but it can make EVERY situation in life better.

Day 34: Challenge Your Routine

Yesterday I noted that I am roughly at the halfway point. So I guess that means that I am in something of a routine now. At least I better be! What is everyday life like out here? Let me try to describe it to you, but I have two disclaimers. First, my sense of time is completely off. I'm not even sure what time zone I'm in now, or what day of the week it is. It's interesting how in the "real" world the day of the week is so important, and out here, it means absolutely nothing. Time is kept by the sun and stars, and my day unfolds mainly by depending on how I feel more than on a strict schedule. Second, for the most part, life is ridiculously boring. The most exciting thing that happened today was hearing another human voice over the VHF radio. Sorry to disappoint you!—but my days are not filled with fighting off pirates or riding on the back of whales or clinging to the walls of my cabin while I ride out huge storms. It's mainly just rowing along, slow and steady. What is that old saying? Slow and steady wins the race. I certainly feel more like a tortoise than a hare right now.

With that in mind, this is my life and routine, sparing few details:

- I wake up around sunrise and first check the GPS. Big smiles when I get "free miles" or have been pushed westward overnight by the winds and current.

- Breakfast is usually oatmeal, cereal with dried milk, rice or couscous topped with dried fruit and nuts.
- I eat my breakfast outside, but I first check for dead fish, and throw them back into the sea where they belong.
- I start rowing until I am hungry again or want to change my iPod.
- I keep rowing until I hear a song so good that it would be rude not to stop and dance. I usually listen to music in the morning and audiobooks in the afternoon.
- If it's too hot, I take a dip in the water and wave to my fishy neighbors (while remaining connected to the boat with a safety line, of course).
- If I'm especially tired, I'll take a 15-20 minute powernap throughout the day.
- Then more rowing. Every day is different but the waves have typically been 3-5 feet and temperatures in the 80s.
- At midday I run the desalinator, which converts the saltwater into fresh water by reverse osmosis. It takes about twenty minutes to produce enough fresh water for a couple days.
- I row until sunset. On a typical day, I see a few fish and birds, especially around sunset and, aside from the odd voice on my VHF radio, there is no sign of other human beings.
- At sunset I stop and have dinner, which is usually a carb-rich meal like pasta and a whey-protein shake.
- I row for one more hour in the dark, and I save some of my comedy audio stuff for night rowing.
- Once I am done rowing, I set the rudder and secure the oars for the night.
- Before I go to bed, I read a letter from home. Before I shipped the boat, my mom gave me 100 letters, one for every day of the trip, which usually brings me to smile, laugh, or, dare I admit, shed a tear.
- And then I check my emails and sometimes do a blog or write in my diary (on waterproof paper, might I add). I use the satellite phone for emails and calls. I have one ten-minute call a week, mainly to keep my sanity intact.
- Right before I sleep, I stuff pillows and dry bags with soft stuff (like my dry bag of clothes) around my bed and wedge myself in between. It helps

keep me secure in a constantly moving boat. Next I strap myself with
three harnesses to my bed.
- I sleep about 8 hours waking up several times to switch positions or let
fresh air in.
- Then I do it all over again!

There you go. This is my life, my reality, and my routine right now.
And the more comfortable I get with it, the more I realize how important
it is to construct a quality routine for yourself. I know, a routine sounds
boring, but in fact it can be liberating.

As you can see, my routine is far from glamorous, but it enables me
to embrace this strange and beautiful life at sea. My routine frees my mind
to confront the physical and mental challenges out here, and without the
pressure of time, I get to experience the "now" without a thought about the
past or future. I learned this on my meditation retreats, where the monks
and nuns lived a very structured, routinized day.

A schedule really helps to put your mind at ease, as opposed to constantly planning or panicking over what's next. With my rowing routine I
know every "what's next" without having to make decisions. I know what
I'm going to eat, what music will be on my iPod, and what my daily activity
will be. No decisions mean I can just do it.

But there are two types of routines. Right now mine just helps me
through each oar stroke. The sad reality is that for far too many people
on our planet, the daily routine is all about how to survive. For them, like
many in Africa, daily life revolves around trying to obtain enough water
and food for themselves and their family. Their only "now" is often a question of *how can I get safe water*?

Consider one African family. Paul Vallely wrote a brilliant article,
"From Dawn to Dusk, the Daily Struggle of Africa's Women," in which he
described a typical survival routine. Letenk'iel lived in southern Eritrea,
awoke before 4 a.m. when it was still dark, and rekindled the embers in the
fire from the night before. After breakfast she gave her children chores,
and then her first big and essential task was fetching water. She was lucky in
that it only took her 25 minutes to walk down a hill to the pump. However,

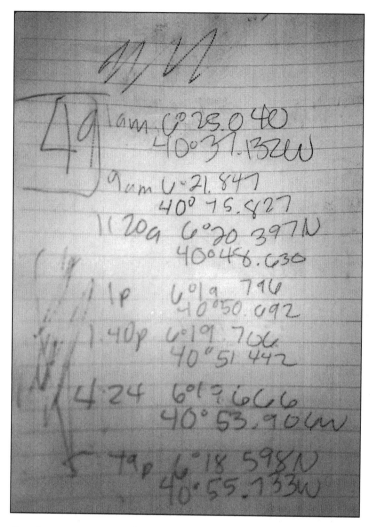

One of my routines was to track my position on the ocean. This is waterproof paper made by a company called Rite in the Rain. They were a sponsor of my row.

trekking back up the hill with five gallons of water, affixed to her back with a rope and old rag, took another 40 minutes.[71] At one point there had been three wells in her village, and now there was just one that flowed so slowly there was barely enough water for everyone to drink.

After lunch, her typical afternoon routine involved helping in the fields, plowing, removing weeds, and sowing seed. Women grow 70 percent of the food in Africa, and account for half of the animal husbandry. However, on this day, instead of going into the fields, she had to take her baby to the clinic because he had caught a bad cough from her. It was a two-hour walk each way. When she returned home more than four hours later it was time to fetch more water and prepare dinner, which consisted of flatbread cooked over the biscuit-tin stove. Despite such challenging routines the beauty and fortitude of women like her as they go about their water-centric days is remarkable.[72]

The lesson today is to evaluate your routine. You can use it to thrive and to enrich your life. How we spend our time is a reflection of our values. Do you spend more time watching TV than quality time with your children? If so, ask yourself what you value more. It is helpful to focus on our routines from time to time and really reflect if they match our value systems. If they do not, then change them.

For many, though, routines are necessary merely to survive, and maintain the health of themselves and their families. This challenge goes out to those who have a routine which enables them to thrive. Use this opportunity to add an element to your routine which gives back to someone in need. You can even make this automatic these days with various ways available to donate electronically. Pick an amount, find a worthy charity, and make that contribution automatic and a part of your life. For example, every Thursday assist at a soup kitchen, or spend Saturday mornings in the summer volunteering for beach cleanup. Or donate your time and energy to another person or organization. As John Andrews Holmes said, "There is no exercise better for the heart than reaching down and lifting people up."

Challenge your routine!

Day 35: You Are the Solution

As you can tell, I believe it is essential for us all to look for ways to propel ourselves through life. We have to keep going or rowing, especially when we are feeling down. That has been the central lesson of the first part of my journey out here. However, that isn't the only reason I'm on the Atlantic. Yes, my running, biking, swimming, and now rowing endurance challenges have been important for me in discovering who I am, but I do not want to ignore the rest of the world. In fact, it's just the opposite. I cannot know myself without figuring out how I can help others. And one of the most significant humanitarian crises on our planet today (the most significant in my opinion), is a lack of clean drinking water.

The sad irony is that we live upon what we call "the blue planet." Our blue water defines the look of the earth from space. It gives us life, as water makes up approximately 60 percent our bodies. Simply put, we are water. We cannot survive much longer than 48 hours without drinking it. And even though the earth has an abundance of it, only a small percentage is drinkable. The oceans hold about 96.5 percent of our water.[73] And the water we can safely consume is diminishing each year, thanks to drought and pollution. That is the first crisis. The second crisis is the vastly disproportionate response to help the huge number of people who are dying of thirst. Many of us like to think our advanced technologies automatically make for a better world. This is not always the case.

In Africa the water situation is dire. Because of ever-increasing shortages, people there spend more and more of their days simply trying to secure water for themselves and their families. Africans spend an estimated 40 billion labor-hours each year collecting and hauling water.

The future appears even bleaker. Some experts predict that by 2025, 5.3 billion people will encounter water shortages. If projections like this seem far off, the current situation is tragic. Worldwide, 1.8 million children currently die each year from waterborne diseases. It is tempting to dismiss these problems as being "over there." I prefer to think of this as a humanitarian crisis, which means it is each person who matters, not their nationalities. A suffering child is a suffering child no matter where they live.

There is hope.

Every day as I row, I reflect not just on the water crisis, but more importantly on the existing hopeful strategies to lessen it.

First, we can overcome the overwhelming statistics and the feeling that a problem affecting so many people is insurmountable. Many refer to this condition as "psychic numbness." In other words, we are bombarded with so much devastating news about pain and suffering every day via our media that we become desensitized to it. We can sensitize ourselves by looking for ways to connect personally with people and communities in need.

We can also lessen psychic numbness by realizing that our actions *can* make a real difference. As for solutions, there are some surprisingly simple ones. For a relatively small amount of money a person in a rural area can have clean water for life, using low-tech strategies that include wells, gravity-fed springs, rainwater harvesting, and bore holes. Important infrastructure investments can have a positive impact on an entire village. In the United States, charity:water is one of the largest non-profits focusing on ways to help bring water to areas in need. It has funded over 13,000 water projects, and this has resulted in more than 4.6 million people getting clean water.[74]

Individuals can also see the benefits of their volunteerism directly. The action of a single person in the United States can bring water to hundreds. Through H2O for Life, Patty Hall and her 900 students raised $12,000 to build a dam in Kenya. The eight-foot structure traps and filters water, thus serving the village year-round. Previously this was a place where girls were unable to attend school because they spent six hours a day walking to find and then carry home giant containers of water on their backs.[75]

This is what I am rowing for.

I row for water.

I row to spread awareness of the problem.

I row to raise funds for the solution.

Robert Redford eloquently brought attention to this crisis in an essay entitled "You are the solution." He ended it with these thoughts: "Water is life. As we share this Blue Planet, we must promise each other that no person will ever again have to live—or die—without clean, fresh water. Fulfilling that promise is within the reach of each of us."[76]

Redford is exactly right. We can solve this global crisis by including ourselves in the solution. This is the lesson for today. Each of us has the power to do something that has a positive impact on this crisis. The smallest gesture is meaningful, because even it can result in a drink of water for a thirsty child. One drop of water can help change the world.

Day 36: Enjoy a Day Off

@KatieSpotz Tweet Log for Sunday, February 7, 2010	
8:33 PM	...By my reckoning, she has rowed a 1,287 miles, and she is just 1,270 miles from Cayenne! [Sam]

You know the famous Beatles lyric, "We all live in a Yellow Submarine." Well if I could compose a tune as catchy, I might sing "I Row the Seas in a Yellow Rowboat." Okay, maybe not.

Liv is very distinctively colored and shaped. Before my row, everywhere I went, eyes were always glued to her. People would look at her with the curiosity of a child, or as if she was a spaceship, whenever I trained on Lake Erie, or took her to fundraisers. They were intrigued by my banana-yellow boat because she looks unlike any other they have ever seen, given there are only two in the world like her (as of 2010). My rowboat didn't just intrigue people. Fish were equally as curious.

Fish are inquisitive by nature. They gravitate towards anything floating on the surface of the water, whether it's a log, a buoy, or debris. Apparently they like the shade, and try to avoid UV rays. And no, I have not seen any applying sunscreen! If you spot anything floating on the water, chances are that a fish isn't far away. With a 19-foot surface underneath me, it wasn't long before the fish found it.

Here is my yummy meal. Quite a feast thanks to Enertia Trail Food!

It started with a couple of small fish. Then more joined the party. And there are always those that crash the party. I mean "crash" quite literally, as the larger fish would pin the smaller ones against the side of my boat, trapping them like it was a wrestling takedown. Then the big fish enjoyed their meal. By the end of week one, my new fish family encircled me. Looking over the side of my boat is like peering into my own little aquarium. And by "little" I suppose I mean "seemingly infinite," with so many unique and brightly colored fish, enjoying the ride. I am also entertained by three large dorados (also called dolphinfish or mahi-mahi) that shoot straight out of the water and land on their sides as if they are clapping for me by doing a belly flop. They have become my friends, I named them Ed, Edd, and Eddy (after the cartoon), and I am never alone with them by my side.

I become even better acquainted with my fishy followers when the temperatures run high. Rowing along the equator means that temperatures above 100 degrees are not uncommon. The one solution for that problem is to jump. I am talking about me, not the dorados. I also try to avoid belly flops whenever I can. Hopping overboard gives me a chance to cool down and also see Ed, Edd, and Eddy up close and personal. Snorkeling alongside my boat, I had moments when I was completely surrounded by hundreds of fish. And yes, sometimes I scream underwater when they sneak up behind and brush against my back. Just as in outer space, no one can hear you scream underwater. That is comforting!

Fish aren't just fun to swim with. They're fun to watch, too. Seeing them freely swimming about always lifts my mood. They make for some of the best listeners, too. Thanks to all those fish for doing what friends do best! They keep me company and remind me to just go with the flow.

Do I sound a little leisurely today? Guilty as charged. I am actually a couch potato . . . or a rowboat potato. I felt like I needed a day off from rowing entirely, and I wanted to get as far away from my oars as possible (which was only a few feet). So I spent the day watching Harry Potter movies on my iPod, and eating chocolate. And of course while immersing myself in the Potterverse I imagined I had some of that magical power to cast spells. If I could choose one which would it be? Well, Aguamenti, of course! Professor Flitwick taught Harry how to perform this charm, and it creates a jet of water from the hand or wand of the person who incants it. How cool is that? With that power I could single-handedly walk around Africa and cure the global water crisis.

Well, you see where my mind wanders when I take a day off. But that is okay, because it's the lesson that the Atlantic is teaching me today. The human body, mind, and soul cannot push hard forever without breaking down. No matter how noble our goals, or how deep our passions, if we do not take time away we will burn out long before we reach our intended goal. The trick is not to be seduced by that time off. Binge-watching movies in a comfortable spot with chocolate, and maybe your favorite person, is a great way to recharge and put your perspectives in order. But if I did this every day, well, then the exact opposite would happen. As with everything in life, find the balance.

What is that old seventeenth-century proverb? "All work and no play makes Jack a dull boy." Did you know that Irish novelist Maria Edgeworth added another line to it in 1825? She said, "All play and no work makes Jack a mere toy."[77] In other words, find a balance between these two extremes. Time for me to add a third line: "Balancing work and play makes Jack a true joy." I am a poet!

Think about your work and leisure balance. How would you ideally enjoy your leisure time? (I know, a private island in the ocean!) How close are you to achieving it? It is vitally important to fine tune that balance for a healthy and happy life.

Now it's time for my seventh chocolate bar today. Shhh. Don't tell anyone! Especially the fish, because they might want some and I am feeling *selfish* (pun intended). I already give them free rent anyway.

Day 37: Never Underestimate a Small Gesture

I had a nice surprise today: the *Los Angeles Times* ran an article about my row. I thought the writer, Kelly Burgess, did a really good job describing what it's like out here. She wrote: "Just thinking about her adventurous endeavor is awe-inspiring. Nothing but ocean in every direction you look; total darkness at night save for the moon and stars and the few navigational lights on board; blisters, rashes and aches and pains in areas never imagined; no fresh foods or cold drinks—there is no refrigeration on board; and the only hot food available is dehydrated—made by pouring hot water heated on a small gas-powered stove into a pouch."[78] Yes, that about describes my life out here.

I like to see articles like this, but not for me. I really don't care so much about publicity or getting my name out there. In fact I feel uncomfortable with a lot of attention. What I do like, though, is that articles like this spread my *message*—water. I appreciate journalists like Burgess who emphasize the cause, and discuss the global water crisis. In particular she mentioned the Blue Planet Run Foundation. It is now the Blue Planet Network and its members have done some amazing things to bring attention to the water crisis. In 2007 Blue Planet coordinated a massive run. How massive? Around the entire globe. It covered 15,200 miles, across 16 countries and three continents, over a period of 95 days, 24 hours a day.

Obviously that was not just one person running. But it was fewer people than you might think—just 20 international runners.

They started in New York City, on June 1, 2007, and ran around the clock and around the world, eventually returning to where they started on September 4th. There were 1,500 baton exchange points, and each runner covered 10 miles per day. The route was really cool. They ran through these major cities (in order): New York City, London, Paris, Vienna, Moscow, Beijing, San Francisco, St. Louis, Toronto, Washington, DC, and New York City. That is an impressive route! Of course they did not run over oceans. They had a plane for crossing those! Now why didn't I think of that?

What was the central message of this amazing endeavor? This was their plea: "we can and must begin today to alleviate the catastrophic burden placed on over a billion people who, every day, must drink unsafe local water, or travel long distances on foot to search for safe water for themselves and their families."[79]

Sometimes as individuals we can look at grand gestures like this (and around the world is the largest possible one) and think, "I can't contribute something like that." It's okay! You don't have to. Small gestures have remarkably profound ripple effects in creating change.

Lisa Nash, the CEO of Blue Planet Run, wrote a guest blog for me while I was rowing. She talked about people who were inspired by my row and wanted to perform athletic challenges to raise money for safe drinking-water projects. Here are some of the cool examples. There is a college student from Oklahoma who is raising funds by having sponsors donate for every mile she rides, and she has already reached 600 miles. Younger students are planning lemonade stands this summer. Other students are preparing school water projects for the fall. A woman about to be married in California is setting up a donation page so her wedding guests can contribute money for clean water projects.[80] I love combining creativity with charity!

It is important to keep in mind that the costs associated with real change are relatively small. Every $30 raised provides a lifetime of safe drinking water to another person. The positive effect does not stop there.

It helps kids stay in school, allows women to start businesses, and keeps people out of hospitals. As of today I have raised $46,147 with my row, with more to come, I hope! If I can do math correctly out here, that means water for life for more than 1,500 people, even if I stopped right now. And I am not doing that! That makes me feel good, and energizes me like nothing else to just keep rowing.

Jeff "Koz" Kozlovich was also inspired by my row, and as an extreme athlete, fitness trainer, and Hawaiian lifeguard, he wanted to do his part for clean water projects. However, he could not take three months off work, so he is charting a run, bike, swim, and paddle course around the Hawaiian Islands that matches the length of my ocean row. Cool idea![81]

What lesson can we learn from this? We can make an impact in this world with gestures both grand and small. There is nothing grander than running around the entire world, and clearly this does a great deal to raise funds and awareness. But keep in mind also what a relatively small gesture like $30 will do. How significant is providing the funds to help someone have safe drinking water for life? A single lemonade stand could earn that amount. For that one person, there is nothing grander than that. It is life-giving. Never underestimate a small gesture, or the power of a few glasses of lemonade. I would pay $30 for a single, cold glass right about now!

An H2O for Life lemonade and cookie stand. The girls (from left to right: Sarah, Isabelle, and Emma Bowles) donated all money to H2O for Life. If only they could have shared some of their cool lemonade with me in the Atlantic!

Day 38: Savor Your Dinosaur Water

@KatieSpotz Tweet Log for Tuesday, February 9, 2010	
10:40 AM	…she is going faster than ever before: 47 miles in 24 hours! [Sam]

I know I talk frequently about the water crisis in Africa, because it's a place that is so close to my heart. However, the water crisis is a significant concern in other parts of the world as well. And I am sure if I were to pay a visit to all of these places and establish personal connections with the people there, I would have the same feeling for them. I look forward to seeing much more of the world. I just have to get to South America first!

In the meantime, let's do this experiment. Go to your kitchen, get a glass, and fill it up under your tap. Now take a close look at it. How old is that water? Let's make a multiple choice question out of it:

A. A few seconds old because that was when you filled your glass.

B. A few weeks old since that was the last time it rained.

C. A few months old since that is the time it took between the last rain and for the water to be stored and treated by your city.

D. None of the above.

The answer is "D" by a large margin. That water in your glass has probably existed on Earth, at least in one form or another, for hundreds

I learned a new appreciation of water, spending time outside Liv, and snorkeling under her.

of millions of years.[82] That means the water that looks clean in your glass actually might have been in a puddle that a dinosaur stepped in. At least it doesn't taste like it! But it is a glass of prehistoric water. I wish we cherished and protected that glass of water as much as we do dinosaur fossils.

Many people think that water is an infinite resource, unlike oil, because it falls so freely from the sky. That is simply not true. Yes, it falls from the sky, but the total amount of fresh water on Earth has remained relatively stable throughout our history. The water is recycled of course, but as our population has exploded there is an increasing conflict for clean water to meet the essential needs of life: drinking, cooking, bathing, and farming.

Something even more troubling is that humans have not been very good stewards of our water supply. You would think that given a finite resource that is essential to life (again unlike oil), we would be very wise and conscientious in how we use it. We quite simply are not. There are many measures to demonstrate this. Here is one that is hard for me to wrap my mind around. How much water does it take to produce a single hamburger? 630 gallons.[83]

What are the consequences of this? You can see it in many parts of the world:[84]

- In Russia, the fish in the Ural River are too contaminated to eat because of industrial run-off and waste pumped into the water.
- In Varanasi, India, millions of gallons of untreated sewage is pumped into the Ganges River every day. This is the same river that 500 million people use to drink, bathe, and irrigate crops.
- The village of Dongjin, outside Shanghai, has such polluted water that the region is known as "cancer village."
- In the United States, the Colorado River is running dry in some places. Lake Mead, which supplies 22 million, people might dry up by 2021.[85]
- Also in the United States, seven states are engulfed in such severe drought that they are running out of water.[86] California is now proposing $1 billion in drought spending.[87]

We hear lots of alarms every time we turn on the news. It's easy to be deafened in the midst of these constant emergencies. We tend to mentally hit the "snooze button" on those alarms and move along with our day. But water is not something to tempt our fate with or be cavalier about. It might not always be there. So what if we run out of oil? We will start walking and biking more, and our bodies and the environment will get stronger. If we run out of water, we die.

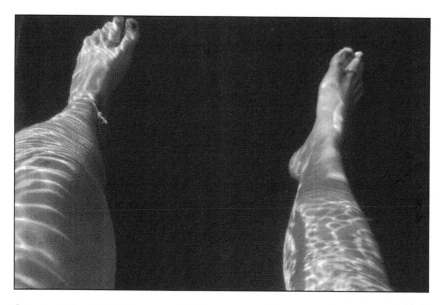

Swimming in the middle of the ocean was like floating in space. The amount of water is staggering, with miles of it below me, and yet none of it is drinkable.

What substance has done the most to improve the health and well-being of humanity? Time for another multiple choice question:

A. Antibiotics.

B. Immunization.

C. Aspirin.

D. None of the above.

Maybe you are catching on to my tricks. The answer is none of them, because the most significant substance for improving health is water. Clean water is the cornerstone in the fight against illnesses like malaria, typhoid, and cholera. Clean water is essential to produce crops that promote healthy and strong immune systems in people. And of course clean water is necessary to keep us alive every day. No more multiple choice problems, I promise.

The next time you take a sip of water think how miraculous it is. It is a clean (likely) life-sustaining resource that has been around for millions of years. Drink it down and truly savor your prehistoric water. It is a commodity rarer than gold, and infinitely more essential to life.

Day 39: Move to Antarctica, or Stay and Conserve

@KatieSpotz Tweet Log for Wednesday, February 10, 2010	
10:22 AM	How did the dolphins know? Back again
7:45 PM	Rowing at night is fun. Hitting mysterious objects while doing so, is not.
8:36 PM	Katie's GPS measures in nautical miles and, from now on, the distance left is in three digits. Under 1,000nm to go!! [Sam]

Yesterday was a little sobering as I talked about examples of how humans are typically not good stewards of our water supply. I know, multiple choice questions are frustrating as well. It is indeed hard not to become overwhelmed and depressed about this. It is something so basic to human survival, and yet on every continent on Earth except Antarctica, poor water conditions have startling consequences. Consider this result: 50 percent of all hospital patients in the world are currently being treated for waterborne diseases. And of course not everyone who is sick goes to the hospital. That means that 80 percent of all sickness and disease in our world is related to contaminated water.[88] I shake my head in disbelief every time I hear statistics like these.

There is good news. Yes, there really is good news! The glass of pre-historic water from yesterday is half full and not half empty.

A reason to be positive is that conservation works! This may not sound like a fun or a glamorous solution, but nevertheless it is an effective one. And it doesn't require you to fly to Africa to make your contributions. You can affect the global water crisis without ever leaving home. In the United States we actually use a lot less water per person per day than we did 25 years ago. Farmers irrigate crops more intelligently and efficiently. Our toilets flush with less water. This is great, but there is much more we can do.

Conservation has a direct and positive effect on our world. As American journalist Michael Specter wrote, "Every drop of water we casually waste is literally a drop of life taken from the mouth of someone else we will likely never meet, but whose fate we will most certainly determine."[89] You can read more from Specter in *The New Yorker*, which ran "The Last Drop" in 2006.[90] Keep in mind he subtitled it "Confronting the possibility of a global catastrophe." Conditions are worse now.

The lesson today is simply a question. Do you want to move to Antarctica or do you want to stay home and conserve water? This question may sound extreme. Perhaps it is not one you will have to answer in your lifetime, but there is a growing chance that the next generation will, especially depending upon where they live.

Therefore, if you want to stay home, and if you do not want to take water from the thirsty mouths of those in need, then consider ways to conserve water at home. First, start by learning what your water footprint is by visiting waterfootprint.org. Once you understand your water consumption levels, you can move to the next stage, which is conservation. Here are examples suggested by the Environmental Protection Agency:[91]

- Turning off the water while brushing your teeth twice a day can save 200 gallons of water a month.
- Take showers and not baths. A bath uses about 70 gallons of water while a shower uses between 10 to 25 gallons (depending on how long you like to luxuriate under hot water).

- A leaky toilet can be like flushing 50 times a day. Fix it! If you're not sure whether your toilets leak, drop some food coloring in the tank. If you see color in the bowl then you have a leak.
- If you have to water your grass, do it in the evening or morning. Otherwise most of your water is just evaporating.
- If you do not want to wait for Mother Nature to give you a free car wash in the rain, then use a bucket of water and soap instead of a hose. A hose uses 6 gallons of water a minute!
- Use rain barrels for gardening. Your water bill will decrease and your garden will love the fresh water. I was able to collect water on the ocean with a tarp and a bucket. If I can do it rocking on a small boat, anyone can do it at home.

You can find many other great ideas at wateruseitwisely.com.

Look at all these simple conservation suggestions as sources of hope for ourselves and our future. Think about ways you can participate, either large or small. Even if everyone just participated in a small way, we would make huge gains in conservation. I challenge you to take on just one of these practices which you are not already doing. Integrate it into your schedule for six weeks, during which time you will make it a habit. Or start with a thirty-day challenge. Tell your friends and family and then encourage them to do the same. Then email or tweet me and tell me how it's working out! There is power in numbers and if we work together we can create positive change in our world, one drop at a time.

Day 40: Failure is an Opportunity

@KatieSpotz Tweet Log for Thursday, February 11, 2010	
5:54 AM	Katie versus the stove. The stove won this time and nearly had my shoes on fire! Did I mention it is an extremely wobbly boat?!
9:46 AM	I must say, I am becoming quite a fan of having a month's worth of food within arm's reach
4:50 PM	I wonder if I stuff dirty laundry under my pillow, the laundry fairy will stop by with yummy smelling clothes. A girl can certainly hope!

I am a Northeast Ohio girl, which means that I have heard all of the jokes about Cleveland being the so-called "mistake on the lake." For many years it deserved that label, especially given its infamous burning river. How could a river burn, you ask? Well it happened because for decades, companies pumped sewage into the Cuyahoga River, and in June 1969 the oil slick on top caught fire. Cleveland was a national joke, and the band R.E.M. even wrote a song about it in 1986, called "Cuyahoga."

Why am I talking about the Cuyahoga River burning? Well, because I thought I was going to set the Atlantic Ocean on fire today! Not really, as the water is clean, but I did have a real fire scare on my boat to contend with. Fire on a small rowboat, alone in the ocean, is not a recipe for success. Here is what happened.

I need to boil water to cook my food, and I do not have a microwave out here. Instead I have an efficient and compact Jetboil stove with a real flame. That means to cook in my oh-so-glamorous fashion, I need to crouch in the corner of my boat and try to keep the waves from putting out the fire, or the wind from knocking me over. Tonight I was cooking dinner in the cockpit with my stove, and I was precariously balanced because it is handheld and I have no place to put it down. So there I was, stove in hand, when I was hit by a wave. I slid off my seat and beans and bulgur went flying every which direction. Oh, bulgur! I nearly caught my rowing shoes (which are bolted to the boat) on fire when the stove landed near them! I couldn't help but have a good laugh once I realized I was not going up in flames. There were bulgur and beans all over the place, though. I looked a little like a two-year-old who had a tantrum with her food. Only my pride was a little damaged. Thankfully, no burning boat and no songs about it either!

I realized after wiping the bulgur off my body that there is an important lesson here. On the way to success, failures are inevitable. Those who do not fail do not try to achieve great things. Failures and setbacks must be overcome to reach any goal, and the more significant the goal, the greater the likelihood that problems will arise. I find that looking at them as a natural part of the achievement process is a great way to take them in stride and move on. I have learned to accept this during my row, and it's something we need to pay more attention to and learn from with water projects too.

An estimated 35 to 50 percent of water projects fail within two to five years.[92] The main reason is not that we are still waiting to invent the perfect approach. There is no perfect approach. Projects fail because we aren't following up to see if our good ideas have turned into long-term successes. Monitoring and evaluation are important in any endeavor. It is not enough to simply install a water project. It must be monitored, with failures documented and recorded. This will enable us to learn from past experience and take corrective actions. Long-term success means visiting the communities time and time again to learn how and why some projects are succeeding, when and why others aren't, and what the sponsoring water organization can do to change that.

Other estimates show that fewer than 5 percent of organizations follow up on their projects post-construction. That means that project failures and challenges aren't being turned into learning experiences to improve the next project. It doesn't matter where the money comes from to fund the solutions—we will never reach a goal of clean water for all if we continue to take two steps forward and one step backward. Sometimes it is even one step forward and two steps back.

The lesson today is this: failure is an opportunity for improvement, but only when that failure is studied and we have the fortitude and insight to learn from it.

Consider my experiences today and my reflection regarding the Cuyahoga River. I learned something about preparing better for waves while I am cooking. The environmental community used the burning river as an incentive for positive change, and Cleveland's mayor, Carl Stokes, played an important role in advocating for the passage of the federal Clean Water Act of 1972. Today Cleveland is rising like a phoenix from these watery ashes, and is even considered a "must-see" travel destination by Fodor's.[93] LeBron James choosing to come home to Northeast Ohio also helps. It seems that in some ways, the size of the failure can be proportional to the potential for success. Take a look at some of the failures you have experienced. How have you responded?

I recommend the strategy I took earlier today. When you're alone on the Atlantic and a giant wave topples your stove, covers you with hot wheat bulgur, and almost sets yourself on fire, take these steps.

1. Put out the fire.
2. Laugh.
3. Clean yourself off (it is more fun to laugh with food on your face).
4. Make a new dinner.
5. Sit and eat and reflect upon how the previous failure can be an opportunity for improvement.

Try these five steps the next time you fail. I predict that good things will come from it! And remember, failure only exists when you stop trying. I may not make it across the Atlantic and land via my own power in South America. But that does not mean I am a failure. I know whatever the outcome, I have tried and given it my all. In the end, that is all that matters.

Day 41: You Can't Hold It Forever

@katieSpotz Tweet Log for Friday, February 12, 2010	
2:06 PM	What a treat! Watching thirty birds fly around right in front of the sunset.
5:20 PM	Sure, rowing halfway across an ocean is great. But, I must say, I am rather proud I have not had conversations with inanimate objects yet. Sorry mini-Wilson.

When I pause from rowing during the day, or at night when I am eating one of my "gourmet" dinners (I have a good imagination), I sometimes look at the sky and let my mind wander. When you live in a city amongst buildings, trees, and hills, the sky is often blotted out and obscured by what we see on the ground. On the ocean, though, there is nothing on the landscape to distract me, and the sky constantly demonstrates its magnitude to me. Like tonight, the only things competing for attention were the birds flying around at sunset. And they complemented, not distracted, from the sight, proving what a wonderful expanse of freedom the sky is! This reminds me of that ancient Chinese proverb, "Women hold up half the sky." I seem to be the only one doing my part out here!

Seriously though, what does this proverb mean? It alludes to the equal significance of women in the world, as we represent half of the human

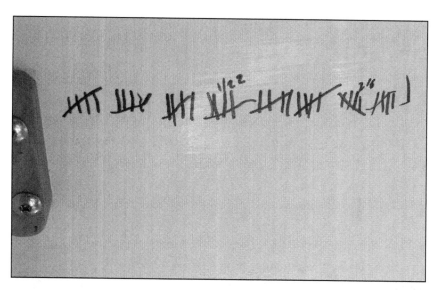

I am marking time like a prisoner! Here are 41 marks written on the inside of Liv, *and the dates I reached milestones.*

population (more now, actually). The sad reality, though, is that women are not treated equally, not then or now. Nothing underscores this point more than the book *Half the Sky*, by Nicholas D. Kristof and Sheryl WuDunn. In the nineteenth century, they observe, the most significant moral challenge to humanity was slavery; in the twentieth century it was the threat of totalitarianism; and in the twenty-first century it is the struggle for gender equality.

Perhaps some people treat gender inequality as simply inconvenient. In the United States we sometimes think about women's rights in terms of equal pay for equal work or in ensuring that women are represented as CEOs of companies. But in poorer nations, the moral challenge of gender equality is far different. Amartya Sen, a Nobel Prize laureate in economics, first brought attention to this crisis in 1990 when she wrote that "More than 100 million women are missing."[94] Every year another 2 million girls disappear. Why? There are many reasons, including infanticide (girls are less valuable than boys in many cultures), forced prostitution, and sex slavery. In some countries, like India, girls are far less likely to be vaccinated or taken to the doctor when sick because a family cannot afford medical care for both sons AND daughters. Male children are the priority.

As the authors of *Half the Sky* wrote, "It appears that more girls have been killed in the last fifty years, precisely because they were girls, than men were killed in all the battles of the twentieth century." This is quite a statement, and it gets worse. Consider the deaths of all the horrendous genocides of the last century. A partial list would include the Armenians in Turkey, Stalin's famine, the Rape of Nanking, the Nazi Holocaust, Pol Pot in Cambodia, Tutsis and Hutus in Rwanda, and "ethnic cleansing" in Bosnia-Herzegovina. Here's another overwhelming statistic: "More girls are killed in this routine 'genocide' in any one decade than people were slaughtered in all the genocides of the twentieth century."[95] You can see why gender inequality is the moral crisis of this century.

While *Half the Sky* brilliantly brings attention to this devastating reality, I wished Kristof and WuDunn devoted more time to a discussion of water. The global water crisis dramatically and disproportionately affects women and girls. In a survey of 45 developing countries across the world, two-thirds of the time that a home does not have a source of water, women are responsible for fetching it. According to UNICEF, in Lesotho, Zambia, Malawi, Mozambique, Kenya, and Ethiopia, merely collecting water takes more than 30 minutes a day (and sometimes much longer), for more than 25 percent of the population. This task typically falls to the women, and therefore it diminishes and threatens their lives in many significant ways.[96]

Let's consider the relationship between water and education for girls. Water takes priority over education because everyone needs to drink water to survive. Women are considered "dispensable," and so they are tasked with retrieval. The effort takes time away from school. And when no water or toilet facilities exist, girls tend to drop out of school when they hit puberty because of the lack of privacy. Also, girls in Africa typically do not have sanitary pads, or tampons, and often only have one pair of underwear. Forced to use ineffectively old rags to manage blood flow, they stay home from school to avoid embarrassment.

Or consider the significance of water on the health of girls. While the lack of clean water poses a risk of diarrheal disease for both men and women, there are unique challenges for women. The strain on the bodies of young girls who carry water long distances often results in injury. In sub-Saharan Africa, women account for 6 out of 10 of all HIV and AIDS cases. Women are usually the caregivers for the sick and therefore at greater risk when treating family illnesses without water and sanitation facilities.

Now consider the safety factor. It is hard to believe that water is essential to safety, but imagine being a woman in a public setting all day long where there are no toilets or secluding trees. The result is a modern "Sophie's Choice," a decision that must be made between two equally horrific options. A 2010 Amnesty International report, "Risking Rape to Reach a Toilet," describes the experiences of women in Nairobi, Kenya, who are too embarrassed to go to the bathroom in public during the day, and therefore only relieve themselves at night. Wandering off alone at night in Kenya is not safe, and exposes women to rape, which is rarely considered a criminal offense by local authorities. One woman said, "Over half of us take 5 to 10 minutes to get to the toilet. . . . If you go out at night you will get raped and assaulted. . . . For women this is unique because it is not just the risk of assault or mugging but sexual violence as well."[97]

Now imagine a brighter world with access to water, and how its availability could contribute to socioeconomic opportunity. Access to water would give girls a better chance at education, which in turn might enable them to gain the skills to escape lives of poverty. Access to water could help reduce the subservient roles women often play in families. Though it is a difficult challenge in patriarchal societies, having water is a start towards empowering women to take active roles in their communities.[98]

As I balance precariously out here on the ocean to go to the bathroom, I am sometimes frustrated with how challenging and undignified it is. And then I think about what my life would be like if I had to do this with a group of men watching me. The humiliation would be devastating, and my self esteem would plummet. I can imagine avoiding the embarrassment by waiting for night and the cover of darkness. What I cannot fathom, though, is how I would make that choice knowing that nighttime brought the real risk of rape and violence. I am not sure how I could live like that. Thousands of women have no choice.

The lesson today is how important it is to be aware of the gender inequality in the global water crisis. If you are a woman, ponder for a moment the ramifications of water in your life and try to envision how your existence would change if it were not there. If you are a man, think about your mother, wife, daughters, or female friends and how that lack of water would change the lives they have now. If education, health, and safety were removed from their lives or yours, what would you do?

Day 42: Give a Crap about Human Rights

@KatieSpotz Tweet Log for Saturday, February 13, 2010	
11:14 AM	Is it more awkward for me or them? Just passed a boat…while rowing in the nude! Oops.
3:26 PM	Feeling a smidgen of jealousy towards the tuna. Apparently, they can travel 100 miles in a day. As for me? Averaging 30-40 miles a day.

I ended yesterday by asking the question *What would you do?* if the global water crisis directly affected you or a loved one. Here is another question: *Why does personal knowledge of someone often dictate whether or not we will come to their aid?* There are so many worthy causes out there, and the spirit of volunteerism, philanthropy, and charitable support is strong in so many people. But today I want to suggest that you lend your voice to participate in solving the global water crisis. This crisis affects people you do not know in devastating ways. Consider for a moment that they are, in fact, family.

Helping out can take as few as five seconds. Other projects could take a lifetime. My hope is that somewhere between those two extremes you might find a way to join us. Here are three suggestions if you have time, money, or talent.

If you have *time* to give, Amnesty International has a campaign entitled "Give a Crap about Human Rights" which focuses on the idea that clean water and sanitation are human rights. They have three rather simple ways for people who want contribute their time to this cause. They include:[99]

1. Tell your senators to support the Water for the World Act (http://amnestyusa.org/giveacrap).
2. Share this tweet with your followers: "I just gave a crap about human rights #giveacrapabouthumanrights"
3. Spread word in your community about these issues. Amnesty recommends taping a flier inside bathroom stalls you visit.

If you have *money* to spare there are many reputable places that can make terrific use of your funds. I have already talked about some of them. charity:water has a number of donation opportunities including Pipeline, which is a unique plan to help communities keep their water pumps flowing freely. The average well has a hand pump that is raised and lowered five million times a year. As you can imagine, breakdowns occur and it can be beyond the skills of a local community to repair them. charity:water has been developing wells with special sensors in them that can self-diagnose problems, send the data to a team in New York City, and they can dispatch locally-trained technicians living in India, Africa, or anywhere a system is in place to fix the well quickly, efficiently, and cost-effectively.[100]

If you have *talent* to offer then you might want to create a team and start fundraising to support a specific community or school in need in places like Kenya. H2O for Life is an excellent non-profit organization that matches schools and groups in the United States with schools in need to help bring water, sanitation, and hygiene. For example, in 2011 three young boys from White Bear Lake in Minnesota decided to put a doggie treat stand in their neighborhood and raise money for H2O for Life. They made posters and doggie treat bags and sold them. All the proceeds went to the Dara-e Zang Girls School in Afghanistan. In total their talent and social awareness raised $640.[101]

Why take time to do this? Because every single human on this planet has intrinsic value and worth. That includes you and me as well as our local neighbors. It includes our global neighbors, people we may never meet in person. Distance and separation does not diminish the fact that these

At one of my stops in Kenya visiting schools. Such infectious, bright, and luminous smiles from all the kids I met, despite their harsh conditions. They were an inspiration.

neighbors have a bright inner light that is being dramatically dimmed by the devastating global water crisis.

Please consider sharing your voice.

Please consider sharing your time, talent, or money.

You can save a life, prevent a rape, or bring a smile to a child.

What more to life is there than that?

As for bright, inner lights, I am sensing a transition point in the row and in my thoughts. Let's see where it leads if we follow that light.

Part Three: Our Bioluminescence

Our children are gifts that are placed in our care for just a short time on this earth. It is our job to nurture and care for them when they are with us. But there then comes that time when they mature and grow into adults. They must make their own decisions and choices.

I had my chance to make decisions in my life; now I must let Katie make hers.

Mary Spotz (Katie's mom), a blog excerpt from midway into her daughter's row.

Day 43: Remember Those Who Have Passed

@katiespotz Tweet Log for Sunday, February 14, 2010	
9:38 AM	So hot. Want to swim but still a bit intimidated by the hungry tunas that like to visit my boat
9:54 AM	Look at that, a Valentine's Day present. Footpiece corroded away from the saltwater and right shoe is now detached

I have reached a potential milestone here, though it is probably wishful thinking. Today marks the two-thirds mark in my journey across the Atlantic Ocean. Apparently the folks at home are paying attention. My mom sent me this email today:

> I know you are in good hands the more I read about your willingness to never give up and your ability to enjoy the moment . . . I need to remember your slogan "no worries." Your marine track is moving right along . . . looks like you are closing in on the 2/3 mark!!! Enjoy the moments Kate. Love Mom[102]

A rower never knows how long a voyage like this will take because unlike the driver of a car, I cannot set my boat on cruise control at a fixed speed and use that handy mathematical formula (rate x time = distance) to know exactly when I will hit the shores of South America. So, for a little mental lift today (which I need after our serious discussions about the water crisis), I will proclaim that two-thirds is complete, and there is only a third to go!

I do not take my progress lightly, nor do the miles I have already rowed make me complacent or less aware of danger. Tom Lynch, the American coordinator of the Ocean Rowing Society (ORS), recalled a Russian toast he often heard, which was simply, "To those at sea . . ." These words did not fully resonate with him until his friend, Peter Bird (who co-founded the ORS in 1983) lost his life trying to row from Vladivostok, Russia, to San Francisco. After that tragedy, on a beautiful night with a full moon, Tom understood the salute honored not just those people currently at sea; it also remembered the spirits of those lost to its depths. To date, seven people have sacrificed their lives attempting to row across an ocean.[103] Though all of their boats were eventually found, rescuers recovered the body of only one rower.

I do not want to dwell on my progress to date, but instead I want to celebrate those who paved the way (or the "wave" as it were) in the history of ocean rowing. Without them I would not be here, and this includes both the successful (340) and the failed (200) rows. The Ocean Rowing Society keeps statistics on all these 540 attempts. They call the first rows, from 1896 to 1981 the "Historic Oceanrows," when rowers had only the most basic technology onboard. In fact their navigational technology was similar to what Christopher Columbus had at his disposal. Of course that meant they had no GPS or satellite phone. Norwegians George Harbo and Gabriel Samuelsen (following in the oceanfaring tradition of Leif Erikson and his fellow Vikings) were the first to cross the ocean in a rowboat. Their 55-day journey in the Fox took place in 1896. Remarkably, it would be 70 years before the next person completed a transoceanic row. Now we are in the "Modern Day Oceanrow" era, which began in 1981 and is defined by the use of the latest and greatest navigational and computer devices (or at least as many as the rowers choose to use). But we still are powering our boats in exactly the same way—human muscle.

This is an activity that has attracted more men than women. If I complete my attempt, I will be just the ninth woman to do it solo, and the young-

D⁰ ₋Fᴏx".

An image of the first two men to row across an ocean in 1896. Their boat was a little different from mine.

est person, male or female.[104] In 1999 Tori Murden became the first woman to row solo across an ocean successfully. She wrote this about her experience:

> Like the epic hero in Homer's Odyssey, women could be clever. We could set out on epic quests of our own choosing. Like men, we could be independent and internally motivated. Women could be tested and not found wanting in trials of courage, resourcefulness, endurance, strength, and even solitude.[105]

I say a big yes to this sentiment!

This brief history lecture is my lesson for the day. No matter how far along you are in your journey (whatever that journey might be), never expect that you will succeed. Yes, have confidence that you will reach your destination, but as soon as you expect to win you can slip into overconfidence and easily lose your winning edge. I call the "Tortoise and the Hare Syndrome." Clearly the hare should have won the race, but his overconfidence led him to relax so much that he fell asleep and lost to the slow-moving, but steady and hard-working tortoise.

I want to be like the tortoise who just keeps moving forward, always with strong intention and ever-vigilant of potential failure. The best thing that can happen if you fall victim to the rabbit's mindset is simply that you lose a race and learn a life lesson. The worst thing is that you actually lose your life if you are engaging in a high-risk endeavor. The last ocean rower to perish at sea, Nenad Belic, died 151 days after leaving Cape Cod while heading east into the Atlantic. Failure can happen at any time, and for any reason. Nothing guarantees my success out here, but I will remain on guard against complacency and overconfidence as a way to give myself the greatest chance to achieve my goal.

Now I take a moment of silence for Peter Bird, Nenad Belic, and the others who gave their lives to the ocean in their rowing attempts. I honor their legacy and courage, and in this silence of the ocean surrounding me, I remember the spirits of those who have died, raise a plastic bottle of warm water, and offer a heartfelt toast: "To those at sea . . ." Your inspiration provides a light for the course I row.

Day 44: Thank the Giants

@KatieSpotz Tweet Log for Monday, February 15, 2010

| 5:53 PM | Katie has less than 1,000 miles to go now; 975 miles in fact. And they're not even nautical miles this time! [Sam] |

I seem to be making good progress today. Sleeping still remains diffi-cult, though, and this adds another layer of complexity to each day's efforts. My hands hurt badly and I have unpleasant rashes all over my body from who knows what exactly—it is likely a mixture of repetitive motions, sun, scrapes, and the salty air. My physical output each day still exceeds the input of rest that I get at night. This is not an equation for long-term success. It does remind me of how much the human body can endure, if you ask it to.

I did finally find something useful to do with the clothes I'm not wear-ing. At night I use them, as well as various other gear, and wedge myself between dry bags filled with clothes and gear on top of my mattress. This is the best position I can find as I attempt to sleep in my stuffy, hot, airtight cabin. I have a small fan, but it provides little relief as it actually just moves the hot air around. Locking myself into place like this allows me to roll better with the waves at night and not to get tossed about and bump into things (a bean bag chair would have been perfect). This gives new mean-ing to "tossing and turning in your sleep!" I know! Hilarious. That might seem a little funny in the daytime, but at 2 a.m., after being slammed by hundreds of waves, my sense of humor is just not there.

While I am not sleeping I can at least think. And I am still reflecting on the ocean-rowing history I discussed yesterday. I am certain my high school history teachers would be happy to hear this. I am coming to appreciate more fully that in most every endeavor in life, pioneers have paved the way. They provide us with knowledge and experience we can build upon to reach our dreams. Some of these people paid with their lives, the greatest price possible. Consider the astronauts who first walked on the moon. Neil Armstrong was the first human to step onto the lunar surface, but he could never have done so without the sacrifice of fellow Apollo astronauts, President Kennedy's authorization to fund the space program, the expertise of decades of scientists and aeronautical engineers, and the daring of stunt and test pilots who pushed the bounds of technology, starting with the Wright Brothers' first flight. Even ocean rowers helped the space program because being isolated in a small boat provided the closest psychological simulation on earth to the conditions astronauts endure in space. Except I think that sleeping in a weightless environment would be easier!

These pioneers are everywhere, in every profession and occupation, and not just in high-profile pursuits like space exploration. Isaac Newton, perhaps the greatest scientist who has ever lived, said it best, "If I have seen further it is by standing on the shoulders of giants."[106] He was referring to his predecessors like Copernicus, Brahe, Kepler, and Galileo, whose discoveries gave Newton a strong foundation for his own work. To Newton's credit he saw himself not as the sole initiator of the Scientific Revolution. Instead he imagined himself standing on these giants' shoulders even as he co-created calculus, developed the science of optics, and articulated the law of universal gravitation. And he also was one of the first to build and use a reflecting telescope. A very cool guy! My point here is that even a giant like Newton had to stand on the shoulders of other giants in order to achieve his dreams. He knew it, and I am more and more aware of this every day.

I am by no means a Newton! That is the last thing I am suggesting. However, this is a really important lesson for the day—a giant lesson, even.

Take a look at the people and things that surround you. It is worth considering those who have helped you on your life journeys. We are all standing on the shoulders of others. Without their direct and indirect assistance, it's impossible to know where we would be today.

I owe a great deal to the giants who came before me. Not just rowers like Tori, Peter, Nenad, George and Gabriel (who I mentioned yesterday), but also boatbuilders, sailors, meteorologists, and the engineers who constructed devices like GPS and Satellite phones. And if there is anyone (or anything I should say) upon whose shoulders I ride and depend the most right now, it is my boat *Liv*. Credit for her goes to the British boat designer Phil Morrison. He has been building boats since 1967 and also had a great yacht-racing career of his own, so he brings a lifetime of experience to his designs.

Morrison designed *Liv* specifically as a one-person rowboat capable of withstanding ocean expeditions. She is strong and lightweight, due to the advanced composite materials she's made of. Technically *Liv* is made of Airex Foam. She has a Nano Shell that is injected with an experimental epoxy, as well as a unidirectional S-Glass. Aquidneck Custom, boatbuilders in Rhode Island, constructed her for Paul Ridley (who I mentioned way back on day 14) and his trans-Atlantic row to raise money for cancer research.[107]

My point in all this is that, like Newton standing on the shoulders of his giants, I also stand on the shoulders of giants, and they allow me to strive for my goals. Consider just the brief list of people technically responsible for *Liv*: Morrison, Ridley, the boat craftsmen at Aquidneck Custom, and the numerous scientists and engineers who experimented with *Liv*'s material shell (not to mention my family and friends who give me emotional support). All of us are standing on the shoulders of giants right now. Who is supporting you? Identify and thank them. Who might be able to see farther by standing on your shoulders? Reach out and help them up. These are critical questions to ask, and I will have plenty of time to continue to reflect upon them tonight as I will battle with sleep. One night I will win!

Day 45: See How We Shine

@KatieSpotz Tweet Log for Tuesday, February 16, 2010

3:53 PM | It's a bird. No, it's a plane. No, another flying fish!

I have no illusions of invincibility, but most of the external threats to my well being out here are entirely beyond my control. I find the best way to deal with this is to try to identify the things in life that I cannot influence and isolate them on one side of my mind. I take a deep Zen-filled breath, and then exhale and attempt to expel these out into the universe. Let the cosmos deal with these problems, not me. It is bigger than I am, and it can handle it. This is not an easy thing to do. We all worry over people, events, and actions we have no control over. Lack of control is the source of all worry, anxiety, and stress. The Zen mind teaches us to move beyond dwelling upon these things to achieve liberation by releasing them into nothingness.

I do not claim to come up with these ideas on my own. Cheri Huber, I have mentioned, is one of the most inspiring Zen teachers in my life. I have attended some of her retreats and they are patterned after the Soto tradition of Zen Buddhism, which she practices. In her fascinating book, *Buddha Facing the Wall*, she interviews several contemporary Zen monks in the United States and discusses an important paradox of existence. We cannot truly become an interconnected part of the world unless we completely separate ourselves from it, at least for a time. When I first heard this I thought, "Whoa, what does that mean?"

It is really about control. Many of us spend our days in a state of angst worrying over things we have little influence upon. We might want to become more popular, taller, shorter, smarter, funnier, or more fashionable. We might fret over someone else's gossip or strive to become something we are not in order to appease someone else. As Cheri says, this is not the right approach to connect with the world. She believes that only through solitude can we have the opportunity to look inward, not only to discover who we are, but to learn to be at home in the world and within our own skins. In other words, and this is the key point, "We already are everything we need."[108]

This relates to the paradox of life. To discover the ways we are connected to everyone, we must also experience being alone with ourselves in silence and solitude. It is in this environment that we gain self knowledge, and learn to differentiate better between that which we can and cannot control in our lives. This teaches us to expel the negativity in our lives back into the universe as we also discern the best way to expend our mental activities. This, Cheri says, is why we have monasteries. They are training grounds that demonstrate we can live without talking or interacting with others, and can rely entirely upon ourselves. Only when we achieve this self-realization, are we free. The Greeks engraved "Know Thyself" on the Temple of Apollo at Delphi for a reason. This is a lesson for all of us, though. We do not have to abandon our lives and move to the inner sanctum of a monastery to begin to achieve this awareness.

I do love paradox. It may seem like this is a different message than yesterday's, when I talked about knowing whose shoulders we stand upon. But both are very true. If we are afraid of being alone, we can wind up spending too long with people who are bad influences. This makes us a prisoner. Abusive or unhealthy relationships can trap us because we are afraid to let go. Learning how to be alone gives us the strength to walk away when it is in our best interest.

As Cheri says, "The separation between us and the rest of existence is an illusion, with sad and destructive consequences." This is a powerful idea. It leads me to wonder how to remove other separations in life.

The sun and water, the vital building blocks of life. If the human body contains roughly 60 percent water, I know that the sun and light also make up a significant, if unmeasurable, portion of what is inside us. Here is a beautiful sunset.

Wow, I am really on a spiritual quest today! Maybe it's the lack of sleep, or maybe it's what Cheri says: being alone promotes self knowledge. I think I have discovered a rowing monastery out here! If our lesson today is that we already are everything we need, then I have just one more example to add to it.

It comes from the life of Thomas Merton, a Trappist monk who died tragically in 1968 (electrocuted by a fan in Thailand while at a Buddhist conference). He is considered one of the twentieth century's most insightful and prolific spiritual writers, and at the end of his life he spent a great deal of time addressing the connections between Zen Buddhism and Christianity. He had a mystical vision in downtown Louisville, Kentucky, on March 18, 1958, a rare day when he emerged from his cloistered home of contemplation at Gethsemani Abbey.[109] (See www.monks.org). I quote him here at length because his words are so passionate and so beautiful. They speak a universal truth, one that Cheri emphasizes on retreats and one I feel here on my boat. Here is what happened to Merton in his words:

In Louisville, at the corner of Fourth and Walnut, in the center of the shopping district, I was suddenly overwhelmed with the realization that I loved all those people, that they were mine and I theirs, that we could not be alien to one another even though we were total strangers. It was like waking from a dream of separateness, of spurious self-isolation in a special world.... This sense of liberation from an illusory difference was such a relief and such a joy to me that I almost laughed out loud.... As if the sorrows and stupidities of the human condition could overwhelm me, now that I realize what we all are. And if only everybody could realize this! But it cannot be explained. There is no way of telling people that they are all walking around shining like the sun.[110]

What a vital message that eloquently proclaims the self-worth of every person on earth! We are all one. We are all exactly the person we need to be. And we all are able to strip away the illusion that there is a wall that separates us from each other. It is also okay that sometimes we need to be alone to come to this realization. It took Merton 16 years in his monastery to realize that we are all "walking around shining like the sun." There is great beauty in this, as well as responsibility. It means we cannot ignore our fellow humans when they are suffering and in need. We are not separate or separated from those that need clean water in Africa, and so many other places throughout the world. We are they, and they are us, and there is a sacred beauty in all of our hearts.

Day 46: Be a Little Paranoid

@KatieSpotz Tweet Log for Wednesday, February 17, 2010	
6:31 AM	Rowing today feels somewhat like one of the wet rides at an amusement park. Lots of waves, lots of splashing.
4:42 PM	Very colorful fish visitors. Unfortunately, my knowledge of marine life is limited by what I've picked up from *Finding Nemo* or *Spongebob*. Have no clue what fish it is!

I find that during the day I tend to enjoy all of the waves in the ocean. Sometimes it feels like the greatest amusement park in existence. Sadly, what seems like a thrill ride for me turned into a disaster for another ship on the Atlantic. Let me tell you the story of the *SV Concordia*.

I embarked on my journey from the Port of Dakar. As the westernmost point in Africa, Dakar is a very popular commercial shipping port. My boat was barely noticeable, hidden under the pier between all the massive freighters.

It wasn't hard to miss the other boat sharing Pier 2 with me. It was a stunning 188-foot yacht with masts more than 100 feet tall. The *Concordia* was a school ship that travels around the Atlantic with roughly 50 students onboard. I eventually met some of the people on the boat, including its captain.

As they showed me around, it became very clear that they knew what they were doing. They had the very best of everything in terms of equipment and they ran the ship like a well-oiled machine. It was hard not to be a little jealous when I saw the comforts onboard (a kitchen and toilet!) that my little rowboat didn't. The day after I left Dakar, the *Concordia* embarked on a similar course across the Atlantic towards South America.

Our companionship and similar voyage is what made a text I received via satellite phone today so shocking:

"Everyone is okay, but the SV Concordia *has sunk."*

My jaw dropped.

I couldn't believe it.

How could such a structurally sound, well-maintained ship sink? The ocean was rough today, but there were no big storms. Tragically, after capsizing, the *Concordia* sank within 20 minutes. Apparently those onboard are now adrift on life rafts awaiting rescue. I will keep an eye out for them, as I'm rowing in their general direction. I can only hope all of them survive this ordeal.

I know I am as ready as I can be for the unexpected on the Atlantic. But so too were the well-trained and experienced crew of the *Concordia*. You can't protect against all of the risks in life. Whether you're in a 19-foot rowboat or a 190-foot yacht, the ocean will take you where it wants to. I know I'm always one moment away from disaster, and even still water has the potential to turn my world upside down.

Today's lesson is about avoiding complacency. Andrew Grove, the founder of Intel, said, "Success breeds complacency. Complacency breeds failure. Only the paranoid survive." I like to approach every challenge with intense preparation, but at the same time I remain just a little paranoid. To me this is another form of fear, and this in itself is not a bad emotion. It's really all in how you choose to use it. You can channel paranoia and fear to make yourself more alert and proactive so as to avert danger when necessary.

Grove said, "I believe in the value of paranoia," and while that sounds a bit crazy, it's a technique that helps me keep my guard up.[111] Well-placed

I am leaving Dakar, Senegal in West Africa in this photo and passing by the Concordia, which sank 45 days later.

paranoia can be an antidote to complacency. It can add an important layer of protection against failure resulting from overconfidence or a lack of attention to details. Consider the ways that paranoia or vigilance has helped you in your life. How might increasing attention to this improve your work, school, or home life?.

I wish all those who were on board the Concordia a quick rescue and safe sailing in the future. I will remain vigilant and a little paranoid as I continue on my course over the undulating arms of the Atlantic.

Day 47: Take Your Ship Out of the Harbor

@KatieSpotz Tweet Log for Thursday, February 18, 2010	
1:40 PM	Eek. Tinkering with the rudder in the back hatch and was hit by a wave. Looks like I am sleeping in one wet bed tonight!
5:14 PM	The 40s look a lot like the 30s which also look at lot like the 20s. Nonetheless, good to reach 40W. Now all I need to do is row one mile 850 more times!
10:09 PM	Took a few extra minutes to gaze into the night sky and saw three shooting stars!

I am fortunate that the only result of being hit with a wave is a wet bed. I am constantly vigilant, and yes, even a little paranoid, as I confessed yesterday, about the possibility of being thrown overboard. The sinking of the *Concordia* is still on my mind. Thankfully, I just learned that after 40 hours in life rafts, all of her crew members are now safely back on land.

Danger is often present in our lives. Threats to our wellbeing surround us constantly, taking various forms, like violence, disease, and accident. Though unavoidable, the person living in constant danger-avoidance misses the fullness the world has to offer. Some might suggest that my row is an example of someone tempting fate, with all risk and little reward. Why attempt to row across the Atlantic? Yes, I have heard that airplanes now make the trip much more quickly! But ask a mountain climber why they court danger and scale higher and higher peaks. The standard simplistic answer is "Because it is there." The reality is that intense physical challenges can help us better discover who we are. They give us confidence that no obstacle is too great for the human spirit to overcome. The price of confidence is the acceptance of some risk and danger.

Although I don't necessarily believe that "the greater the risk, the greater the reward" always holds true, I do believe there is much I have gained by taking calculated risks (at least "calculated" from my perspective). Risks force you to make things work. When you put your life on the line you're engaging natural problem-solving abilities. Risks empower you to establish new limits and boundaries, and can lead to higher levels of achievement. And once you make a habit of taking well-measured risks, you begin to live a life greater than you imagined.

Having said that, I'm not into taking risks for the sake of taking risks. I have tried other more extreme activities—skydiving once, white-water rafting, and some adventure sports like bungee-jumping while I was in New Zealand—but it's not something I feel I need to do constantly. And when I do, I prepare for the risks as best as possible. For example, many ocean rowers have issues with sunburn, saltsores, etc. I have not so far, and I think it is a matter of anticipating the dangers. If you're going to take some risks, planning and preparation are key.

Of course this applies to every endeavor in life. John Shedd, the second president of the Marshall Field Company, expressed my philosophy on risk much more eloquently than I can. He said, "A ship in harbor is safe, but that is not what ships are for."[112] Ships fulfill their purposes when they are sailing free, at one with the risks of the waters. Yes, there is always the chance of capsizing, as happened yesterday to the *Concordia*, but the rewards of traversing the ocean outweigh the risks. A ship languishing in a harbor would have no purpose.

The same is true for humans. We can all construct safe harbors for ourselves. While there is nothing wrong with caution, those who never leave the shelter of their safe harbors are in danger of missing out on more life experiences. We might tell ourselves we aren't strong enough to try out for a sports team, so we stay in our safe harbor at home instead. Perhaps we think we aren't smart enough to take a new class and we shut off a learning opportunity. Maybe we're unhappy with a job but think ourselves too unqualified to strive for a better one by learning new skills. It's risky to sail our human ships out of safe harbors, but we'll miss opportunities to discover what we *can* do if we don't. The way I look at it is that the risks of failure are no different than staying in the harbor. Either way a dream is unrealized. However, when you do assume risk you have a chance to succeed. And that is the reward.

The lesson for today is to take some time and identify the harbors you have created for yourself. Some are of course essential, like having a place to call home. But imagine where you might like to sail if you ventured into open waters. Then prepare your ship, accept the fact that some risk in life is healthy, chart your course, set the sails (I recommend them over rowing), and launch your boat. In other words, leave the comforting lighthouse, and let your own light guide you into the darkness and uncertainty of the future. There is great adventure in the unknown which propels us to discover powerful parts of ourselves we didn't even know were there.

If you fail, so what?

Count your successes, not your failures. I would have never seen those three shooting stars this evening, streaking across the night sky, had I remained in Ohio.

Day 48: Focus on the Present and Presence

@katiespotz Tweet Log for Friday, February 19, 2010

8:28 AM	Most peculiar creature of the sea just floated by. It's purple, it's lumpy, it's a man-o-war.
4:06 PM	The milestones are falling day by day. [Sam]

Though I am typically optimistic, today my glass is half empty and not half full. I have already talked about the virtues of solitude over loneliness. Sometimes I don't know how to take my own advice because this seems like a hollow idea to me today. It's a struggle to accept even the best theories at times. Today I have a major case of the lonelies.

It is gray and overcast, and you would think I would celebrate a respite from the sun. Instead, the grayness outside has seeped inside. I have not seen land in almost seven weeks, and even though I have gotten into a rowing routine, it feels different right now. This morning I rowed for what seemed like at least an hour, and when I checked my watch only ten minutes had passed! This sense of time slowing to a standstill stayed with me all day. On top of that I have a palpable sense of being alone. At home if I felt this way there would be easy fix with a meet-up or even just a jog in the park. That is not going to happen any time soon!

I know that at any stage of a long row (or any long journey) you can lose the willpower to continue on. I can certainly see why. Momentary thoughts like, "Isn't rowing seven weeks on the ocean far enough?" invade my own mind. This has been my battle all day. It's not so much wanting to quit. It's more like just not wanting to continue on any longer. And then finally, at sunset, out of the blue something glorious happened.

On the horizon I saw something move that seemed unusual. I kept looking, trying to focus my eyes at that distance. When I finally was able to make out the shapes, I realized there were sharp fins breaking through the water. My first, and immediate, reaction was "Sharks!" I froze, stopped rowing, and watched as they came closer. It was not my imagination. They were actually swimming towards me. My fear rose as they approached, and then suddenly I heard a blowing sound, a soft whistle over the constant white noise hum of the ocean. My fear vanished in a heartbeat, replaced with excitement. "Dolphins!"

It was like coming home to a dog. It was not so much that I was excited to see them (which I was), but they were excited to see me. And they were not just passing through. Instead someone must have told them that there was a party on *Liv*, because they started circling my boat. And as if I were at the most elaborate aquarium-touching tank in the universe, I could have leaned over my boat and made contact. Their silky smooth skin looked so soft and comforting. How different they were from my rough and calloused rowing hands.

It was then that I experienced the most wonderful sense of being connected to the universe. I was grateful to be here. I was thankful to be alive. And I was humbled that these dolphins came to share their presence with me at the moment when I needed it the most. Maybe that is why the words "presents" and "presence" are homonyms. The dolphins' presence was a gift.

Eventually I could ignore my surge of energy no longer, and for the next 20 minutes I rowed at full strength. My dolphin friends kept pace—or should I say, since they can swim 20 miles an hour, that they slowed their pace to match mine! I could tell they wanted to stay with me because they

One of the playful dolphins coming close enough to touch. This one seemed much more hungry than playful though. I do not think I will be swimming today.

weren't just swimming, they were playing. It was my private Sea World show, with the dolphins jumping completely out of the water, turning flips, and interacting with me and my boat.

Eventually, they left my side. But they no longer left a girl alone in the ocean. Instead I had regained my sense of solitude. My case of the lonelies was gone. I was connected to the universe and one with my oceanic surroundings. Most importantly, I regained the feeling that I would be okay. I will have the mental and physical strength to continue my row and I will proceed as far as the Atlantic lets me. I am good for another day.

I know that some endurance athletes spend their entire journeys envisioning the end, and that helps them get through. But for me, the secret is to focus on the moment, and that is the lesson today. It is this present moment in time that matters most in our lives. Funny, there is a third word that sounds the same: presence (state of being), present (gift), and present (time). How different and yet how similar all of those are!

It is only in the *present* moment that I can have total awareness of being connected to the sun, the weather, and the waves. That is a *present*, or a gift, from the universe itself. And today, the best day of my life, a connection with the *presence* of the dolphins![113]

My final thought today is this—we are similar to flashlights. When they dim, it is typically because the batteries have run down. The bulb itself is usually still strong. And so we do not discard the flashlight, we simply change the batteries. This is a metaphor for how to re-energize our lives too. How lucky am I that dolphins brought me some special batteries today? Who in your life can recharge your batteries when you need it the most, through either their *presence* or *presents*?

Day 49: Share a Moment of Time

@KatieSpotz Tweet Log for Saturday, February 20, 2010	
7:43 AM	If it is possible to have an endorphin high like the "runners high", I may be having a "rowers high" right now.
6:39 PM	Cool! Can see more glowing under the water from night rowing. Brief flashes of light right below the surface but nothing like that glowing plankton.

My spirits remain higher today after my dolphin encounter from yesterday. I realize that after experiences like that, I have a completely new appreciation of the natural world and the creatures living within it. Before I left home, people often warned me about a long list of dangers. This did not just include the waves, the weather, and the months of being alone. They gave much well-intentioned advice about being fearful of a number of sea creatures as well. The list was frightening and it always included sharks, but there were also jellyfish, eels, and whales on it, among others.

Certainly caution is never bad. The ocean is a mysterious place and much of it is unknown. It's the largest habitat on earth and remarkably, 60 percent of our globe is covered by ocean that is at least a mile deep.[114] Give that much watery volume billions of years to evolve, and you wind up with some incredible inhabitants. Almost every time an oceanographer goes on a deep sea dive, they discover a new species of creature. How cool is that? As far as spooky creatures go, forget about *Jaws*. Instead take one look at the phronima and I promise you will cringe. It was the visual inspiration for the *Alien* movies. This translucent creature is just plain creepy.

Along with creatures like these, the ocean boasts stunning geographical features. The Abyssal Plain is an underwater world on the deep ocean floor that extends 28,000 miles in length and covers more than 50 percent of the earth's surface. Its mountains are larger than Mount Everest, and despite their size they are some of the least explored regions on our planet. What we do know is that the Plain is home to a great many unusual creatures. For example, the Pompeii worm lives there in hydrothermal vents. These are known as the most heat tolerant creatures, thriving in an environment of 80 degrees Celsius (176 degree Fahrenheit). They live so far underwater they have never seen the sun, and do not require it to live.

Needless to say, these and other frightening stories about the mysteries of the ocean swirled through and flooded my mind before I left. Now they are starting to unravel as I begin to see these creatures differently. The oceanic beings have never been taught to fear a girl in a yellow rowboat, and so I am trying to unlearn the fear I have of them. That does not mean I want to stick my head into the mouth of an Orca. I do have some sense about me. Instead, the general fear of this blue unknown is leaving me. I see myself honored to be welcomed into it, watching these creatures existing in the habitat in which they belong. What I see around me right now is the product of billions of years of natural change. This makes everything back at home seem so transient, temporary, and new. The United States is not even 250 years old. My rowboat is like a time machine, taking me into an epoch before humans roamed the earth. Perhaps that's the storyline for a science fiction novel: "Girl goes on ocean row and returns to find she is the only human alive on the planet." I sort of feel that way right now.

Clearly my greatest danger is getting too involved in observing the ocean! At the moment I am enjoying a turtle who has decided to accompany me for a little while. While it's fun to watch, I find that he (or is it a she?) lessens the urgency I feel to row. I tell myself that it's because I don't want to hit him with an oar. In reality, I just like seeing him swim. Didn't I tell you way back on Day 4 that I have a weakness for procrastination? Here it is on display for you!

And now the turtle decides to swim off without warning, as if it remembered a previous engagement it had. It floats gently away, almost gliding upon the water, getting smaller and smaller in the distance. Now the speck disappears and is gone. I will never see him again, but he has given me a small gift (another present of presence)—to watch an animal so free and wild and experience a shared present moment of time with him. I have no excuse now but to get back to rowing.

This is the lesson for the day. Share a moment of time with someone (or something) you perceive as different from you. When you do, what often happens is that the illusion of separation or difference is revealed as exactly that, an illusion. No, I do not now think I am a turtle! But I am learning to see how all the creatures on this planet coexist in a delicate ecological balancing act. We all share one home. This is true not just for animals and humans, but also between humans and each other. Oftentimes we create artificial distinctions, categorizing people by race, ethnicity, in different categories like racial, ethnic, age, gender, religion, economics, physical appearances, intellectual abilities, etc. Do these distinctions really exist objectively, or are they just subjective stereotypes and culturally constructed illusions? Either way they block us from seeing each other as we really are and appreciating the unique aura that emanates from within each of us.

I think we are far more similar than different, and sharing a moment with people we've placed in these perceived categories helps us to fully dispel this illusion. A thirsty child in Africa suffers the same as one in the United States. *There are no "others." There is only us.* Thank you, Mr. Turtle for sharing a moment with me today. I wish you well on your journey! And now it is back to mine.

Day 50: See the Sublime

@KatieSpotz Tweet Log for Sunday, February 21, 2010	
9:17 AM	I'm convinced someone wrote "hit me" in permanent marker on my back. Just got hit by two flying fish at once!
8:00 PM	Wow. Wasn't sure it was possible to see more than a thousand stars at once until now.

I feel like I am floating between two impossible giant universes: one above in space, with infinite stars, and one below me in the sea. It's difficult to wrap my mind around how much volume the ocean makes up on our planet. Consider this comparison. When you are flying on an airplane and looking out the window, think about how far the earth is away from you. Planes attain altitudes between 25,000 and 40,000 feet and there is a remarkably comparable distance between the ocean's surface and its floor.

The average depth of the ocean is 2.65 miles, while the deepest part is in the Mariana Trench in the Pacific Ocean (36,000 feet). The Atlantic is a little shallower at 27,400 feet, but this is still deeper than the altitude of some planes. I am not sure if it's possible to get vertigo on board a boat while considering how far away I am from the ocean floor, but it's best not to dwell on that. At least where I am, the depths reach only 6,000 feet, but that's still more than a mile!

There is nothing as sublime as the daytime passing into night.

Along with its sheer size, the ocean is full of mystery, and it has enticed dreamers and adventurers to explore it as long as humans have roamed the earth and constructed boats to venture off dry land. This is no wonder because the ocean is a part of us. As evolutionary theory states, life emerged billions of years ago within the depths of the ocean. Today many of us long to return, if only to its shores on vacation or to cruise to an exotic location.

Creatures who still make the ocean their homes are in many ways as mysterious and unique as we are. Take for instance the blue whale. It is not only the king of the deep, but it is the heaviest creature to have ever existed on earth. These creatures can extend up to 90 feet in length and weigh about 170 tons (remarkably the largest dinosaur weighed 90 tons). Their hearts are as large as an average automobile, and the offspring drink up to 150 gallons of milk a day. Oddly, adults only eat one of the smaller sea creatures, krill. It is amazing something so big hunts a creature only one or two centimeters long, but they make up for it in quantity, eating up to

40 million krill a day. Some of the blue whale's veins are so big, humans could swim down them. That is one river I have no plans for swimming!

Why am I reflecting on all of this today? The Atlantic is teaching me to see the mystery of life and to be astonished by it, even when I'm struggling to move forward. That is my lesson for today. It sounds trite certainly, and we have heard the suggestion to "stop and smell the roses" all our lives. But sometimes simple phrases contain a deeper meaning.

There is sublime[115] beauty surrounding all of us. To see it, though, we should consider pausing to look with new eyes. Try to emulate the way children explore new things with joy, focus, and complete immersion. I know I certainly need to take a moment away from my daily responsibilities and see life like a child.

Often our routines can blind us to the awesomeness of life. We think we have no need to look, because we have already seen. The author Amy Tan expressed it well: "You have to be displaced from what's comfortable and routine, and then you get to see things with fresh eyes, with new eyes."[116] I think she is right. Taking myself out of my daily life has given me a remarkable new perspective. Remember my Proust quote on *Liv's* walls? "A real voyage of discovery lies not in finding new landscapes, but in having new eyes." I am starting to see with new eyes. Now as long as the sun does not blind me by the end of the voyage, I will be okay!

The lesson today is really a suggestion to take time and find just one thing to look at with new eyes and wonder at its mystery. In the words of playwright Henry Miller, "The moment one gives close attention to any thing, even a blade of grass, it becomes a mysterious, awesome, indescribably magnificent world in itself."[117]

Be astonished with life! See the sublime. Consider the beauty of a single tree in the landscape, the patterns of the stars in the night sky, the sound and feel of a summer rainstorm, or the taste of cold water on a hot day. I think the sensation of an ice cube in my mouth might induce euphoria. Learn to appreciate the sublime reality that surrounds us. Mine today is the blue whale. I will leave you now while I ponder more of its mystery, as you find a mystery of your own to explore.

Day 51: Be Careful What You Touch

A word of advice. When you are gazing in wonder at the sublime, do be careful what you touch. I will tell you why in a moment.

All the cool stuff happens at sunset and sunrise. They are the transition points in life, between day and dusk, and darkness and dawn. Time always seems to stand still a bit during those moments when the sun is either disappearing under the horizon or christening a new morning. The sunset today was certainly memorable. Dorados, for some reason, seem to like to jump out of the water at the end of the day, and the only dive they know is a belly flop. Sunset is always a nice time for a break, so this was a perfect entertainment opportunity. I decided to row closer to them because I do find it so funny.

After getting close I got out my waterproof camera. Leaning far over the boat and partially into the water, I slid the camera beneath the surface. At the same time I realized that my hand was stinging intensely. I looked down in disbelief and saw a jellyfish had tangled its tentacles around me and my oar like a vicious piece of seaweed. Screaming, I flung it off me into the water and felt the panic rising as the stinging red pain increased.

Thankfully, I prepared for something like this and I remembered my first aid kit. I only had to recall what nook on the boat I had crammed it into. I dove into the front cabin and found it relatively quickly, opened it with one hand, and pulled out the manual. The pain was spreading by that point and reading a book was the last thing I wanted to do. But a calming breath helped me discover a relevant passage. First I needed to remove the tentacles and any remaining stingers. It looked pretty clean so I was fine there. Then I had to rinse with saltwater. Check! That was certainly easy—after making certain that I had drifted away from the jellyfish. Finally I had some hydrocortisone cream I could apply.

Then I remembered, of all things, an episode of *Friends* when Monica, Chandler, and Joey were at the beach and a jellyfish stung Monica. Joey recalled a TV documentary explaining that human urine helped eliminate the sting. So I thought, if it was good enough for *Friends*, it was good enough for me. I was glad I was in the middle of the ocean where no one could see me! I dabbed the painful skin dry, applied the cream, and rested in the cabin until the pain subsided.

That helped a little, and so I decided to read the poison control section in my first aid manual more carefully. It started, "Stings usually cause severe pain to humans. . . ." I thought, "Yeah, great insight there." Then it explained that the sting would leave a whip-like red welt on the skin for a few days. That was indeed what was appearing. I should have just stopped reading at that point. There was nothing more I could do, but I read on.

> . . . the venom may cause, depending on the amount of venom, a more intense pain. A sting may lead to an allergic reaction. There can also be serious effects, including fever, shock, and interference with heart and lung action. Stings may also cause death. . . .

That was just terrific. Of all the heroic and dramatic ways to give your life to the ocean, a jellyfish sting was not one I had in mind. All I could do was direct my mind elsewhere. I knew I could deal with the pain. My concern was what to do if I started to show symptoms of a reaction. A doctor's appointment was not in the near future, and so I taped my arm up, and just kept rowing.

These Portuguese man-of-war are creepy looking, and it's even worse if you get tangled up in them.

It turns out that this was not a common jellyfish—it was a Portuguese man-of-war. *National Geographic* comforted me with the words that "Anyone unfamiliar with the biology of the venomous Portuguese man-of-war would likely mistake it for a jellyfish."[118] I also learned that I should stop cursing "it." I needed to reword that to a "they." This animal is composed of an entire colony of organisms that work together. The unusual name comes from its gas-filled bladder which sits on the surface of the ocean, looking like a warship's sail. Having no propulsion capabilities, they just drift with the current, or catch the wind with the "sail." It is amazing that the tentacles, the tendrils, can extend up to 165 feet. If I would have gotten wrapped up in one that big I could have looked like a mummy! Luckily mine was a smaller one. They kill their prey by wrapping these tendrils around them, and paralyzing with their venom. I guess I spoiled its—or I should say *their*—dinner. The good news from *National Geographic* was that though the stings are "excruciatingly painful," they rarely cause death. That wording was much more reassuring than my first aid manual's.

My lesson today is simply to be careful what you touch, but there is a deeper meaning to this. During the last few days I have had some remarkable experiences, sharing a moment with a turtle and being with the dolphins. Perhaps these joyful encounters caused me to lower my guard a bit, and relax about the dangers out here on the ocean. No matter how comfortable we are with our surroundings, we have to be careful, literally and figuratively, what we stick our fingers into. It might be a jellyfish or a Portuguese man-of-war on the other end. Figuratively it could be putting yourself in harm's way, hanging out with the wrong crowd, engaging in careless activities like drinking (or texting) and driving, or imposing your opinions where they do not belong. I am keeping my fingers and other body parts to myself from now on, unless invited by a friendly dolphin.

And the other moral of the story that I learned? Well, it turns out that urine on a jellyfish or man-of-war sting does nothing but intensify the pain, and has no healing properties. Well done, Katie. Well done!

Day 52: Music Touches Our Essence

@KatieSpotz Tweet Log for Tuesday, February 23, 2010

11:18 AM	Rain and shine, at the same time. The first good rain since I have been at sea and oh-so-refreshing!

I really needed that refreshing rain that I tweeted about! It was a perfect mixture of fresh water and sun. Is there a better combination? I think about moments like this: we associate rain with tears and sun with smiles. Yet whenever it rains and shines at the same time, it reminds me of happy tears, those moments in life when you are so moved emotionally that they bring on tears of joy.

Why did I especially need this today? I am having one of those good news/bad news experiences. The bad news is that yesterday's man-of-war sting adds an entirely new level of pain to all of my daily activities. It's not just rowing with this injury that adds a new complication. Sleeping is even more difficult now because it's even harder to get comfortable (or what I currently approximate as comfortable). I thought I was diligent in preparing and packing for every scenario and challenge. If I ever do this again (and I am pondering a circumnavigation right now) I will bring along more sleeping pills. I ran out weeks ago, and long for a few hours of uninterrupted sleep. However, I would rather be tired than overly reliant on sleeping pills. Sleep medications can make for a slow response to the sound of my AIS emergency alarm. So it is sort of a catch-22.

I said there was good news, right? There is. *I am not dead.* Apparently yesterday's sting has not triggered a reaction in my body. The redness is just painful, but thankfully there are no red streaks running up my arm. So, no more tweeting today or blogging. I am just going to row and listen to music. Thankfully I have music!

While I will never tire of the ambient noise of the ocean, the music of Mother Nature, I often drown her out with my waterproof speaker box and iPod. Music energizes me, and the song's beats and my oar strokes blend into one as the hours pass. I brought one iPod for audiobooks, another for lectures and comedians, and two more for music. I have a lot of music! If I had only listened to the Gorillaz' song "Superfast Jellyfish" yesterday!

Music is much more than entertainment. The ancients believed that music was essential to understanding the universe. Pythagoras studied the musical scale and determined the lengths of vibrating strings that produced specific "notes" or tones in 500 B.C. This was not just about how to tune an instrument! He was exploring how music and the power of numbers revealed hidden truths about the universe.[119] Music has continued to influence scientific thought ever since.[120]

Music is a force, which is why I think I listen to it when I row. It is fuel for my spirit, just as food is for my body. I am not sure how that actually works in terms of human biology (I am not sure anyone is), but all you have to do is observe the number of headphones at a gym or on a running track, and you will see the relationship between music and movement. It helps us propel ourselves forward physically and intellectually.

I find it to be such an important component of this row that I do not listen to music when I am done rowing for the day. I do not want to lessen its effectiveness when I need it the most. Just like my chocolate bars, music is a treat and I need to use its power wisely.

What music most conveys power for me? I like all of the following artists, especially when they use their music to talk about water. Zero 7, a trip-hop group, has a wonderful instrumental piece called "Salt Water

Sound." These smooth, mellow, electronic tones are a perfect tonic for sore muscles. Kate Havnevik's silky voice also calms me, especially when her lyrics talk about "slumber in water." If you like otherworldly ethereal voices I put Bat for Lashes in this category too. The French duo Air falls into this soothing genre too, and their first album, *Moon Safari*, really is the perfect soundtrack for nighttime rowing. My favorite song so far has been from Morcheeba, another electronic pop band that has a similar sound. The song that resonates most with me? "The Sea."

If I need something to energize me, I might turn to DJ Miguel Migs with his deep house music. The theme of his first EP, *Underwater Sessions*, is a wonderful electronic inspiration. The fuzzy electric guitars of Imogene Heap's song "Daylight Robbery" help me to soar, especially when she sings about "happiness and silhouettes, revolving in the deep water." She is so right, there is "pleasure in the wave."

If I am in a fun mood I will listen to the Gorillaz, which is actually a virtual band. Their song "Clint Eastwood" always makes me smile and gets me dancing. When they rap about a "panoramic view" they should see what I do. And maybe they do, because they share my philosophy that "you don't see with your eye. You perceive with your mind."

Other artists who get frequent plays include: Sia (who used to sing for Zero 7), Kaskade, Jem, Natalie Walker, Radiohead, Olive, Jamiroquai, Garbage, Swayzak, Thievery Corporation, Coldplay, Emiliana Torrini, Fiona Apple, Flunk, Hird, One Republic, Lily Allen, and lots, lots more.

My lesson today is that we should not underestimate the power of music. It can elevate our moods, and help us to push forward in life (especially when dealing with a jellyfish sting!). Music captures the beautiful essence of life in ways that pictures, books, paintings, and even some experiences cannot. It's a window into our existence that is like no other. And it also unites us together in remarkable ways. Think of people gathering around tribal drums in Africa, a Native American pow-wow, or even the heightened sense of love and unity at a rave or a rock concert. The intricate beauty of Beethoven's Ninth Symphony, composed by a man that could not hear, reinforces this point. Music can be an "Ode to Joy" that has the capability to touch our essence.

And believe me, it is much more fun to touch music than a jellyfish.

Day 53: Dance Like No One is Watching

If there is music, then there must be dancing. I shared my musical obsessions yesterday, and so today I want to share my thoughts on dance. The band Generation X had a hit with, "Dancing with Myself." If they saw me out here on *Liv*, they would find me standing precariously, balanced in the middle of my rowboat, alone on the ocean, and dancing like no one is watching.

Why am I dancing out here? Many reasons!

I dance to stretch my legs after rowing.

I dance to celebrate a milestone on my journey.

Most importantly, I dance because it is a shortcut to happiness.

I hear a great song and just cannot help it. It is not about being a great dancer by any means. According to self-help guru Wayne Dyer, "When you dance, your purpose is not to get to a certain place on the floor. It's to enjoy each step along the way." This means a lot to me, for several reasons. It reminds me that I do not always need to be getting from Point A to Point B. As the expression goes, "Life is a journey, not a destination."[121] Dancing is a way for me to really let go. I relax my determined focus because there simply is no destination in dancing. It ends when the music is turned off, and you might find yourself standing in exactly the same place where you started. But that journey in between, if mind and body move with the music, can be glorious.

Dyer's quote about "enjoying each step" is also important because, as I have already said, the present is the only moment that exists for us. We can either enjoy it, or not enjoy it. I would much rather opt for the former! I can't really take too many steps out here, but I can try to enjoy each oar stroke. Think about being in the middle of a wonderful, soul-enriching dance. Are you thinking about the future, or reflecting on the past? I am not! I am living the moment, and this is what happiness is all about. The only place you can truly feel it is in the present.

I agree that this is much easier said than done. Not only is it difficult to appreciate each moment of the day, it is also challenging to stop focusing upon the destination. And that is okay. Life is difficult and a challenge. Many days are neither easy nor enjoyable. However, if we keep striving to enjoy the journey, in the long run we will be in a much better place.

What is the best advice I can offer to achieve this? *Dance like no one is watching.* That is the lesson for today. I am not the first to make this suggestion. There was a *30 Rock* episode named this. Jon Stewart even had a "Moment of Zen" clip with this title.[122] And there is a lyric by Susanna Clark and Richard Leigh in their song "Come from the Heart":

> You've got to sing like you don't need the money
> Love like you'll never get hurt
> You've got to dance like nobody's watchin'
> It's gotta come from the heart if you want it to work.

Think about the times when, as a kid, when you were dancing alone in your room. It was so freeing because no one was watching. What if we could live life that way, with every moment a true expression of ourselves, not caring if we were being judged or evaluated? Experiment with this sometime. Go through your day and ask yourself, "What would I be doing right now if no one were watching?" Obviously, this does not mean taking off your clothes and running through a crowded park. Nor does it mean doing or saying something hurtful. Instead the experiment is a way to become more *in tune* with your inner thoughts, desires, and longings.

That is the tune we should be singing along with and dancing to. My promise is that I will not judge your dancing if you do not judge mine. As David Bowie's album title so succinctly says, "Let's Dance"!

Day 54: Step Up from Rock Bottom

I tweet to the world that there are no worries out here, and I try to pass discomfort off with a little quip or joke. But then again I have never really been one to share my darker thoughts of despair openly. I often feel like this: What gives me the right to share my moments of sadness when, compared to so many people in this world my problems are minor? I mean, what is more tragic than watching your child die from drinking water that's so scarce that you had to spend half a day walking to get it?

That said, I am requesting permission to speak openly, kind of like military subordinates do in the movies when they want to tell an officer something they might not want to hear. If I am honest, things have been really difficult lately. Unbearable even. Instead of revealing that truth to the world via social media, I simply share my happy times and sort of hide behind ideas like I'm dancing like no one is watching. While that is true, it is also true that I am not always dancing out here. There are tears and feelings of hopelessness. Sometimes I simply cry. I have one person to thank for pulling me through dark times, and that is Sam Williams. Let me tell you about him.

I initially contacted Sam nearly three years before I began my Atlantic journey to discuss the rowboat he used to cross an ocean.[123] He lived in London and we emailed for months. When my family and I took a family trip to

England and France, Sam and I arranged a meeting in London. It was a great first encounter, and I guess you might measure that by the fact that we ended it not with a handshake or even a hug, but a kiss. Over the following months he became my main supporter, and time after time pushed me through and beyond technical hurdles. We discussed logistics, planning, project management, social media, and so on. He was a close mentor who helped me see the forest when I was stuck focusing on the trees. He believed in me before anyone else did, and at a time in my life when most people opposed my idea. And he was there with me in Dakar when I started my row.

My mom and his mom, Kit Williams, shared emails of support with each other during the first days of my row. For example, two days into my journey my mom emailed Kit and said: "I wanted to make sure to compliment you and your husband on the great job you did raising your son, Sam. I can't believe what a great friend he has been to Katie over these past days. I am sure she wouldn't have been able to do it without all his help and moral support."[124] Kit responded to my mom later that same day: "Sam and Katie are both very special young people—they have a spirit and courage which only very few have—either through birth or life experience, probably both. Doesn't make them easy to parent or live with, but they do bring a lot to the world."[125] Yeah, I know my mom would agree with the "Katie not being easy to parent" part! Sorry, mom!

Sam has continued to support me in remarkable ways even while I am out here on the ocean. The most important moment for me, though, was yesterday when I reached rock bottom. Even one more oar stroke seemed like a monumental task which I had neither the energy or will to initiate. All I wanted to do was curl up and disappear. I wanted to get away from the ocean and from everything. I thought I was done.

What I really lost sight of was *why* I was out there. I felt like the ocean no longer held the meaning it once did. I started asking myself, "What's the point?" Even though I never lost sight of the fact that the water crisis was the most significant cause I could imagine, I questioned how much good I was doing. Donations were not coming in at a consistent rate and nothing guaranteed that I would reach my target fundraising goal. I thought perhaps I was so focused on taking care of others that I had ignored my own needs so deeply that I could not recover. The bottom line? I felt overwhelmed and lost in a darkness of my own creation.

It was not just my body that was at a breaking point. I thought my boat was too. The rudder was acting up, and that meant steering was problematic. It seemed symbolic to me. I had lost my direction and so had *Liv*. Furthermore the rudder continuously reminded me that it was broken because it banged constantly during the night, making sleep even more impossible. I barely cared enough to even ask for help, nor did I think anyone could actually get through to me anyway, given my state of mind. I hated the idea of talking about it because it simply took too much energy. I remember wanting to cry, but I didn't even have the energy for tears. I had become a lifeless zombie. I felt so alone.

Also, I really could not tell most people how I felt. I certainly could not tell my parents because their worry would make me feel worse. I already felt guilty because my decisions and dreams were making it hard for them to sleep at night. So I hid, put on a good face in tweets and emails, and tried to just keep rowing. I was sleep-deprived, exhausted, in pain, and ready to make an emergency call asking to be rescued from this madness I had gotten myself into.

I was not thinking straight anymore. My mind flashed back to an interview I gave before the row and I was asked what I would do if I reached my breaking point. How much money it would cost to rescue me and how many lives I would put at risk? I did not want to jeopardize someone else, nor did I want to face sponsors, family, and donors after letting them down. I also did not think I could live with the humiliation of not "being strong." Not coming back at all seemed preferable to me to being carried back like a baby. And, it was not just the row that I wanted to give up on. It was life itself.

Instead of an S.O.S. call I made a S.A.M. call.

I was in the cockpit because there was better satellite phone reception there. I lay there, staring up at the night sky, rocking aimlessly in my boat. I was at the lowest point possible, so deep that I could barely verbalize my sadness. I do not think I actually had to speak the words: Sam knew how

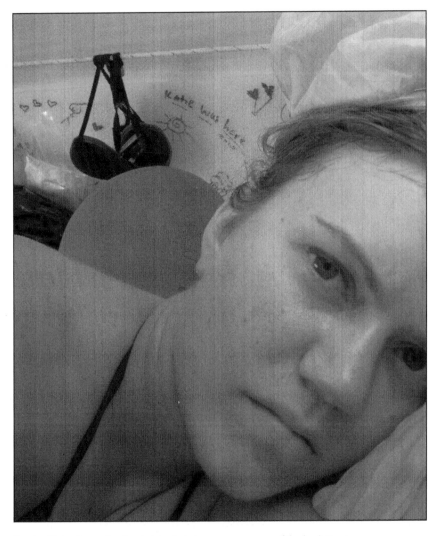

I took a photo at one of my low points. Perhaps you can see some of the desolation in my eyes. Normally bright blue, they looked as dark as I felt here. You can see behind me some smiley faces and heart doodles that I drew on the side of Liv *in happier times.*

to get me out of that dark place, just by being there as a friend. But, he did not know how deeply I had fallen into a dark place. What did he say to me? I don't remember what he said, but I remember how I felt. It was like Maya

Angelou said, "People will forget the things you do, and people will forget the things you say. But people will never forget how you made them feel."[126] That is exactly what happened with Sam that night under the stars.

Suddenly I was sobbing. The tears were rushing so strongly that my entire body was shaking. My emotions rolled through my body and I had no control. And though Sam and I were very far apart physically, he made me feel like he was with me. The true meaning of the word "compassion" is "to suffer with." In Sam I had someone who could suffer with me and ease my pain.

Sometimes you are in a situation that cannot be analyzed, and you simply need someone to take your hand and understand. Sam listened to what I am certain was incoherent babble most of the time. He did not preach or judge. He heard me. The fact that he acknowledged my feelings as legitimate somehow made them seem okay. He had been where I was before, having crossed the Atlantic two years earlier. He had felt the same thing and that meant that I was not deficient or a failure, I was just experiencing what others had. I no longer felt "weak" or "wrong." I felt like a human, perfectly imperfect, just like everyone else.

Sam has been more willing than me to convey publicly some of the struggles I have been enduring. For example, he gave the following interview to NPR:

> Reporter: So how's Katie doing?
>
> Sam: It's a struggle. She's getting sore limbs and blisters and everything like that. But it's the head that falls apart first. She's been holding up mostly pretty good. There's been a few days when she's been struggling, but Katie has a way of getting through that and the next day she's on form and rowing toward Guyana again.
>
> Reporter: When you say struggling, do you mean mentally?
>
> Sam: Yeah, absolutely. You get into a mindset and everything is just so difficult. You have incredible lows because you feel a bit down and there's absolutely nothing there to stop you. You're just spiraling down into huge depression because you're

by yourself, you haven't seen anybody for two months, there's
no one to help you out and basically kick you in the backside
and get you smiling again. So you have these massive lows and
incredible highs.

My lesson today is Sam, or really the importance of having a Sam in
your life. Everyone has dark moments. You can't go through life without
periods when you feel down or unable to complete your goals. It is essential
to have someone special in our lives who has access to our hearts, someone
we trust enough to let deep inside where their special light illuminates
our darkness. If they truly listen to you, they can help you take the first
step in overcoming an obstacle, which is acceptance, instead of avoidance
or denial. Even though you may feel powerless, you *can* step up from rock
bottom.

Let me use a boat metaphor. You would not think of taking a boat out
into an ocean without a life vest. Of course you do not plan to sink, but
you think ahead, prepare for a worst-case scenario, and have that safety
precaution in place. Our lives are like boats on an ocean. We get very lonely
and lost sometimes. We don't plan on this, nor do we know when it might
happen. But the only way to survive is to have a lifeline. Sam was my tether
to sanity. I now know that, with less than two weeks to go, I at least have the
mental power to continue until the ocean tells me to stop. I have Sam to
thank for that. It's time for me to begin to climb up. That is the beauty of
hitting the bottom: there is nowhere to go but up.

Day 55: Take the Albatross off Your Neck

@KatieSpotz Tweet Log for Friday, February 26, 2010

| 9:41 PM | Usually only spot one or two at a time but today saw 6 albatross floating one by one. |

I love to watch the albatrosses gliding over the surface of the ocean. They are so graceful and precise in their movements, and efficient in the air. The birds soar and glide such great distances using what appears to be a minimal effort. When they dive for food it's also amazing how fast they snatch fish, squid, and krill. These birds are like martial arts experts on the ocean. They should be wearing little black belts!

It is hard to believe they can also symbolize bad luck. This association began with Samuel Taylor Coleridge's 1798 poem "The Rime of the Ancient Mariner." Legend has it that if an albatross follows your ship it is good luck. But in the poem, the mariner shot an albatross with a crossbow, and a curse fell over his boat. The crew blamed him for their ill fortune, and he felt like the dead albatross was hanging around his neck for all to see. Today we use the term "albatross" as a metaphor for a psychological burden or curse.

Because of those birds, and Coleridge's sea poem, I find myself thinking about things that feel like psychological burdens in our lives. For example, I used to believe that being naturally more introverted was a curse instead of a blessing. I no longer look at it this way.

Carl Jung first popularized the psychological theories of introversion and extroversion, and from that point on, popular culture stereotyped people sorting them into one camp or the other. Some think that introverts are people cowering in the corner at a party, while they imagine extroverts as revelers standing on a table at that same party singing, gregariously. Psychological reality is much more complex and "No man is simply introverted or simply extroverted," according to Jung.[127] Instead, he suggests, everyone has both of these tendencies, and depending on the situation one or the other is dominant. Those who lean towards introversion often find large groups of people mentally and physically draining after a period of time. Those who drift towards extroversion are likely to feel energized by such situations.

I tend towards introversion, as I suppose one might guess, given that I've chosen to be in the middle of the ocean all alone! What has helped me, though, is understanding that my introversion is not an albatross. It does not prevent me from making deep and meaningful connections with the people I meet as I travel the world. More importantly, I now realize how essential it is to look for those connections. Yesterday's story makes that case perfectly.

For me, expanding my psychological comfort zone could mean making friends with a stranger. For an extrovert, it might be retreating to a quiet spot, spending time alone and deep in thought.

My lesson for today is this. It's very important and necessary to spend some time understanding who you are. Accept that person. If you're more of an extrovert and prefer being with groups of people, don't lament that reading poetry by yourself is not your thing. If you tend towards introversion that's okay too. It's not an albatross around your neck! Don't be ashamed if you're not always the life of the party. I have found I sometimes quite enjoy being a party of one.

Day 56: Expose Yourself

@KatieSpotz Tweet Log for Saturday, February 27, 2010	
5:06 PM	No more cookies or edamame or gum. And the nearest store? Over 500 miles.
5:16 PM	Katie has reached her goal of $50,000 for Blue Planet Run!!!! But let's not stop there... [Sam]

Thankfully I still have plenty of food. I'm not going to run out of that because I packed for 100 days, and given my progress, I should hit land well before that. My water supplies are fine. I have fresh water as ballast and my solar-powered desalinator is still working like a charm. I even have a backup hand-pumping desalinator should this fail. I should be content with my abundant storehouse ... but no cookies? I have run out and I feel like Cookie Monster shouting "Me want cookie!" But, as I said in my tweet, the nearest store is more than 500 miles away. And I also know this about myself: I am not one for asking others for directions. I do not like to show weakness, even though I know being lost is not a personal failure.

My lesson today is that there is great value in exposing yourself. No, I am not talking about the illegal kind. Instead, I mean that humans can experience incredible personal growth by exposing a vulnerability to another person. I learned this lesson over and over again preparing for this row. It can often be humbling, but I prefer to look at it a different way. Perspective is key. Exposing one's weaknesses can be an opportunity for growth.

For me, this process started at almost the same moment that I decided I wanted to row the Atlantic. There is not an *Ocean Rowing for Dummies* book out there. Even though those *"Dummies"* books cover more than 2,500 subjects, there probably won't be one on ocean rowing because it might sell only a dozen copies!

So my first challenge was learning what I needed to learn! The second was finding people who could help me. I soon discovered there was more to comprehend than I ever imagined. I had to understand the mechanics of rowing and the weather patterns on the ocean. I needed to become a boat mechanic, a nurse, a nutritionist, a project planner, and a website manager. It was a matter of training the mind and body, sorting out the logistics of shipping the boat, learning first aid, completing survival-skills training courses, negotiating with sponsors, building a website, drafting press releases, spreading awareness of the water crisis . . . and the list went on and on. I started writing notes on the back side of gift-wrapping paper because I could use it as a giant scroll for my lists! I was trying to put together a million-piece puzzle without knowing what the final picture looked like— other than me rowing from one side of the Atlantic Ocean to the other.

I have already talked a little bit about this in my lesson "Life is a Team Sport." But there is another component I need to address, which makes this team concept work. I had to expose my vulnerabilities and uncertainties to people I didn't know very well. It was hard for me to admit that I didn't know all the answers.

It's true that I'm guilty of not asking for directions when I appear to be lost. I rarely take the time to read the instruction book when I buy something new. I enjoy the thrill of having limited knowledge and using my intuition and imagination to figure things out. This approach can also result in a long path to what, in reality, is a nearby destination. This row challenged my "I-can-do-it-on-my-own" mentality. People like to say there is no "I" in "TEAM." True, but there is a "ME" in "TEAM," and sometimes I rely on "me" to a fault.

My list began with questions like, "How do you go to the bathroom?" and moved on to more complex ones, like "How do you use celestial navigation?" (I assure you that learning about how to navigate by the stars is much more fascinating than figuring out how to go to the bathroom.) It was a matter of quieting my somewhat stubborn tendencies and opening up to others. There's an infinite amount of knowledge available to us if we're willing to listen, expose ourselves, and trust the idea that vulnerability is the path to growth.

I sought help and advice from rowers, sports psychologists, sailors, engineers, web designers, nutritionists, oceanographers, personal trainers, mechanics, publicists, fundraisers, and sometimes my mom. The list grew as one person introduced me to the next. The Buddhist proverb that "when the student is ready the teacher will appear" couldn't be truer to my experience.[128] Thinking that I knew all the answers had prevented me from learning in the past. The time for that was over. It's much more difficult to learn with this mindset, and my time was not unlimited.

"He who asks a question is a fool for five minutes; he who does not ask a question remains a fool forever," goes a Chinese proverb. There is tremendous wisdom here. It offers a path to the vulnerable fool, exposing herself, asking a question, and walking confidently towards knowledge. This requires an implicit trust that the teacher's own light of wisdom will shine into you.

Now, if only I could find one of those teachers right about now. I have a non-life-threatening question. Can someone please show me the way to a cookie? I openly admit I have no clue how to get one!

Day 57: Make Friends with a Stranger on a Bus

My dreams out here are very strange. I am sure this has more to do with sleep deprivation and constant exhaustion than my movie selections (as I mentioned in my tweet). Perhaps I should have thought through the effects of my entertainment options a little more carefully.

As you can see from my writings these past few days, I have been thinking about who I am deep down, and how important it is to celebrate who you are. You may be shy or gregarious, funny or solemn, sensitive or stern, but there is no one right way to be in life. The only absolute rule, found in all the world's religions, is simply to treat others as you would like to be treated yourself. In other words, be kind, and as long as you are that, be yourself.

And sometimes, as I suggested two days ago, you need to go a little beyond just being yourself and push the boundaries of your comfort zone. Let me tell you a story about a time when I did just that. It happened when introverted Katie opened up to a stranger on a bus. It is odd how life works:

that unexpected interaction with a complete stranger significantly changed my life in a matter of moments. Making friends with a stranger is actually the reason I am out here on the Atlantic Ocean.

I was on a bus in Australia, and it was one of those times in which I had my headphones ready; I was planning for an introspective ride. I might have listened to music, or simply put on the headphones as a sign saying, "Don't talk to me please." However, the person sitting next to me had other plans.

So with a little hesitation, I pushed introversion aside and we shared stories about how we ended up in Australia (he was from Britain). One thing led to another and I eventually started talking about endurance events I have participated in. This seemed to spark more interest from my companion and he said the strangest thing: "I have a friend who's into that endurance stuff. She just rowed across the Atlantic with her mother." What!?!?

That one statement brought a million questions to mind. I was intrigued and yet skeptical that anyone would try something that seemed so impossible. At that point in my life there weren't many adventures I hadn't heard of: climbing the tallest mountains, biking across a country, running through a desert, skiing to the poles, or sailing around the world.

Rowing an ocean? That was completely new to me. It was also the most difficult challenge I could imagine. Although my companion on the bus told me about a rowing team of two, my introversion kicked in. I tried to imagine what it would feel like to be alone on an ocean. I wanted to know what it would feel like to make it back to land after months at sea. I wanted to find a challenge that would push me to the limit, with only one option. To overcome.

I didn't just *want* to row the Atlantic. I *had* to. My more logical side tried everything it could do to persuade me to ignore this dangerous desire. But I was curious, intensely, and the more I learned, the more I wanted to do it. No matter how hard I tried to ignore it, arguments against it simply faded away. I was sensitive to the fact that it would take a huge toll on my friends and family, who would worry about me. I knew death was a real possibility.

My desire did not go away. There wasn't a day that went by after that bus ride that I didn't think about the row. I wanted every bit of that experience. I couldn't ignore it. It was like dropping a ball from the sky. The ball has no choice but to fall to earth. Gravity takes it. The Atlantic Ocean had me in its gravitational pull—all because I decided to talk with a stranger on a bus. Or maybe it was just the universe doing its thing and setting me on a path I was destined to travel.

Perhaps making friends with strangers is what you do on a daily basis. Maybe you may think I am excluding you a bit in this lesson, but actually I am not at all. Be patient with the people you interact with, because their reluctance to talk might not signal a lack of interest, but rather discomfort with the social situation.

We all have something to learn from each other. Differences in psychology, geography, society, and culture do not have to become dividing lines that dictate who we can and cannot talk to and learn from. Huston Smith said it best, in terms of describing the world's religions. He wrote that we should think about how all belief systems are interrelated, like "stained glass window[s] whose sections divide the light of the sun into different colors."[129] What a beautiful way of seeing all people on earth! It makes me want to reach out to the next person I see, to discern their uniquely colored window glass. What an adventure to discover how each person reflects the light of the sun.

And that sounds much more enticing than calling the person next to me on a bus a "stranger."

Day 58: Look Beyond the Shell

@KatieSpotz Tweet Log for Monday, March 1, 2010	
4:49 AM	Woke up at 6am to see the bird visitors. Stayed four nights in a row now! If they come again, I'm charging for clean-up services.
3:42 PM	Cool fact—it takes a drop of ocean water more than 1,000 years to circulate around the world
6:41 PM	I'm having trouble figuring out where the water ends and sky begins with tonight's rowing. It's like rowing into a black hole!!

As the old saying goes, you can't judge a book by its cover. Some of the best books I have ever read were old cloth bound hardbacks from the library, their pages torn and underlined by previous readers. Contents and substance are what matter, not packaging. Rough edges can conceal something special within. Remember what a piece of coal can hide deep inside. The same is true of people, but it's so easy to fall into the trap of judging by what we see. Psychologists have studied our tendency towards judgment and how quickly our brains form opinions of other people. Nonverbal cues can have a vastly greater impact and impression than anything you say.

I experience this all the time. People have offered their impressions of what an ocean rower should look like, and I did not fit their expectations. A piece about my journey that ran in *New York Times* before I left suggested that

I "seem[ed] an unlikely addition to the list of ocean crossers." The reason? My looks. The story continued, "Even now, she displays none of the exotic musculature—mammoth shoulders, triceps shaped like lobster claws—that one might expect of a person who expects to row 2,500 miles."[130] I am not sure I want my triceps shaped like lobster claws!

The reality is that I look a lot like most women my age. I do not spend all my time at the gym trying to perfect an image. My goal is not to develop muscles or a physique that wins me a beauty pageant. To me, fitness is about performance. My body is a tool to get from point A to point B efficiently, whether I'm running, biking, swimming, or rowing. Getting a high score for perfect muscle tone is not for me. There's nothing wrong with that for some. It's just not what drives me.

My body is more than just something to squeeze into skinny jeans. It's a biological machine capable of feats even our own minds cannot imagine. How amazing is it that I can get a sunburn (if I forget sunscreen) and my body knows how to repair it on its own? If I get a blister, a rash, or a sore muscle, my body knows what to do. My mind has no clue! Our bodies are capable and strong. They are miraculous in so many ways—and that's true of all bodies. Judging someone purely by surface appearance does not do justice to the miracle within.

Not just endurance athletes are subject to critiques about body type. This is a significant problem for many people, especially young girls, who are bombarded with the "Barbie ideal" body-type image from a very early age. Modern media defines a type of female body that best sells products, and then perpetuates that image over and over. Today, human physiques are judged more on how they look on the outside, as opposed to how they are on the inside.

For example, I once did a print campaign for a jewelry company which will remain nameless. My body was capable of amazing feats of endurance, just as it is now, but I was a little surprised not to see my body when I opened the magazine. My friends and family said to me, "Wow, Katie you have lost a lot of weight." I said, "Yes, it's called Photoshop." I was certainly surprised to see my body airbrushed, since no doctor has ever told me I needed to lose weight. Apparently a body strong enough to row across the Atlantic Ocean is not the correct shape to sell jewelry.

As Pema Chödrön, an ordained American Tibetan Buddhist nun, says, "It's . . . helpful to realize that this very body that we have, that's sitting right here now . . . with its aches and its pleasures . . . is exactly what we need to be fully human, fully awake, fully alive."[131] Notice that she did not say that this requires airbrushing, nor did she mention anything about how that body looks. We all have this innate gift within our tall or short, thin or wide, bodies. Looking beyond our outer shells, and each other's, will help us to better appreciate this gift.

Give it a try sometime. Walk around during your day, intentionally blind to how people look. Then try to truly engage with everyone you meet based solely on what is inside both of you.

Day 59: Understand Instinct

@KatieSpotz Tweet Log for Tuesday, March 2, 2010	
7:38 AM	Breakfast on land: organic fruit with greek yogurt sprinkled with wheat germ. Breakfast at sea: Dirt and worms chocolate pudding. Slightly different, but no worries, lots of oatmeal on board too.

Another late night entertaining guests. Noisy and messy ones. They flew by a bit after sunset, fought over spots to perch, and turned my boat into their nest for the night. It's nice to meet these birds up close and personal. One picked a spot less than six inches away from me while I was rowing, clearly displaying no fear for humans. These late night visits have been more frequent and further proof of my theory that it is simply not possible to sleep on this boat!

With less than two weeks until landfall, I have been kicking it up a notch, and I've had my best week yet. One day I rowed more than 60 miles. I am not sure if I am "zoning in" or "zoning out," but I have certainly found a mental and physical space where I can just row and row and row. Despite the frenzied pace, I'm still making time at day's end for the beautiful sunsets. Today there were tons of dorados jumping out of the water as the sun went down. Every thirty seconds or so, I would see one, sometimes several, emerge from the water and make a huge splash. They still aren't graceful.

Come on dorados, learn a new dive technique! They're big fish, too, so I hear their splashing all the time.

How do I drown them out? Music, of course!

There is an old Pretenders song (Chrissie Hynde, who fronts the band, grew up in a town about an hour south of me), called "Thin Line Between Love and Hate." That's the irony about love. Common sense says that there should be a large divide between these two emotions. But our experiences tell it a bit differently. Sometimes it can be hardest to see the intrinsic beauty in those you love the most. And maybe there *is* a thin line between these two most powerful emotions. Or perhaps there are some people who elicit such deep passions that describing it all with just one word is too limiting.

So, let's talk about my mom. Bet you didn't know where I was going with this!

I already shared with you the strongly worded email she sent me when I told her I wanted to row the Atlantic. I still think about this line: "Dad said if Katie goes on that adventure you might as well kiss her good bye . . . she won't make it." There are very few parents on the planet who think letting their child face an ocean alone would be a good idea. My parents were clearly not among them.

My mom and dad didn't even like the thought of me being a few hundred miles from home, let alone a few thousand. They much preferred that I would get the adventure bug out of my system in less extreme ways. Because I care so deeply about them, it hurt to know that my decision would make things difficult for them. In some ways, this row is harder on them than on me.

As I prepared for the row we struggled to see each other's points of view. Perhaps that's putting it too mildly. But when I made this decision I was over 18 and legally of age to do what I wanted without their approval. On the other hand, they were legally welcome not to support me. This adversarial situation continued for quite a while.

Time does have a way of bringing change. My beliefs started to shift. I was still as committed to the row as ever, but I began to see it more from their perspective. I realized that it had been their job from the day I was born to protect me. Their fear of my getting hurt far exceeded their desire to see me make it across. My instinct was to row. Their instinct was to keep me safe.

From that point on, I saw beyond my perceived lack of parental support. It was not "My parents don't understand me or care about what I want." That was the little girl inside me talking. Just slightly wiser, I instead saw something much greater. It was love. Every "don't do it" was their way of expressing a genuine feeling of love for me. I saw that they loved me so much that they wouldn't want me to face the challenges of the ocean by myself.

The lesson here is that it's essential to understand more than your own instinct. Your instinct is the default way in which you see life. Knowing your instinct is critical, but you also need to step outside yourself from time to time and appreciate the instincts of the people around you. As long as it does no harm to others, one instinct is no better or worse than another. They are just different. Once you can appreciate and respect that difference, you will have a much better perspective from which to see the love that shines through.

Do you want to see an example of my mom's love shining through? I have on board with me 100 sealed letters she wrote to me, one for each day I might be out here alone on the ocean. Every day I can pretend the mailman comes, and I open and read one of her letters. How cool is that?

I think I will let my mom actually have the final word today. That's a first, right, Mom? She wrote a blog posting for me to share with the world during my row and here it is. She may get the last word today, but I'll be back tomorrow!

Guest blog—A Mother's Point of View by Mary Spotz

Last week I received an e mail from Katie asking me if I would like to write a "guest blog" for her. I immediately wrote back to let her know that whatever she needed me to do, I would be glad to do it. I began to wonder what she would want me to write about. I know people are often curious and like to ask Katie questions like, Why are you doing this?; Aren't you scared ?; and What will you eat? Katie is always so prepared to answer these questions but there comes that one question that usually stumps her. . . . What do your parents think??

Well let me begin to address that question . . .

I wish I could say that both her dad and I gave her a big hug and told her that whatever she wanted in life, we were behind her 100%—even if that meant rowing an ocean!! That is farthest from the truth. I remember getting this e mail from Katie two years ago while she was participating in a student exchange in Australia. She matter-of-factly stated that she knew what she wanted to do next in her life. . . . she wanted to row an ocean!! I quickly responded, "Oh no you are not!! That's crazy and that's way too dangerous!!"

So from that moment on the battle began. A battle between a mom who selfishly wanted to keep her daughter close and safe forever and a daughter who wanted to go after her dream. The more I tried to think of every reason for her not to do it, the more Katie found every reason to do it.

Eventually I began to realize a few things. First, that our children are gifts that are placed in our care for just a short time on this earth. It is our job to nurture and care for them when they are with us. But there then comes that time when they mature and grow into adults. They then must make their own decisions and choices. I had my chance to make decisions in my life now I must let Katie make hers.

Well, I know this all sounds good in theory but some days are easier to live by this than others. December 18th was the day that I forgot everything about Katie doing what she wanted to do and Katie making her own decisions in life. For December 18th was the day Katie would leave for her adventure!! It was terrifying enough saying good bye to someone who would be at sea for 70 to 100 days but it was even more scary knowing she would be ALONE at sea. No one to help you if you needed a shoulder to cry on or no one who could lend a hand rowing.

I should say, I thought she was alone at sea. I was so wrong. Let me explain. . . . The night before Katie left, we were get-

ting many calls from news agencies who wanted to interview
Katie. After speaking with many of them Katie decided to go to
bed. During the night, however, I could not help but hear the
telephone ringing on numerous occasions. The next morning
I checked the messages to see if anyone left one—NONE. I then
began to look at the caller I.D. and discovered one call that
really caught my eye!!

Before I tell you what it said, I must explain something to
you. Six years ago Katie's grandmother passed away. She had a
very special nickname... "PAL". She got this nickname from
her grandson who repeated the term she so lovingly called him,
"My little Pal".

Well on the caller I.D. were the words "OHIO PAL". I
showed Katie and she immediately pulled something out of
her back pocket. It was the note that was found next to her
"Grandma Pal's" chair the day she died. It read...

To my family
If I don't get a chance to say good-bye
Remember—"I will be on 24 hour call"—
Call me anytime.
Mom

At that moment I knew Katie would not be alone and Katie
knew this as well.

We did give Katie a proper "send off" at the airport. After
good byes were given, Katie turned to us with tears in her eyes
and said,

"I am going to give this all I got!!"

With that she proceeded in line and we all watched her as
she disappeared from our sight...so we thought. Katie then
ran back and looked at all of us one last time and gave us that
smile and wave!!

I think she finally realized...

We were behind her all the way and she would not be all alone
on this journey!!

Day 60: Remember a Hug Forever

@KatieSpotz Tweet Log for Wednesday, March 3, 2010	
4:56 AM	Noticing more and more boats showing on my GPS. A sign I am getting closer to South America!

I screamed a long and dramatic "Noooooo!" followed by a "Why?!!!" The reason for my outburst? There it was, a few miles away: a potential chat with a human. We might have played a game of poker. We could have bartered and exchanged energy bars (though in reality I would not have done this because I would have been disqualified by the Ocean Rowing Society for "unsupported" help . . . but a girl can dream). I'm not really sure what the appropriate mid-ocean etiquette is, but anything to break up the six hours of rowing ahead would have been very welcome.

This afternoon, I saw my first sailboat of this journey. Unfortunately, after several failed attempts to contact the boat on my VHF radio, it disappeared like a passing cloud. Maybe it's for the best. It might leave me with a smidgen of jealousy to watch as the wind propelled it effortlessly on its journey, while I inch my way along, pulling at the oars. So, for now, it's just me and the dorados.

It feels like I'm slowly returning to consciousness after a long, undisturbed dream. Yes, I have been in contact with the outside world through email and my sat phone. The difference is that now, for the first time, I'm seeing signs of human life around me. Sure, they might be in the form of blips representing ships on my GPS, but they signify that humans are actually more spatially present than they have been since I left Dakar 60 days ago. This means South America is approaching, my quest is nearing its end, and I have some confidence that I might actually complete what I set out to do. I am not counting my oar strokes before they are completed, though!

Oddly, as I approach land I'm feeling more homesick, and not less. For so many days I put actually being with my family out of my mind. Now that the reunion is coming closer, I'm thinking about who I want to hug. Maybe I should say who I need to hug. Arranging the landing party is not an easy task. It's not like driving from Ohio to Pennsylvania to meet me after my Allegheny swim. Traveling from Ohio to French Guiana is a bit more complex, to say the least. There are many people I want there, but I felt compelled to write my mom an email today about my younger sister, Maggie. I will share it with you:

Hi Mom

I talked to dad tonight and I desperately wanted to see if Maggie could come. It would mean so much to me. She has been part of this journey from the beginning even helping with some of the events, packing food in my room, for advice, comments to media articles, etc. You know how much we laugh and have fun together. Every time you mentioned Maggie in your letters it would get me all teary-eyed realizing how much she means to me. And I'm sure you too understand with your bond with Aunt Kath how important it is to have a sister.

This is a once in a lifetime experience and the first steps back on land will never be able to be reproduced. The first hug will be remembered forever. I so desperately want that to be Maggie. I know she too will remember it forever. I have been alone for so long now and the one thing I realized I miss the most is just laughing. The kind where you can hardly breathe, you are so happy. Today I was thinking about all the times Mags and I laugh like this, over the silliest, smallest things. I know as soon as I arrive, there will be lots of work ahead (media demands, shipping the boat, having the cradle built, etc.) It's so much to handle and the one thing that will help me through is to have a few good laughs with Maggie. We enter our own little world!

I know it is a lot to ask. But I took off a few days for the Bahamas in high school and there is enough time where she could plan around tests and assignments. I'm guessing most of her teachers know about this, so I'm sure they would be supportive. It would probably be 4 days off because I'm arriving on the weekend. Can you please let me know? I know I should be excited about arriving, but I feel like I'm rowing into a big pile of work and no fun.
Love
Katie

One thing this row has reinforced for me is how special some people in our lives are. My sister Maggie is one of those people for me. We really can and do enter our own little world where our souls sort of mystically entwine. What is the natural response when that happens? Joy and laughter, the sound of life being lived right. That's why I want her to be the first person I hug on land.

Perhaps I had forgotten how much hugs matter in life. Hugs were something I could not pack along with my Clif bars. I really never thought about what being devoid of hugs for 70 days might mean for my psyche. I can tell you now that it's hard. An embrace with a loved one is a gift of life we need to enjoy many times a day. The problem is that we sometimes take hugs for granted, much like a handshake. But they are far more than that. They are that brief moment when two people open their arms in a sign of vulnerability, compassion, love, and welcome. Entwining arms with another person brings our inner lights together. Think about two candles burning apart from each other. What happens when you bring them together and the flames unite? The single point of light becomes much brighter. That's how it feels when Maggie and I hug. As I said in my letter to mom, "The first hug will be remembered forever."

This is the lesson the Atlantic is teaching me today: the power of a hug is not reserved just for a select few. Hugs are for everyone! This reminds me of Mata Amritanandamayi, a 60- year-old Indian guru, known simply as "Amma," meaning "mother." Others call her "the hugging saint." She challenges us with one simple question, "If it is one man's karma to suffer, isn't it our dharma (duty) to help ease his suffering and pain?"[132] She heals suffering not as a physician, but with her love and deep hugs. These are not just random hugs; they are the focal point of her life. She schedules worldwide tours where she will sit onstage for 15 hours, hugging thousands of people, each one special. She has embraced more than 34 million people in her lifetime.[133]

Whose suffering might you ease with a hug? Whose love might make your light shine brighter with an embrace? Do not take this gift for granted. I know because you learn to truly appreciate something the moment it is taken away from you. On this hug-less row of mine, I have learned the value of touch. Take a moment and really hug someone. If you try to be truly present in that moment and remember that hug forever, you experience a special union, the ways humans are meant to be, in complete equality and love.

Now if only these people represented by blips on my GPS could actually hug me!

Reuniting with Maggie after my Big Ride Across America. Our reunion after this row will be even more special. I cannot wait for that hug!

Day 61: Learn to Say, "Hello, Friend"

@KatieSpotz Tweet Log for Thursday, March 4, 2010	
7:07 AM	Nothing, nothing, nothing. Hey, that's not nothing. A tanker!

Remember that I ended yesterday's message, saying I wouldn't mind if one of these people out there who show up as blips on my GPS could come over and share a hug? Well, I didn't really mean that literally. And yet it almost happened today. Here is the story. . . .

This morning, for some reason, I actually decided to row with clothes on. I have not done this very often because it makes the fabric so salty and rough. If you rub something rough over your skin 10,000 times over the course of a day, you can guess what will happen. So you can see why naked rowing was not about exhibitionism, but instead about self-preservation! My decision to wear clothes this morning came perhaps because I saw a tanker off in the distance, or maybe I wanted to introduce an item of civilization back into my life now that I am approaching land. I don't know. Either way, I was wearing clothes and was glad of it.

So, there I was rowing along lost in the rhythm of my muscles and the music on my iPod, when over my shoulder I glimpsed a boat! I could tell it was not nearly the size of a tanker, nor was it a sailboat. Instead it looked like a medium-sized fishing boat, and it was coming closer to me. The scary thing was that I should have been warned of its approach. All boats are required by law to carry GPS transponders with them, alerting all other ships to their presence. This boat did not have one, which could mean its crew hoped to travel undercover. That was not only dangerous; it was also very suspicious. Maybe they just could not afford a GPS. I had a lot of questions! And it was coming closer.

Lots of thoughts raced through my head. I had heard about people starting to hallucinate and I wondered if the boat before me was imaginary or real. I decided to assume it was real, and quickly ran though these questions:

What was that size of boat doing way out here?

Pirates? No, I had not heard of any activity in this part of the ocean. Should I find a weapon?

I quickly alerted my support team by satellite phone that a boat was approaching—not that they could do anything, but it felt good letting someone know. I just kept rowing and eventually saw 15 tanned men, hanging over the side of the boat, coming still closer, all of them looking at me. I did a double-check to make sure I had indeed remembered ALL of my clothes, and then, instead of a weapon, I discreetly reached for my camera. Based on their facial expressions, they seemed not to believe what they were seeing, a girl all alone in the middle of the ocean, rowing a boat. I was checking them out to ensure they were not pirates, but I realized there was no way to tell just by looking! There were no peg legs, parrots, or eye patches. While I was going through my visual inspection, I think they were looking at me to see if I was a mermaid at best, or, at worst, a mythological Siren, luring sailors with enchanted voices into shipwrecks.

They got very close and then started shouting at me. They did not speak English, but there were a few words that I could pick out, like "Venezuela" and then "Guyana." I understood one man ask if I had a "problem." I simply shook my head no, and tried to smile. I kept at my rowing and noticed some dolphins swimming by. I secretly wished I could join them and escape underwater for a while. I wanted to hold my breath and disappear.

The silence persisted a few more uncomfortable minutes and I started rowing. Oddly they continued next to me with their motors on, just staring. Most of the men even moved from the bottom of the boat to the top and just sat watching. Eventually, after what seemed forever, they turned their boat around and motored off. It has been a while since I have heard an engine or smelled the burning of gas and smoke. The scent was much stronger than I remembered. It was so foreign and unnatural that it gave me a moment of sadness about what I was rowing toward.

Anyway, I breathed a sigh of relief when the boat disappeared over the horizon and I kept at my rowing, quickly forgetting the encounter. A couple hours later there was again something over my shoulder. It looked like the exact same boat with the men from before. Why would they be coming back towards me? This time I ignored my camera and grabbed a flare and a pointed tool I could potentially use as a weapon. I knew I didn't have much of a defense given what I had. I never felt comfortable taking a gun onboard with me.

As it got closer I realized that although it looked identical from afar, it was a different fishing boat. We had the same language barrier and a remarkably similar interaction followed with words like "Venezuela" and "Guyana" again exchanged. This time though they kept saying over and over, "Loca, loca, loca." I remembered enough from my Spanish classes that this meant they thought I was crazy.

Thankfully they eventually left me alone, and as they continued on their way, the last thing I saw was one of the men staring at me with his fist pounding at his chest. Either he was having a heart attack, or was trying to flirt with me. Either way, I was quite glad to see them motor off, and I hoped there would be no other visitors.

My lesson for today is the importance of preparing oneself to communicate with other people. If we want to convey our benevolent intentions, we need to learn at least the very basic greetings in the languages of the different people we might come in contact with. I had actually planned to do this, bringing Spanish lessons on my iPod. This was kind of like bringing schoolwork along on vacation, with good intentions. I never got to the language lessons because I preferred listening to music and comedians. Had I taken my studies more seriously I could have maybe said something valuable like:

Mi nombre es Katie y estoy remando en solitario a través del océano!

(My name is Katie and I am rowing solo across the ocean!)

This boat and its crew were my first human contact in 61 days. Luckily they were just curious what the "loca" girl was doing out on the ocean by herself.

> Estoy levantando dinero para la crisis mundial del agua. (I am
> raising money for the global water crisis.)

Sadly, none of that happened. I believe there was goodwill between the fishermen and me, but the language barrier prevented us from the exchange of our intentions. The lesson is that you never know who you'll pass by on the journey of life. Learning a simple "hello, friend" in a few different languages is enough to open up new friendships and prevent unintended enemies. I will be better prepared next time!

Here is how I might say "Hello friend, how are you?"

Dutch: Hallo vriend, hoe gaat het?

French: Bonjour ami, comment allez-vous?

German: Hallo Freund, wie geht es dir?

Indonesian: Halo teman, bagaimana kabarmu?

Irish: Dia duit chara, conas atá tú?

Italian: Ciao amico, come stai?

Latin: Salve amicus, quid agitur?

Polish: Witam przyjacielu, jak się masz?

Spanish: Hola amigo, ¿cómo estás?

Sudanese: Salam sobatna, kumaha damang?

Day 62: Be a Zen Mirror

Behind door number one (or wave number one) is . . . *Holsatia Express.* Door number two . . . *Omega Emmanuel.* And number three . . . *Jose Breeze.* I have officially entered tanker territory! With larger waves around seven to ten feet, this makes for a slightly unnerving experience. My boat is easily tucked away between the waves, so that I am barely visible. Even with technology onboard for communicating with and viewing other boats (AIS/VHF/GPS), playing involuntary hide-and-seek in the waves still ranks high on the "Why ocean rowing is frightening" list. I would have a greater potential survival rate wrestling a shark than passing in front of a freighter. I think I'll be sleeping with one eye open, just like the dolphins do, until I reach land! My close call with the tanker during my first night at sea is still fresh in my mind.

Remember my dorados who have been following under my boat—Ed, Edd, and Eddy? Today was not a good day for Edd.

As I started to dig around in the hatches for my next meal, I noticed two hungry dolphins. They were more interested in Ed, Edd, and Eddy

Playing hide and seek with a tanker. This game on the Atlantic is not nearly as much fun as it was when I was a kid.

than in entertaining me. They circled around my boat, and one dolphin emerged minutes later with a dorado in its mouth. It was Edd! I wasn't going to get in the way of their mission, even though they were eating a friend of mine. They were quite possibly the largest dolphins I have seen, longer than my boat, and I wouldn't be surprised if they weighed as much too, especially given the way one seemed to inhale a twenty-pound fish.

Ten minutes later, after they swam off, about seven more dolphins came for dessert. Some swam so close to my boat that I could have easily touched them. Eventually the dorados came back, doing their belly-flop-style splashes. Perhaps it was Ed and Eddy doing a little victory dance (or splash) after escaping those dolphins.

This is the way of nature, though. It's not good or evil, it just is. The dolphins weren't evil, they were just hungry, and following their instincts. As I watched this today I was like a mirror, just reflecting what I saw, and not judging or "fixing" it. There is a classic Zen story about approaching life like a mirror because it, unlike humans, is a perfect reflection of what it sees. The mirror offers no critique. The mirror does not judge. A modern Zen writer, Zenkei Shibayma, put it like this:

> The mirror is thoroughly egoless and mindless. If a flower comes it reflects a flower. If a bird comes it reflects a bird. . . . Everything is revealed as it is. . . . If something comes, the mirror reflects; if it disappears the mirror lets it disappear. . . .[134]

This is a perspective on life that I would like to emulate.

Today's lesson? Become a Zen mirror. There are great benefits when we strive to wholly become "egoless mirrors." It's a worthwhile experiment to take an hour, a day, or a week, and really try to see the world in this way. There are lots of areas in our life where we can do this. For example, when you see a street person who looks homeless, just reflect back with a smile and no hint of judgment. If there is a person at work or school with whom you don't get along, and you find their mere presence churns up feelings of impatience or even anger, then be a Zen mirror. Just let them be. Don't try to "fix" him or her, and do not give that person the keys to your emotional kingdom either. Does a mirror change its composition if someone is making silly faces at it? Just breathe and exist. Try it sometime! Then reflect on how this perspective changes, alters, or re-informs how you perceive life and the people around you.

This helped me today while watching nature take its course, and Edd's demise. Now my plan is not to become an "Edd" and succumb to one of these tankers!

Day 63: See the Bioluminescence in Everyone

@KatieSpotz Tweet Log for Saturday, March 6, 2010

| 6:16 PM | The subject of my email tonight: "Is this normal?" with a picture of the latest and greatest rash development. It keeps getting worse! |

As I near the end of my journey (it's so odd to think this) I am fully accustomed to the sameness in my surroundings. The sky remains blue, occasionally shaded by some fluffy white clouds. The ocean reflects that blueness with its constant movement. The sun and my boat offer a bright yellow contrast. The scene is beautiful for sure, but I know tomorrow will be the same. Mixed in with the sameness, though, if you look carefully, is something unique about each day. This is true even of something as similar as blades of grass. This was on my mind back on Day 50 when I shared Henry Miller's thoughts on grass, that paying close attention to anything, even a single blade of grass, reveals an indescribable beauty and mystery. Look at a field of it and it appears like a limitless sea of similar green blades. Crouch down to look at just one and let it reveal the "mysterious, awesome, indescribably magnificent world."

Compare that to a stadium of people, or the citizens of a far-off country. Each of those people are unique with their loves, sorrows, dreams, and abilities.

I am striving to see something new every time I look out at the world. Some days this is a real challenge, but when I let my mind quiet, the calmness helps me appreciate it. It can be the way the sun glistens off the water, or how the clouds are reflected by the waves themselves in a beautiful merger of sea and sky. The way the water splashes against my boat, or drips down from my oars can be remarkably complex. I am always rewarded when I take a moment and visually explore the world around me.

Some days, or should I say nights, this is easier than others. Tonight I would have had to have been blind not to be amazed. I was peering into the water after dark. At first I thought my mind was playing tricks on me, because I saw something unlike anything I had ever seen before. It looked like the ocean was catching fire as glowing plankton began to swirl around my boat. I thought of Tinkerbelle's fairy dust, and it seemed like I was rowing to Never Never Land as *Liv* glowed from the magical light. While it was mysterious to me, oceanographers have a name for it: bioluminescence.

This beautiful phenomenon is exactly what the name describes—biological (bio) light (luminescence). It happens when a chemical reaction within a living organism produces light. Most of the organisms capable of producing this light live in the ocean and they include bacteria, jellies, and fish. But most have encountered them on land too.

Think back to how magical it was seeing a firefly when you were a kid. There was such joy in running and trying to capture one in your hands. The problem was that they always seemed to blink out right when you approached them, so you had to anticipate where they were flying. Once you caught one, you gingerly encased it within your hands, tentatively looking inside, and waiting for it to light up. Magic! Imagine a thousand of them flying around you at night. That was what my experience was like. It was beautiful and surreal as I watched the ocean light up underneath me.

Bioluminescence is *sublime*, to reuse a word I defined back on Day 50.

Sometimes we can be blinded to the beauty in everyone around us. The reality is that we all have a beacon of light that shines forth from within, projecting our inner radiance. It might not be as obvious as a firefly punctuating the night air with a fleeting moment of light, or as breathtak-

An example of the sublime beauty of bioluminescence.

ing as a swirling light show from glowing plankton, but we all, unmistakably, glow. This is particularly evident in the human capacity to express unconditional love for each other. How are pregnant women described? As "glowing." No, that does not mean we are all pregnant. But it does mean we all glow with beautiful light. Some New Age gurus believe that humans have luminescent auras or energy fields. Thomas Merton saw that we are all walking around shining like the sun.

In our daily lives we can strive to see the ways in which everyone around us glows. Of course there are people with whom we click and become friends. It may be easier to see their glow, but it's worth taking time to look for it in everyone. The reality is that we each have a beauty and a glow unique to us. Everyone has gifts to share. When I get home, I am going to practice seeing the bioluminescence in everyone and understanding the truth that all living creatures are sublime.

So as I feel like I am starting to say goodbye to the ocean, this light show of life has burned a message deep into my soul. It is one I will never forget.

Part Four: Climbing the Ladder

I sure wish she would finish this trip as soon as possible. Maybe she should just take up fishing for a while.

Mary Spotz (Katie's mom), email to Sam on March 2, 2010.

Day 64: Smile When You Reach Your Lowest Point

I'm in the home stretch now. The final leg. I feel both numbness and pain. I am tired and yet wide awake. I am ready for this to be over, and yet I want it to continue forever. I know I'm a tangle of contradictions, but somehow both emotional extremes feel correct. For so long this journey has defined me. I have planned every detail of this row, except for one thing. What happens when I see land and it comes to an end? What's on the other side? What will it be like to see people again? I am 22. What am I going to do with my life? For now, I am going to put those questions aside and just keep rowing.

I feel a little like a mountain climber at the last camp before the final ascent to the summit. I imagine looking down the mountain, seeing how far I have come, as I prepare for the last, and most difficult push.

How far *have* I come? Further than just Dakar, actually. I have not revealed to you what was perhaps my lowest moment before I started this voyage. Just two months before my scheduled departure, while I was training on Lake Erie, I crashed *Liv*. For a moment I thought all was lost, not just my boat, but my life. Settle in for the story!

Rowing on Lake Erie was an important part of my preparations for the Atlantic. Not only was it a place I could train my body on the mechanics of rowing in open waters, it also helped me learn how to operate my equipment, although I didn't anticipate using my distress signal. On Lake Erie I also adapted to living on my boat, if only for a short time, and with land always in sight. It was there that I learned how I would eat, how I would navigate, and what I would do about injuries or equipment failures.

Two months before reaching the Atlantic, I planned a 40-mile row from Cleveland's west side, heading east to Mentor, the suburb where I grew up and where my parents lived. I expected a ten to twelve hour day, approximately what I planned to do every day on the Atlantic. After checking the online weather forecast I began to row. The winds were light and waves were rough, but I thought the more challenging conditions would be good practice for me. It certainly seemed very manageable at the start.

My expectations changed as night fell and panic set in. Some might think the Great Lakes are easy and safe to navigate. Nothing could be further from the truth. Those are unpredictable waters, especially in the fall and winter, with dangerous weather conditions that have taken the lives of many sailors. Remember that Gordon Lightfoot song called the "Wreck of the Edmund Fitzgerald"? Once the largest ship on the Great Lakes, all 29 of its crew died in 1975 when hurricane force winds and 35 foot waves capsized her on Lake Superior.

What makes Lake Erie particularly dangerous is that it is shallow and the conditions can change quickly and unexpectedly. That's exactly what happened during my training session. The day's winds were stronger than forecast and the waves continued to grow and spike. I was slowly losing the ability to control my boat with the oars. The waves were becoming too powerful and the winds were pushing me towards the dangerous, rocky cliffs. I knew I needed to forget about my destination and instead simply find a place of safety. It was a battle against time and I was losing fast, becoming more and more fatigued by the moment.

I tried in vain to use my sea anchor to stop me from getting closer to the rocks, but it was also powerless against the strong wind and waves. And in the sand, the anchor simply didn't hold. The undertow was winning the battle and my life was in real jeopardy. My last resort was now my only option. I reached for my VHF radio, and trying to sound calm I said, over the wind, rain, and waves: "This is ocean rowboat, *Liv*. Coast Guard, do you read?" No one responded. Again, but shouting louder, "This is ocean rowboat, *Liv*. This is ocean rowboat, *Liv*. This is ocean row boat, *Liv*. Coast guard, do you read?" I heard a response, and they were on their way, but I knew it was too late.

The wind pushed me in all directions, but mainly towards land, and the rocky cliffs were coming nearer. "Is this it?" I wondered. "Does it all end here on Lake Erie?"

The rocks were so close. Impact was unavoidable even if the Coast Guard arrived.

All I could do was brace for it.

Then a giant wave lifted me high in the air, as if my boat and I weighed nothing. Towards the rocky cliffs we traveled, faster and faster, surfing, completely out of control. I tried to use the oars at least to guide the boat, while also minimizing the impact of the inevitable crash, but they were more like toothpicks in this gale-force wind. I closed my eyes, gritted my teeth, and the sickening sound of the crash filled my ears. We hit the rocks hard. Even though I was harnessed, whiplash jerked my neck forward. Then came the sound of scraping as the undertow pulled us backwards. It was not over. I could not believe it, but we were being drawn back into the turbulent lake. A new panic set in. We could be thrust back and forth against the rocks and into the lake, until there was nothing left of my boat or me.

Remarkably an even larger wave decided to lift us higher this time, and it javelined my boat into a rock crevice above the waterline. We were stuck in the rocks, and the waves were not pulling us back out.

It was such a surreal experience. It was like I forgot how to breathe. My body was shaking from the adrenaline pumping through my veins. It was hard for me to get my harness off because I was trembling so much. On top of all this it was a cold fall night, and being drenched intensified my shaking.

Here is where Liv *wound up after my crash on Lake Erie. She was more broken than I was.*

Eventually I unfastened myself and began to climb up the steep rocks. Once I started to climb out I felt more in control of my body. Now the adrenaline was my ally, giving me a surge of energy to climb the challenging cliffs. Once on top I was greeted by the flashing lights of a police car and an ambulance. I learned later that the officer stopped because he saw my distress light.

The officer asked me if I was okay, and in my shock all I could say was, "My boat." The paramedics wanted to take me to the hospital. I signed a form stating I refused their help, but they did a basic check while I stayed in the back of the ambulance. I was safe from the storm but *Liv* was still fighting it. She was pinned against the cliff wall, being smashed anew with each wave. My dad and brother arrived while I was in the ambulance. No towing company would risk getting *Liv* out that night because the conditions were so rough. I cared little about my injuries in that moment, which consisted of a badly bruised body. My mind raced, thinking the journey was over before it ever really began.

In the morning, after a sleepless night, I immediately wanted to get back to the cliff, but my mom was waiting for me. She was so relieved that

I was okay, but she seemed to have an even greater sense of satisfaction in thinking that this was the end of it.

All I could do was go back to *Liv* and assess the damage. I was devastated by what I saw. Calling her a boat would be generous. It looked as if a group of sharks were hungry for lunch. The entire bottom of the boat appeared to have been ripped through with ravenous jaws, cracking my boat as if she were balsa wood. My hope shattered with my boat, thinking my dream was finished, and I was a complete failure.

I could see the headlines now: "Ohio Girl Dreamed of Rowing Ocean, But Couldn't Survive a Lake." It was my lowest point. All I could do was find a new perspective.

This taught me an important lesson. It was not going to get any worse than this.

True failure, I realized, is not having the courage to try. That was not me. I gathered my resolve and did everything I could to find a way to repair my boat and continue with my plans to get to the Atlantic. I had just two months. Within 24 hours of the accident, I was on the road, driving more than a thousand miles back to the original boat builder to see what he might be able to do. To my relief, I found him and his crew ready to work hard. Sure, I endured a few good-natured jokes about learning how to row before I got to the ocean. But I took those in stride because implicit in the jokes was the assumption that I was going to the ocean. It's not about the falling that matters. Everyone falls. What matters is what you do when you are on the ground (or embedded in the rocks). As long as you can get up, you can keep going. As long as you keep going, you will get there. . . . Now, about that summit I have to climb.

Day 65: Be Open to the Ride

@katiespotz Tweet Log for Monday, March 8, 2010

| 7:11 PM | Yes—we're making sure that Katie has people to welcome her in to land and provide the celebration she has earned. [Sam] |

If you ever plan to climb a mountain there are several camps and stages you have to go through to reach the top. For example, if you attempt Mount Everest, the largest mountain on Earth, these are well laid out by the many climbers and their sherpas, who have scaled it over the past decades. This includes the Base Camp, Icefall, the Valley of Silence, Camp 2, Lhotse Wall, and The Deathzone. From that final point, when you are on the edge of the atmosphere, you are ready for the final summit. I am ready for the final push now. I can almost see the top of the mountain, except instead of looking up, my "peak" is in the opposite direction—at sea level. Land is just 100 miles away.

But guess what? Imagine if you were a climber ready for the final push to the top and the mountain suddenly grew much, much taller? This is not a hallucination, either. This is what has just happened to me.

I am so close now, really just a couple of days away. I could be in a warm shower and a dry bed. Instead I feel like I am stuck in my own Everest-like Deathzone out here. I am battling the largest waves of my voyage so far, at over 30 feet. My previous average was just between 3 and 5 feet. The reason? I have just rowed over the Continental Shelf, where the ocean's depth changes from 6,000 to 600 feet. The result is that the waves are now spiking from out of nowhere and dwarfing me and my boat, making rowing almost impossible.

Based on conversations with my land support team, if I continue rowing as planned to French Guiana, I will never make it. Or as they put it to me, "It would be certain death." I don't care for odds like that! Remember what I told you yesterday about my crash on Lake Erie? I do not want to duplicate that situation, especially in a much more dangerous environment. There are cliffs in Cayenne, French Guiana, far larger than those *Liv* and I crashed into a few months ago in Ohio.

What exactly is happening to make the conditions so unfavorable? Right now the current is coming up the South American coast, the waves are moving down from the north, and the wind is blowing from the east. I am currently experiencing winds gusting at 20 knots with even stronger forces ahead. Imagine what all of this would do to a tiny rowboat! Really I do not want to imagine it at all.

So now it is on to Plan B. Here are the givens in my decision-making process: a) I can no longer trust the sea a few miles out from Cayenne; b) I refuse to be towed in because I want a completely unsupported crossing; and c) Certain death is not an appealing option. Where does this leave me?

I am kind of like a pilot flying around a storm, and I have made a decision to tack an additional 400 miles onto my journey. This means rowing two countries to the northwest, through a part of the ocean where the current has died down and I will have a much better chance of landing without assistance—or loss of life. My new target is now Georgetown, Guyana. To put that distance in perspective, it's almost like rowing from Cleveland to New York City!

Although the route to Cayenne is much shorter and would end my journey sooner, if I divert further west and follow a track to Georgetown, the seas should be less aggressive. Weather permitting, my hope is that this course change will allow me to conclude my journey as I have conducted it: solo. And it will give me a better chance of completing it alive and in one piece!

What is the lesson from this? It is exactly what I said in a radio interview I gave last week over my satellite phone. The question was "Are you in any way a different person now than when you left Dakar two months ago?" I answered, "I am definitely more patient. I know myself a little bit better." Patience is more than a virtue, as the old saying goes. It is perhaps our greatest survival tool. I concluded my radio interview with this thought: "No matter how prepared you are, the ocean will give you something to challenge you. There is nothing you can really do except be open to the ride."[135]

Whatever your "ocean" is, no matter what journey you're taking in life, be open to the ride. Sometimes the summit gets farther away even if you are making progress on the climb. Be patient. The ride is really what life is all about, and it would be pretty boring if everything was flat. You earn the downward coast only by pushing through the hard work of climbing the hills.

Day 66: What Does Not Kill You Makes You Stronger

@KatieSpotz Tweet Log for Tuesday, March 9, 2010

| 7:34 AM | Weeeeeeee. Just hit 7.7kt surfing down a wave! |
| 12:00 PM | It feels like rowing through glue when I'm going into a headwind. At least I have some help from the current. |

As you can see from my tweets, the waves are picking up, and I made a good choice in redirecting my landing. I'm also starting to understand the thrill of surfing big waves! Hitting a speed of 7.7 knots is scary, but also so very exciting. My boat is built for these conditions, and she's able withstand the force of the water and wind. Until this point, though, she hasn't been tested. It's kind of like buying new hiking boots and only getting to wear them in the city. Each step on the flat concrete tempts you to get out and test them in the wilderness or on a mountain. So I welcomed these big waves today, as they were a wonderful break from the three-to-five foot norm, and they let me see a little bit of what *Liv* was designed to do. It was also a reawakening for me.

What do I need to be reawakened from? Well, I will not lie. It's been hard out here. Speaking of mountain hiking, my struggles out here remind me of something Bree Lowen wrote in her book about being a climbing ranger on Mount Rainer (which is a special place for me because I officiated at the wedding of my best friend there). She wrote, "The greatest skill I ever had, though, was the one I started with: being able to suffer for long periods of time and not die. In exchange, I got to see some amazing things."[136]

I completely relate to this.

As I am approaching land, let me reflect back on some of the small, daily challenges I have been enduring. This row is not just about easy, breezy days in the sun, gracefully cruising along the ocean—after all, that's what motor-boating is for! I have mentioned sunsets, wildlife, and starry nights, but just in case there's a rush of readers who want to row an ocean too, I should mention that it's not all sweetness and light. Check these off your list if you are thinking about rowing an ocean.

- ✓ If pushing a thousand pound boat once sounds daunting, perhaps the 10,000 daily strokes may not be for you.
- ✓ No strawberries or apples or fresh salads. Say goodbye to fresh foods for a few months. Cross ice cream and cold drinks off the list too, because there is no refrigerator onboard.
- ✓ Feeling well rested will be but a distant memory. And you may wake up several times during the night, feeling as if you are suffocating and need to open the hatches for fresh air (I have a ventilator for air but it's only a couple inches wide).
- ✓ This is fun to describe: Your nighttime ritual will start to match that of an infant, and it's not the bedtime story I'm talking about! Having a seriously sore bum will take on a new meaning and the nickname "baboon butt" might be fitting.
- ✓ If bullriding does not sound fun to you, neither will using the toilet (a.k.a. the bucket). Hold on tight!
- ✓ No matter how clean you are, it won't last. You can expect to be a lightly-salted and greasy sun chip.
- ✓ That last meal may disagree about staying in your stomach and decide that over the edge of the boat is a better place to be.
- ✓ The color white no longer exists. The grime has a way of getting into everything and never coming out.

✓ Some days it will be so hot, you may wonder if you are melting away. So hot, almost to the point of fainting. And no shade, all day.

✓ One step further . . . on those hot days, you probably won't feel like eating and without eating you soon won't feel like moving. It's a vicious cycle.

✓ You may look at your GPS to see a boat coming alarmingly close, leaving you to wonder if you are about to become nothing more than fish food.

✓ Forget about good-smelling clothes or hair or bed.

✓ Think of your worst hair day, multiply that by ten, and expect to see that in the mirror every morning.

✓ If you do not like fish, you especially won't like cleaning up the dead, smelly ones that land on your boat. You also may not be fond of the occasional "hit-and-run" or, better yet, "hit-and-swim" by the flying fish.

✓ Medical tape will become your new best friend, as you play doctor and tape yourself back together every night.

✓ You may get a rash from the constant movement in rowing that is so painful, it may feel like you are reopening the wound with even the slightest touch.

✓ Just when you are all nice and dry, expect Mr. Big Cold Wave to drop on by. Being dry is a rare luxury!

✓ Expect everything you do to take five times longer on a constantly moving boat.

✓ Sometimes the satellite phone will connect, and sometimes it will not, which means no human interaction.

✓ You may find yourself becoming overly emotional about things you would never dream of, say, realizing your last Snickers bar was spoiled by water. (I assure you, I would never let this tragedy happen to me.)

✓ You may wake up at night and wonder if your fingers are broken because of the pain from simply moving or bending them.

✓ Say hello to a sore lower back and knees. Your knees may be especially confused in the morning.

✓ The newfound liberation of being able to literally "dance like no one is watching" may leave you to cause yourself further harm, especially with the loss of your leg muscles, which enable you to stand. Sadly, my dancing days are numbered.

✓ And then there is that one blister that seems to always want to remind you that it's there.

✓ Winds may push you eastward, meaning those hard-earned miles are now lost.

✓ Expect days where you will have an abusive relationship with your boat, causing jammed toes, bumps, and bruises. And if you are really lucky, a quick jab-jab to the ribs or pinch-pinch to the fingers by the oars.

Dirty, hot, tired, smelly—I think I have covered my bases here. Although most things listed here are minor inconveniences, repeat any number of them for the tenth or hundredth time and they no longer feel quite so small.

But I don't need anyone who reads this to come away feeling sorry for me—pity isn't welcome here. For where there is a will, there is a way and I have been able to work with these opportunities to practice patience. I honestly would not trade this experience for the world and feel so lucky to be on the ocean, bad hair days and all. So let me raise a toast to Bree Lowen and share with her the joy of enduring suffering for the reward of amazing things like dolphin visits and shooting stars!

Consider your own life for a moment. Sometimes the fear of suffering prevents us from trying a new experience. Have you found yourself in that position? As Lowen says, and I second her, you can suffer for long periods of time and not die. It's worth it! And in return you might find rewards that makes your life more meaningful. The often-quoted words of Friedrich Nietzsche (the self-proclaimed "Buddhist of Europe") rings true, "What does not kill me, makes me stronger."[137]

Day 67: Float Like a Bumblebee

@KatieSpotz Tweet Log for Wednesday, March 10, 2010

6:56 AM	Katie has just entered the final 200 miles of the journey. [Sam]
8:04 AM	I take my safety seriously, but there's still time for fun. Started talking on the VHF with an accent. Everyone else is!
5:56 PM	Eek, 1 mile from a freighter. A little bit too close for comfort.

I had an interesting new encounter with nature tonight. I was rowing the evening shift with my nav-light on. I usually only leave it on while I'm sleeping, as it can be difficult to watch for waves with it shining, but since I am entering freighter territory, this visual beacon gives me a little extra security. While I'm hopeful the light alerts tankers, it also seems to have attracted attention of a different kind: a bird came to visit. It was flying rather awkwardly, almost like a bat, and found itself a spot in the cockpit.

Midnight . . . 2 a.m. . . . 6 a.m. . . . 8 a.m. . . . it was still there. Most other birds leave by sunrise so I knew something must be up. And I realized the problem when it attempted to move. It hobbled around, unable to fly. Perhaps its wing was broken. With a cockpit about 4 feet long, I debated whether or not this was the right place for an injured bird. But, I couldn't bear to put "Hobs" (I mean he was hobbling, so what better name?) overboard, so I let him stay.

Poor Hobs. Though he did not live, he at least spent his last moments comfortably on Liv with someone who tried to help him as best I could.

After 10 minutes of rowing, I feared running him over with the sliding seat, so I fenced him in the corner of the cockpit with some snacks; they remained uneaten. Humans can go three days without water and possibly ten without food; if that is the standard for birds too, I'm afraid Hobs' days may be numbered.

With less than 150 miles to go, it's now my personal mission to do what I can to save Hobs. I guess I've always had a soft spot for any creature that appears too weak to survive. Support does not always need to be something physical, like food or a strong shoulder to lean upon. Often survival, or success at accomplishing a goal, is achieved through a mental boost.

When we think we are too small, slow, weak, old, or young to accomplish something, then we fail before we even try. And so the first step in any journey is simply to conquer the weaknesses that exist within ourselves. In other words, we need to acknowledge when we are weak in body or mind. Accept it. And then work towards overcoming our personal limitations in whatever way we can.

In the mid-nineteenth-century, the passion for mountain climbing swept through Europe. Leslie Stephen wrote eloquently about this 1868 when he said, "The history of mountaineering is, to a great extent, the history of the process by which men have gradually conquered the phantoms of their own imagination."[138] Aside from the fact that this ignores the conquering capabilities of women, I find it to be such an important message. How many of our goals are defeated not by what is out there, but instead what is inside our mind? Mountain climbers know that reaching the summit is not just a physical feat, but a mental one as well.

As I near the end of my journey, I have certainly had to conquer some real phantoms out here on the ocean. But I was as ready as I could have been to tackle them head on because I had prepared my mind.

I first learned this on my Big Ride Across America. After one long day's ride, I wrote a letter to my grandfather: "The more I ride the more I realize it is not about the miles or heat or wind. Today I also realized about the power of attitude. Forty people are all doing the same ride. We go through the same hills, wind, mountains, heat, and storms. But those who carry a positive attitude can tackle the day better. It is all about how each person perceives the day. I am learning lots on this ride and I know it's just the beginning!"[139]

Now, how to encourage Hobs to believe he can fly? Believe and achieve! There is an old saying that the bumblebee is actually too heavy to fly, based on the size of its wings. But no one ever told that to the bees—they believe they can fly, and so they do.

As an aside, scientists have only recently discovered the mechanics of how a bee flies. It has to do with stretching its wings out wider and thus the bee doesn't require an impossibly fast wingbeat frequency for its mass.[140]

Forget the science for a moment! We all feel like bumblebees from time to time. Our bodies may appear too big, slow, weak, or frail for the task ahead of us. But that is okay. The great boxer Muhammad Ali once said that in the ring he would "float like a butterfly and sting like a bee." I would actually rather float like a bumblebee because its mind and its wings overcome a body that's too big to fly. In what areas in your life can you overcome bodily limitations with a positive mindset?

Come on now, Hobs! Fly like a bumblebee!

Day 68: Scale the Mental Wall

@katiespotz Tweet Log for Thursday, March 11, 2010	
7:46 AM	Over 2 months at sea and I'm still seeing the same white birds and strange-looking fish.
8:55 AM	Katie is now at 6d41N 56d02W and into the final 150 miles. [Sam]
12:33 PM	Another sign I'm closer to land...trash.
5:25 PM	Katie is currently perfectly placed to approach Georgetown, at 6d40.068N 56d26.612W. [Sam]
7:29 PM	Perfect day for rowing. Waves not too big, not too small. Wind not too strong, not too light. A nice mix of sun and clouds and so bright moonlight.

Though my options are not like the entertainment extravaganza on a cruise ship, I did bring along some things to do to pass the time when I'm not rowing. I've mentioned some of them, but I also wanted to tell you about my audiobooks. They're great because reading while rocking in the waves can be a challenge! Among the books I've listened to out here are *Eat, Pray, Love*, *Three Cups of Tea*, and *Blood Diamonds*. Above all, though, what brightens my mood the most are the comedians (although they complain because my stage is so small!). And for special milestones or on bad weather days, I have movies loaded onto an iPod Touch. I've shared my day-off story with the

Harry Potter movies, but I also brought *Twilight, Borat, The Two Towers*, and some episodes of *Curb Your Enthusiasm* and *Sex and the City*. Maybe I should have planned in advance but I really just took whatever movies my friends lent to me. The public library was also great for downloading audiobooks and comedy. I might have just a *little* late fee!

If you told me a few years ago that I would be rowing solo across an ocean, I would have found it difficult to believe. To be honest, it was only recently that I learned to row, but even more significantly, I didn't understand that the mental challenges are far more difficult than the physical ones. That didn't occur, as I mentioned yesterday, until, my Big Ride Across America. It was from endurance challenges like this (and running, swimming, and now rowing) that I learned how to confront and scale the "mental walls" that arise. Here are my five scaling tips, or tools, for overcoming those inner obstacles.

- *Don't question.* During some of my first endurance challenges I wasted too much energy questioning whether or not I could complete the goal. The truth is that you never know until you try, and the worst thing you can do is not try. I learned to redefine failure, not as a failure to finish, but rather as failing to try. Fear of failure was one of the most difficult "mental walls" I faced.
- *Break it down.* You don't row across an ocean in a day, so it is important for me to break it down into daily, sometimes hourly goals, and to focus on that one step (or oar stroke) ahead. If I lose sight of that one step, I become overwhelmed by the magnitude of the challenge.
- *Know all things will pass.* No matter how tired, hot, seasick, bored, lonely, etc. I get, it will pass. For some of my more grueling one-day challenges, like my ultramarathon (100k run), I expected to go through all sorts of highs and lows in a matter of hours. All you can do is ride out the highs and the lows.
- *Do not make it personal.* Here on the ocean the weather will do what it wants, equipment will break, and things will not go according to "plan". But it has nothing to do with *me*. So often I can think and feel that things are happening "for," "against," and "to" me. In reality, life just happens, and it's a waste of time to define things as good or bad. Just deal with them and move on.

• *Understand the real challenge is me.* The only thing that holds me back is *me* and it's not about what happens but how I chose to react.

I can only speak of my own experiences but, above all, endurance challenges have taught me about what it means to be present. When you set off on a 3,000-mile row, the scale is so immense that you are truly forced to focus on that one stroke, one moment at a time. The present is like a fulcrum. Behind you is the past and ahead is the future. If you walk too far in either direction, away from the fulcrum (the present), then you lose your balance.

The lesson for today is how important it is to have a toolbox of techniques for scaling mental walls. Not all techniques work equally well for everyone, so experiment with these tools and start building your own toolbox. You can use your tools for any task in life. This is especially true for the global water crisis. It's a problem whose scope is sometimes unfathomable—at least as big as an ocean. But that does not mean we cannot overcome it. All it takes is the willingness to try, persistence, and an acceptance of the highs and lows that come with the challenge. Be in the present moment and you will endure. At least this is what my toolbox enables me to do.

What are some of your mental walls that prevent you from achieving your goals? Once you identify them, consider borrowing some of my tools: all discomfort will pass, break the wall down into bricks, and don't waste energy questioning yourself. Quite possibly these will help you scale that mental wall just like the tools expert mountaineers use on Everest. So grab a metaphorical backpack, rope, crampons, helmet, and carabineers and start that climb. The view from the summit, atop a personal mental wall, is breathtaking.

Day 69: See What Your Body Can Do

@KatieSpotz Tweet Log for Friday, March 12, 2010

12:54 PM	No one seems to understand when I speak to them on the VHF that I'm actually on a rowboat!
5:13 PM	They've gone too far this time. Flying ninja fish invading my jam out session to Best of MJ. Shame shame!

What was the first thing Sir Edmund Hillary said to his teammates at base camp after he and Sherpa Tenzig Norgay, became the first men to summit Mount Everest? "We knocked the bastard off."[141] I understand his feeling, but I actually do not share his sentiment. Maybe I'm in good company here, as Junko Tabei, the first woman to climb Everest commented, "I can't understand why men make all this fuss about Everest."

Personally, I have little interest in climbing mountains. I love the heat and I'm not a huge fan of the cold, especially for adventuring. Besides what attracts me the most to swimming, biking, running, and rowing is the freedom of movement. With mountain climbing? Not so much. I feel held back hiking with a 50-pound pack on my back, concentrating more on not tripping instead of the beautiful scenery.

That in part is why I love the Atlantic Ocean. I am grateful for the lessons from it. I respect its power and its beauty, and I'm thankful it allowed me to be a quiet passenger upon its waves. So instead of knocking off a bastard, I feel like I've been given a wonderful gift as I nearly reach land.

There I go, getting a little overconfident at this late stage.

It's ironic that in life, just when you start to let your guard down, something threatening happens. That's how it was this morning, when I smelled something burning. At first I was half hopeful a passing boat was having a barbecue gone wrong. When nothing appeared on the horizon that sinking feeling set in: it was *my* boat that was on fire. That could mean *literally* sinking. I heard an explosion before I got to the cockpit, which was a bit startling, but although there was smoke and fire, at least my worst fears were not realized.

My tracker unit has been acting up recently, and it finally decided to go up in smoke. I grabbed the fire extinguisher and was able to stop the flames from spreading. There were no holes in my boat, I was not taking on water, and the fire was out. I'm close to land, so I figure I can make it the rest of the way without a tracker. Not reaching land now would be so difficult. I might just swim it!

The tracker was a "nice to have" and not a "need to have." I didn't use it to navigate. It was more like those sensors parents can secretly put in their kids' cars to know where they are. So my family, friends, and followers of my website used it, but not me. Everyone just needs to know I have not disappeared in the Bermuda Triangle, which is well north of me.

These final days have been similar to the first ones, with generally calm seas. After the fire scare, today was an especially nice day. The water sparkled as the sun glistened off the undulating waves. I'm hopeful these conditions will allow for a safe and successful landing, unlike the conditions in Cayenne. I'm so glad I extended the journey 400 miles, as a part of me is holding on dearly to the simplicity of the sea. I was asked during an interview what I think about while rowing. Although my mind wanders here and there, for a large part of the journey I felt present; there's no need to think beyond the moment. I also know that when I land it will be a challenge to stay in the moment. There will be the plans for the next interview, the next place to fly to, and the next challenge to prepare for.

I'm going to do all I can to resist the anxieties of the future, and try to take the lessons I have learned with me into all my endeavors. The ocean taught me about being patient, open, and accepting. . . . The list goes on and on. But with land just beyond the horizon, I'm most looking forward to good food (that means watermelon!) and good company.

I find it interesting that I'm not the only one who looks at a journey like this as an opportunity for life lessons. I mentioned Junko Tabei at the start of my writing today. Maybe, as she said, men make too much out of scaling Everest, but that doesn't mean the experience does not grant wisdom. "The mountain teaches me a lot of things," she writes. "It makes me realize how trivial my personal problems are. It also teaches me that life should not be taken for granted." Let's substitute "Atlantic Ocean" for "mountain." Every life is so special, especially one's own. Never take it for granted. It's like the way it feels to get behind the wheel of a luxury car. What do they always say in the movies? "Let's see what this baby can do!" That's how we should feel about our bodies, minds, and souls.

I'm expecting to arrive in the next 24 to 30 hours, and my dad and brother are in Georgetown now. It's time to wrap up this row.

Day 70: Show Your Inner Soul

@KatieSpotz Tweet Log for Saturday, March 13, 2010	
12:41 PM	Not long now until Katie hits land. [Sam]
9:15 PM	Katie is currently heading slowly towards Georgetown, hoping to avoid a night-time arrival. Less than 30 miles to go. [Sam]
11:24 PM	Katie is spending her last night onboard *Liv* less than 20 miles from her destination. [Sam]

I am getting close now. The ocean feels different somehow. I have left solitude behind and I'm rowing into what will be a maelstrom of people, media, and events. It's going to be like getting out of a hot tub and jumping into a frozen lake (which is something I have done). Seeing people will be a shock to my system! I know there will be lots of questions, and one of them will be, "Why did you row the ocean?"

I need someone like Maya Angelou to explain it. She was once asked in an interview "Why do you write?" and she responded: "We write for the same reason that we walk, talk, climb mountains or swim the oceans—because we can. We have some impulse within us that makes us want to explain ourselves to other human beings. That's why we paint, that's why we dare to love some-one—because we have the impulse to explain who we are. Not just how tall we are, or thin . . . but who we are internally . . . perhaps even spiritually. There's something, which impels us to show our inner souls. The more courageous we are, the more we succeed in explaining what we know."[142]

Please go back and read Angelou's words again. They are that important.

I admire those who say such beautiful things in interviews. Her words are so incredibly true. They inspire us all to reflect on the things we do in life that matter to us the most. By engaging in our passions we reveal something of our inner soul to the world.

I am savoring these last moments here as best I can.

So I watch the ocean. I watch the sky, the wildlife, my mind and my body. I've watched the day turn into night, and the days turn into weeks. And they wonder why I would ever want to row an ocean! It is just as Angelou so eloquently said.

I row an ocean for the same reason a mountain climber stands on the top of the world at the peak of Mount Everest.

I row an ocean for the same reason a painter transforms a piece of white paper into a beautiful image.

I row an ocean for the same reason an author tries to express innermost thoughts in written words.

We are all called by our passions and compelled to expose our inner souls. The process makes us vulnerable, and strong, and human. The Atlantic Ocean has exposed my soul in ways nothing else could. It stripped me naked, literally. It broke me to the point that I was ready to quit. And from that point of utter rawness, it showed me the absolute beauty of what life is all about.

I look up at the lines from Proust that I scrawled onto *Liv* before I departed: "A real voyage of discovery lies not in finding new landscapes, but in having new eyes." I did not find any new landscapes. I did not "discover" the New World, like Columbus. Nevertheless, I rowed the ocean because it was a voyage of discovery for me, and I took it all in as best I could with my new eyes. I will now adopt that attitude every day of the rest of my life on land.

The reality is, life happens. I am likely to forget much of this tomorrow when the microphones are in my face. And that is the beauty and ben-

I was all smiles at the end of the row. Nothing shows your inner soul like a smile!

efit of solitude. I will someday return to it and reconnect with the lessons the ocean taught me. The quiet and alone times have enabled me to look within deeply, and really see who is there. And before the questions start flying for real, let me turn one back to you: *What have you done in life, or what can you do, to share your inner soul with the world?*

Zen is "seeing into one's own nature."[143] This, to me, is our highest calling in life. It is the central lesson that the Atlantic has taught me, and I encourage you to explore your own way of seeing into the true you. That person is utterly beautiful . . . I promise. There is nothing to fear about meeting the person you find in solitude. That was a huge fear of mine, because I equated alone with loneliness. Now I can see the gift of being "with myself."

And so for now, the observant one is signing off. Civilization awaits. . . .

Welcome to Guyana!

@KatieSpotz Tweet Log for Sunday, March 14, 2010

1:39 AM	Hello land. Haven't seen you in awhile. It started as a glow in the night but now I see shining lights.
9:45 AM	The Coast Guard have spotted Katie—she has 4 miles to row. [Sam]
9:49 AM	Katie has been rowing for 70 days, 3 hours and 3 minutes so far! [Sam]
11:15 AM	Apparently the welcoming team can see Katie. Minutes to go! [Sam]
12:23 PM	SHE'S FINISHED!!!!!
4:08 PM	Oh my! I nearly fell over walking down a set of stairs and everything still feels like it's moving.

"Welcome to Guyana!" This was a sentence I have been waiting to hear for 70 days, 5 hours and 22 minutes! It's hard to believe I'm on land now! In fact, it's so hard to believe it's over that my body still thinks it's moving even though I'm on solid ground. This might make me more seasick than actually being on the ocean! Let me tell you about my final moments of the row.

South America first appeared as darkness fell. It was subtle at first, starting as a soft glow on the horizon. Then, as the night progressed, it

I was overwhelmed with the generosity of the people waiting for me at the end of my row. Here is the welcome sign they created.

turned into dotted lights and, in the morning, it materialized into trees and buildings. Even hearing sounds I hadn't heard for two months was a revelation. As relieved as I was to see land, I didn't allow myself to become too excited until my feet were planted on terra firma, as I knew these final miles could be the most treacherous. I remembered all too well crashing into the rocks of Lake Erie. I did not want to end this trip with a bang.

When I was within four miles of the shore my excitement started to build, especially after a helicopter appeared overhead and waved to me. Most importantly, though, was the boat full of friendly faces, including my dad's and my brother's, that appeared to greet me officially. But that wasn't the end of the challenge, as the final approach into the Demerara River proved as difficult as any other. It started to rain, and at times I was rowing as hard as I could just to stay in the same spot. Worst of all, I wanted to make sure I looked like I knew what I was doing for all the interested onlookers! Suddenly I had an audience of humans, and not just fish and birds.

It was a wonderful welcoming party in Guyana, especially because my dad and brother were there to greet me!

If the entire Atlantic Ocean hadn't defeated me, then I was determined this final obstacle wouldn't either. Eventually, I began making progress towards the land and I found myself rowing up to the pier. However, the relief of landing was quickly replaced by fear, as I spotted my final obstacle. I would not be rowing onto a nice sandy beach, where I could gracefully slide my tired legs over the side of my boat. No, just the opposite. I was rowing up to a pier and there was a ladder they expected me to climb up!

I questioned whether this was really the best place to land, as I was expecting to not be able to walk, at least not straight, once on land. Could I even climb a ladder? There was no choice but to try.

I grabbed onto its lower rung, and looking up, I simply asked, "Are you sure this is a good idea?" Apparently the landing party thought this was a rhetorical question, so I relied on my tired arms and somehow I found the strength to take one rung at a time, even though my foot missed the first step. It seemed like one of those giant fireman ladders, although I knew it was not. Eventually my eyes, my entire head, and at last my body emerged over the base of the dock. I slowly stood up and I was in the arms of my dad and brother.

As we made our way out and into a mob of media, I could only think of one thing—finding my way to that desperately wanted, long-awaited watermelon. As tempting as it was to karate-chop my way through the masses, I practiced patience. And then there it was, waiting for me! Sweet, heavenly watermelon!

After the interviews and welcoming party, we made our way to the Princess Hotel. When I opened the door to my room I discovered the next wonder. A bed. A bed where I didn't have to worry about being run down by freighters. A bed where I didn't have to gasp for air as the night wore on. A bed that was completely dry. A bed where I could sleep for an entire night without constantly being thrown into the wall by a rogue wave. And a bed that smelled so fresh it almost overwhelmed me.

Climbing that ladder meant everything to me. It did not just mark the end of my long journey. It stood as a symbol for me and an icon of what all humans strive to achieve. In the book *Ordinary Wisdom*, I found the following words: "We persist in climbing the ladder of human development, step by step, hoping that, like Jacob's ladder, it will one day lead us beyond the human condition to the stars. . . ."[144]

Find your ladder.

Climb it.

Never stop.

One day you will reach the stars.

This was the hug that I was so anxious to give and receive. Here I am with my sister Maggie who met me in the Cleveland airport on my return home. I was finally home.

Epilogue: A Half Decade Later

As I write these words, in January 2015, exactly five years have passed since I departed from Dakar in my row boat. Half a decade may seem like a long time to write a book, and I suppose it is. But I needed the temporal distance to put my experiences into perspective. If you have made it this far in the book, ultimately you are the one who will decide if that perspective holds any value for you. It does for me.

My hope is that you enjoyed joining me on my adventure, and that along the way you learned some useful lessons about propelling yourself towards your own goals, and how to climb the ladder when the going gets toughest. I also hope you take away a deeper awareness of the global water crisis and its impact on the lives of so many people around the world. Finally, I also wanted to share my realization that all of us matter on this globe. We are all connected, and each of us has a beautiful inner light that shines like the sun. This is what my journey taught me, and perhaps a lesson or two that I shared will help you to see life with new eyes.

Glamour Woman of the Year

Now, let me catch you up on where life has taken me since I completed my ocean row. Upon my return I was immediately thrown into a media

The "red carpet" at the Glamour Awards. Left to right: Editor-in-Chief of Glamour Cindi Leive, Katie Spotz, and Bill Wackermann, EVP and Publishing Director of Glamour.

spotlight. This was not the most comfortable place for me (to say the least), and if it did not ultimately raise awareness about the global water crisis, I'm not sure I would have stepped into that spotlight. It all happened very fast.

On March 14 I ended my row, and five days later I was in New York City being interviewed by Katie Couric on the *CBS Evening News*.[145] The next day I was in CNN's studios with Anderson Cooper for another interview.[146] Over those two days I also did interviews with *World News*, Diane Sawyer, NPR, and the Discovery Channel. I even went to Rosie O'Donnell's home and did an interview for her radio show. It was really a blur and sometimes I forgot who I was talking to. Sam and my PR team helped keep things together and supported me through it all. Then I went to the *Glamour* magazine office to get some big news. Each year in their December issue, they

A photo shoot on Lake Erie for the Glamour Awards.

highlight women leaders from all around the world as their "Women of the Year," and it was a huge honor to be on the 2010 list! Other winners were Melinda Gates, Queen Rania of Jordan, Malala Yousafzai, and a long list of other dignified and important women.

In November I was honored at *Glamour's* star-studded award ceremony at Carnegie Hall. I met lots of cool people, including Kate Hudson, Fergie, Julia Roberts, Mia Hamm, and even Oprah! I was nervous going onstage because I was most worried about falling over in my heels and messing up my acceptance speech. After Diane Sawyer introduced me, I tried to impart some wisdom about what I learned on my row.[147] When the December 2010 issue of *Glamour* hit the newsstands, it was surreal to see my article and photos, sandwiched between Fergie and Julia Roberts. Diane Sawyer provided insight about why *Glamour* selected me. I was a woman of the year, she said, because "[Katie] used her raw courage to row the Atlantic, all alone, for 70 days, to make sure people who will never know her name have clean water to drink."[148] I am so glad she brought the water to the forefront!

Speaking Around the Globe

For the past five years I have focused on speaking engagements and working to raise money to mitigate that water crisis. Along the way I have raised nearly $275,000 for water projects in Haiti, Honduras, Guatemala, Nicaragua, India, South America, and Kenya. In 2011 I visited some of these projects in person and saw how these funds are helping people in tangible ways. That journey sparked a campaign to challenge ten schools in the United States to help ten schools in Kenya. To date, they raised more than $100,000, which means that 10,000 students have access to safe drinking water. Along the way, all the students gathered and earned a Guinness World Record for the most people carrying water jugs on their heads!

I was also an ambassador for Kinetico and Giant Bicycles, speaking at events and races across the country. I started graduate school, and enrolled in a program for Social Entrepreneurship at Goldsmiths, University of London, as part of a Rotary Ambassadorial Scholarship.

I am also an ambassador for H2O for Life, a nonprofit organization, which educates, engages, and inspires youth to learn, take action, and become global citizens. In 2014 we launched a three-year partnership to reach out to 210 schools in major cities across the U.S., including Minneapolis, Nashville, New York City, Phoenix, and Seattle. In my spare time there are radio interviews and other speaking engagements, including one at the United Nations' Annual Youth Assembly. I have also spoken in Mexico, India, and Sri Lanka.

My Stolen Oars

It has not been all bright lights and glamour, though. In September 2010, as I was about to head off to work, I noticed my trusty Dodge 2000 minivan, helpful for towing around a certain rowboat, was not where I had parked it. After calling a few of my friends who might think this a good prank, I realized it was truly gone. Stolen. Poof.

Who would have known that my particular year, make, and model of van was the most stolen vehicle in Ohio? Minivans come and go, but there were a few items inside that were priceless—oars and a bike. Not any oars or any bike. The oars that I rowed 3,038 miles across the Atlantic with and the bicycle that I pedaled 3,300 miles across America. I'd left them in the van after a local magazine's photo shoot around Lake Erie the day before. Keep in mind that I no longer had *Liv*. I sold my rowboat because she was expensive and my ocean-rowing days were over for the foreseeable future. Those oars, though, were like extensions of my arms for 70 days, and they were gone.

Several days later the police informed me that they had found the van on a side street in Cleveland and taken it to an impound lot. When I got there my first question was: Were the oars and bike still inside? Negative. The van was empty.

Incredibly, the Chagrin Valley Rotary Club teamed up with Giant Bicycles and Century Cycles to replace my stolen one. No more peering around dark alleys in search of my missing bike. No more posting flyers with pictures of the long lost one. They gifted me with a brand-new carbon-fiber 2011 Giant Defy Advanced 1 road bike. For those of you who don't know bicycles, it's quite simply the cream of the crop. At 17 pounds, I could lift it with my finger. It felt like Christmas morning. Nope, better! It's a day I will never forget. I wasn't really sure how to say thank you to everyone who had gone so far above and beyond anything I could possibly have asked for. So as a small token, I gave one of the rowing gloves I used to cross the Atlantic to Century Cycles, and the other to the Rotary Club to thank them for giving me a hand when I needed it the most. Oh, and it wouldn't be right to have a bike without a name! I call it "Phoenix"—a person or thing regarded as uniquely remarkable in some respect. Or, in classical mythology, a bird that lived for centuries and rose from ashes with renewed youth to live through another cycle (yeah, that's a pun). To break it in, a friend and I decided on a little ride from sunrise to sunset. We made it from Cleveland to Niagara Falls, 211 miles—and just in time for some french fries!

That new bike was the seed that planted the next adventure. It was very much "the adventure found me." The same day that I received my bicycle, a local bike team invited me to dinner to ask me about my fundraising efforts for clean water. They, too, wanted to raise funds as part of a bike race they were planning.

Race Across America

During the dinner, I talked about the water crisis and I learned about this race. Not just any race! It was the Race Across America (from Oceanside, California to Annapolis, Maryland) and it was described like this: "During this marathon attempt, riders will have to climb over 100,000 feet (more than three times the height of Everest.)" The riders cover 3,000 miles, which is longer than the Tour de France, at 2,300 miles. They don't call this the "world's toughest bike race" for nothing.

I was immediately intrigued. I learned that my new friends were part of a four-person team, but one of the riders was about to drop out. They asked if I would be interested in taking his place. Each rider would have to cover about 85 miles a day—something I had already done during my 2006 ride across America. I liked the idea of trying something new and more challenging. I was honored that they asked, but I wanted to see about doing a two-person team, covering 200 miles a day instead.

That night, I texted Sam to see if he'd be interested. I knew him well enough to know that adventure is deep in his blood. He was all about it, and it was an instant "yes." Sam and I were all set to be a two-person team, and one of us would have been riding 24 hours a day. There was a problem though: seven days before I was to begin, I broke my pelvis in a training accident. Seriously, what is wrong with me and my bad luck right before big endurance events? Remember, I crashed *Liv* shortly before my ocean row.

This time it was me, and not my vehicle, that was broken. That is more difficult to fix. Not only was the injury excruciatingly painful, the doctors forbid me from riding a bike.[149] So I had two alternatives, either quitting or finding a solution. Quitting is not typically my thing, so I went with the latter option and eventually found a hand-powered bike I could use (the bike had done an around-the-world-trip more than a decade earlier). We had others join our team, though, because quite obviously the distances possible on a hand-bike were much more limited. It was extremely difficult, and I felt like I was cycling with an elephant on my shoulders because the only arm exercise I had been doing was passing the dinner plate! I persisted, slowly and with great frustration, and tried to remind myself, *it's not where we get in life that defines us—it's what we overcome along the way that truly matters.*[150]

I had to add an extra wheel to make up for my broken pelvis.

We raised $25,000 for water projects, with a film team following us the entire time, sharing our journey.

Triathlons

My next endurance quest was a triathlon, which was something I had wanted to do since my first marathon at age 18. I had very little experience in triathlon, and after the adventure's accident, I wanted to do this one just for me. I was pleasantly surprised to have finished in second place! It was such a high for me and I regained that confidence in my body again. I completed a 2.4 mile swim, a 112 mile bike, and 26.2 mile run in 10 hours and 48 minutes.

Since then I was invited to be on the Ironman Foundation-Newton Running Ambassador Triathlon Team—to join 50 other triathletes from across the country who combine their passion for the sport with a greater purpose behind it. Everyone who participates does so with a charitable mission. My goal is to help at least one school get clean water as a result of each Iron Man I do. In early 2015, I qualified for the Boston Marathon and in the summer placed 1st overall female in the 29th Annual Cleveland Triathlon!

The Atlantic Teacher

What is the one sure way to overcome any obstacle that you face? I hid that secret in the title of this book. *Just keep rowing.*

All you have to do, no matter what challenge confronts you, is to *just keep rowing.* Simply replace the word "rowing" to match your challenge. Having trouble in school? Just keep studying. Can't raise your foul-shot percentage? Just keep shooting. Can't learn to play a guitar? Just keep practicing. Can't get out of debt? Just keep trying, budgeting, and saving. Life is all about persistence. As Thomas Edison, a native-born Ohioan like me, famously said, "Genius is 1 percent inspiration and 99 percent perspiration."[151] Perhaps someone once told him, "Just keep inventing."

When it's all said and done, if I had to use one word to describe the Atlantic, it would be "teacher."

I learned a lot from rowing those 70 days alone at sea, facing everything from 30-foot waves, sharks, and extreme isolation. Each day brought on new challenges, and the person who began that journey in West Africa was not the same person who reached land in South America one million oar strokes later. The ocean had many lessons to share, and I have now shared them with you.

Most importantly though, the Atlantic taught me how to hold onto hope when I felt like quitting.

I learned patience when, despite rowing all day, my hard-earned miles were lost by opposing winds.

The ocean taught me acceptance when equipment broke, bumps and bruises happened, and weather changed.

I learned what it meant to be alone for 70 days and yet still feel connected.

I learned how to keep going, at times, without physical support from the people I love the most.

I learned to appreciate nature more by having a front seat to the sublime beauty of the Atlantic's amazing wildlife, ocean creatures, and stunning sunsets.

But most of all I learned that you don't need to be extraordinary to achieve incredible things, and that even former benchwarmers can break world records.

These lessons live beyond the Atlantic. I hope you carry some of the lessons I have learned while crossing *your* ocean. *Just keep rowing* and you will make it to the other side, where watermelon, friends, and family await.

Notes

1. John F. Kennedy, Eric Freedman, and Edward Hoffman, *John F. Kennedy in His Own Words* (New York: Citadel Press, 2005), 76.

2. Roz Savage, *Rowing the Atlantic: Lessons Learned on the Open Ocean* (New York: Simon & Schuster, 2009); Kevin Biggar, *The Oarsome Adventures of a Fat Boy Rower: How I Went from Couch Potato to Atlantic Rowing Race Winner* (Auckland, N.Z.: Random House, 2008); Toni Murden McClure, *A Pearl in the Storm: How I Found My Heart in the Middle of the Ocean* (New York: Collins, 2009); Sarah Outen, *A Dip in the Ocean: Rowing Solo Across the Indian Ocean* (West Sussex, UK: Summersdale, 2011); Adam Rackley, *Salt, Sweat, Tears: The Men Who Rowed the Ocean* (New York: Penguin Books, 2014); David W. Shaw, *Daring the Sea: The True Story of the First Men to Row Across the Atlantic Ocean* (Secaucus, N.J.: Carol Publishing, 1998); Sally Kettle, *Sally's Odd at Sea* (Gardners Books, 2007); Rob Hamill, *The Naked Rower: How Two Kiwis Took on the Atlantic—and Won!* (Auckland, N.Z.: Hodder Moa Beckett, 2000).

3. Jay Famiglietti, "California has about one year of water left," *Los Angeles Times*, 12 March 2015, http://www.latimes.com/opinion/op-ed/la-oe-famiglietti-drought -california-20150313-story.html.

4. John Burroughs, *The Breath of Life* (Boston: Houghton Mifflin, 1915), 231.

5. Email from Pascal Vaudé to Rick Shema, December 31, 2009.

6. Email from Pascal Vaudé to Katie Spotz, December 31, 2009.

7. Paul Sorrentino, *Stephen Crane: A Life of Fire* (Cambridge: Harvard University Press, 2014), 230.

8. Lao-tzu, *Tao-Te Ching* (Maine: Weiser Books, 1991), 73.

9. Chrisoula Andreou and Mark D. White, *The Thief of Time: Philosophical Essays on Procrastination* (New York: Oxford University Press, 2010).

10. Howard R. Pollio, Tracy B. Henley, and Craig J. Thompson, *The Phenomenology of Everyday Life* (Cambridge: Cambridge University Press, 1997), 167.

11. Susan Ratcliffe, *Little Oxford Dictionary of Quotations* (Oxford: Oxford University Press, 2012), 382.

12. Jill Haak Adels, *The Wisdom of the Saints: An Anthology* (Oxford: Oxford University Press, 1989), 31.

13. Jalāl al-Dīn Rūmī, and Coleman Barks, *The Essential Rumi* (San Francisco, CA: Harper, 1995), 3.

14. Email from Rick Shema to Katie Spotz, January 9, 2010.

15. Quote is inspired by German philosopher Martin Heidegger. Andrew Mitchell, "Praxis and Gelassenheit: The 'Practice of the Limit," as found in François Raffoul and David Pettigrew, *Heidegger and Practical Philosophy* (Albany, N.Y.: State University of New York Press, 2002), 322.

16. Mother Teresa, *Where There is Love, There is God: Her Path to Closer Union with God and Greater Love for Others*, (New York: Doubleday, 2012), 213.

17. Daniel Malloy, "Take Me To The River," *Pittsburgh Post-Gazette*, August 22, 2008, http://www.post-gazette.com/local/city/2008/08/22/Take-me-to-the-river/stories /200808220174

18. http://swimforwater.blogspot.com/2008/06/why-swim.html

19. Simon Hartley, *Could I Do That?* (United Kingdom: John Wiley and Sons, 2014).

20. Huston Smith, *The World's Religions: Our Great Wisdom Traditions* (San Francisco: Harper Collins, 1991), 129.

21. Thomas Merton, *Mystics and Zen Masters* (New York: Farrar, Strauss and Giroux, 1967), 15.

22. Michael Boylan, *The Extinction of Desire: A Tale of Enlightenment*. (Malden, MA: Blackwell Pub., 2007), 171.

23. Svafa Grönfeldt and Judith B. Strother, *Service Leadership: The Quest for Competitive Advantage* (Thousand Oaks: SAGE Publications, 2006), 69.

24. These suppliers include: H2Row.net, GMN, South African Airways, Sprout People, JetBoil, Sailrite, Rowing Sport, OLM Gifts, JL Racing, Mariner Insurance, TIPOSI, GU Energy Gel, Headsweats, Kakadu Australia, GreatBoatStuff.com, Yak-pads, Aqua Signal, Nuun Active Hydration, Rite in the Rain All Weather Writing Paper, and H2O Audio.

25. These individuals include: Rick Shema and WeatherGuy.com (weather support); Betty Yopko Weibel, Yopko Penhallurick (Public Relations); Jack Lesyk and the Ohio Center for Sport Psychology (sports psychologist); Ryan Valentine, Aetomic Web + Print Marketing (web design); and a host of others including Mentor Harbor Yachting Club, Lakeside Yacht Club, Eric Knudson, Greg Spooner, Sam Williams, Chris Martin, Sarah Kessans, John Zeigler, Kelly Ryan, Big Ride Team, Cleveland Rowing Foundation, Titan's Gym, Jaime Cordova, Adam Fuller, Ann Netzel, Doug and Jane Price, and Bill and Joan Ziegler.

26. Marshall Berman, *All That Is Solid Melts into Air: The Experience of Modernity* (London: Verso, 2010).

27. Arthur M. Schlesinger, *A Thousand Days: John F. Kennedy in the White House* (Boston: Houghton Mifflin, 2002).

28. Robert Reid, *Architects of the Web: 1,000 Days That Built the Future of Business* (New York: John Wiley & Sons, 1997).

29. http://wfpusa.org/what-wfp-does/1000-days

30. Malcolm Gladwell, *Outliers: The Story of Success*. (New York: Little, Brown, and Co., 2008).

31. Email from Katie Spotz to Mary Spotz, January 25, 2010.

32. http://www.got-blogger.com/cherispracticeblog/?p=31

33. Peter Kivy, *Sounding Off: Eleven Essays in the Philosophy of Music* (Oxford: Oxford University Press, 2012), 9.

34. http://healthysleep.med.harvard.edu/healthy/matters/benefits-of-sleep/why-do -we-sleep

35. http://magazine.seymourprojects.com/2014/07/a-case-for-kon-tiki/

36. Virginia Woolf, *A Room of One's Own* (New York: Harcourt Brace Jovanovich, 1929).

37. http://swimforwater.blogspot.com/2008/07/day-5-finally-progress.html

38. Thomas Merton, as found in *Cloud of Witnesses*, ed. Jim Wallace and Joyce Hollyday (Washington, DC: Orbis Books, 2005), 257.

39. Paul Reps and Nyogen Senzaki, *Zen Flesh, Zen Bones: A Collection of Zen and Pre-Zen Writings* (Boston: Tuttle Pub, 1998), 103.

40. Email from Rick Shema to Katie Spotz, January 26, 2014.

41. It is a Katadyn Survivor 35 Watermaker.

42. Alan Beattle has also made this point in his book, *False Economy: A Surprising Economic History of the World* (New York: Riverhead Books, 2009), 94.

43. Rachel Nall, "Why Do We Need to Drink Water?" *Livestrong*, January 11, 2014, http:// www.livestrong.com/article/30860-need-drink-water/.

44. Charles Lee, *Good Idea. Now What? How to Move Ideas to Execution* (Hoboken, NJ: Wiley, 2012), Chapter 25, second paragraph.

45. http://www.who.int/mediacentre/factsheets/fs391/en/

46. World Health Organization (WHO). (2008). *Safer Water, Better Health: Costs, benefits, and sustainability of interventions to protect and promote health*; Updated Table 1: *WSH deaths by region*, 2004. United Nations Development Programme (UNDP). (2006). *Human Development Report 2006, Beyond Scarcity: Power, poverty and the global water crisis*. Estimated with data from *Diarrhoea: Why children are still dying and what can be done*. UNICEF, WHO 2009. Estimated with data from WHO/UNICEF Joint Monitoring Programme (JMP) for Water Supply and Sanitation. (2012). *Progress on Sanitation and Drinking-Water*, 2012 Update.

47. http://www.who.int/water_sanitation_health/publications/factsfigures04/en/

48. Irena Salina, *Written in Water: Messages of Hope for Earth's Most Precious Resource* (Washington, D.C.: National Geographic Society, 2010), 162.

49. http://www.charitywater.org/about/mission.php

50. W. Bernard Carlson, *Tesla: Inventor of the Electrical Age* (Princeton: Princeton University Press, 2013), 262.

51. http://www.cdc.gov/healthywater/global/assessing.html

52. http://www.charitywater.org/whywater/

53. http://www.who.int/water_sanitation_health/publications/factsfigures04/en/

54. http://www.smithsonianmag.com/smithsonian-institution/how-do-astronauts-go
-to-the-bathroom-in-space-2174968/

55. John Duffy, *The Sanitarians: A History of American Public Health* (Urbana: University of Illinois Press, 1992).

56. http://www.pbs.org/wgbh/americanexperience/features/general-article
/death-numbers/

57. Jimmy Stamp, "From Turrets to Toilets: A Partial History of the Throne Room,"
Smithsonian June 20, 2014. http://www.smithsonianmag.com/history/turrets
-toilets-partial-history-throne-room-180951788/

58. Claire Suddath, "A Brief History of Toilets," *Time*, November 19, 2009, http://
content.time.com/time/health/article/0,8599,1940525,00.html.

59. http://www.unwater.org/worldtoiletday/home/en/

60. Carol Off, *Bitter Chocolate: Anatomy of an Industry* (New York: New Press, 2014). Kevin
Bales and Ron Soodalter, *The Slave Next Door: Human Trafficking and Slavery in America Today*
(Berkeley: University of California Press, 2009), 153.

61. http://www.cocoainitiative.org/en/about-us/child-labour-in-cocoa

62. http://fairtradeusa.org/products-partners/cocoa

63. "New Living Wage Benchmark for Kenya," http://www.fairtrade.net/single-view+
M54659d5f66b.html.

64. https://www.rotary.org/en/about-rotary

65. Nancy Lutkehaus, *Margaret Mead: The Making of an American Icon* (Princeton: Princeton
University Press, 2008), 261.

66. https://www.rotary.org/en/about-rotary/history

67. http://www.bartleby.com/73/484.html

68. http://aquaclara.org/what-we-do/training/

69. Richard S. Gilbert, *The Prophetic Imperative: Social Gospel in Theory and Practice* (Boston:
Skinner House Books, 2000), p. 14.

70. Louise L. Hay, *Life!: Reflections on Your Journey* (Carson, CA: Hay House, 1995), 145.

71. http://www.independent.co.uk/news/world/africa/from-dawn-to-dusk-the-daily
-struggle-of-africas-women-416877.html

72. For other examples of women and water in Africa visit here (http://www
.charitywater.org/blog/khadija/) and also here (http://www.charitywater.org/blog
/ethiopia-11-2011/). Also visit: http://www.charitywater.org/blog/womens-day-2012/

73. http://water.usgs.gov/edu/earthhowmuch.html

74. http://www.charitywater.org/projects/

75. Lynn Rossellini, "Quenching a Thirst in Kathungu," *Reader's Digest*, June 2008,
http://www.rd.com/true-stories/inspiring/quenching-a-thirst-in-kathungu/

76. Robert Redford, "You Are the Solution," Rick Smolan, Jennifer Erwitt, Diane
Ackerman, Robert Redford, and Fred Pearce. *Blue Planet Run: The Race to Provide Safe Drinking*

Water to the World (San Rafael, CA: Earth Aware Editions/Against All Odds Productions, 2007).

77. W. Gurney Benham, *Cassell's Book of Quotations, Proverbs and Household Words* (London: Cassell and Co, 1907), 754.

78. http://latimesblogs.latimes.com/outposts/2010/02/katie-spotz-youngest-to-solo -row-across-atlantic-ocean.html

79. http://blueplanetnetwork.org/BPR/

80. http://rowforwater.com/archives/1392/

81. http://dailynews.openwaterswimming.com/2012/03/koz-paddles-for-cause.html

82. http://environment.nationalgeographic.com/environment/freshwater/freshwater -crisis/

83. Ibid.

84. Rick Smolan, Jennifer Erwitt, Diane Ackerman, Robert Redford, and Fred Pearce, *Blue Planet Run: The Race to Provide Safe Drinking Water to the World* (San Rafael, CA: Earth Aware Editions/Against All Odds Productions, 2007), pp. 58, 60, 61, and 75.

85. http://thewaterproject.org/water_scarcity_in_us

86. http://www.usatoday.com/story/money/business/2014/06/01/states-running-out -of-water/9506821/

87. http://abcnews.go.com/US/wireStory/california-governor-propose-1b-drought -plan-29755288

88. http://savethewater.org/education-resources/water-facts/

89. Michael Specter, "We're All Downstream," *Blue Planet Run: The Race to Provide Safe Drinking Water to the World* (San Rafael, CA: Earth Aware Editions/Against All Odds Productions, 2007), 95.

90. http://www.newyorker.com/magazine/2006/10/23/the-last-drop-2

91. http://www.epa.gov/watersense/our_water/start_saving.html

92. https://improveinternational.wordpress.com/handy-resources/sad-stats/

93. http://www.cleveland.com/travel/index.ssf/2014/12/cleveland_makes_fodors _must-se.html

94. Amartya Sen, "More Than 100 Million Women Are Missing," December 20, 1990, http://www.nybooks.com/articles/archives/1990/dec/20/more-than-100-million -women-are-missing/.

95. Nicholas D. Kristof and Sheryl WuDunn, *Half the Sky: Turning Oppression into Opportunity for Women Worldwide* (New York: Alfred A. Knopf, 2009), xvii.

96. http://www.unicef.org/esaro/7310_Gender_and_WASH.html

97. http://www.amnesty.org/ar/library/asset/AFR32/006/2010/en/6eab2ee6-6d6c -4abd-b77c-38cfc7621635/afr320062010en.pdf

98. http://water.org/water-crisis/womens-crisis/

99. http://www.amnestyusa.org/sites/default/files/pdfs/how_to_give_a_crap_about _human_rights.pdf

100. https://www.charitywater.org/pipeline/

101. http://www.h2oforlifeschools.org/index.php/about-h2o-for-life/success-stories/item/205-who-knew?-dog-treats-help-afghan-girls

102. Email from Mary Spotz to Katie Spotz, February 14, 2010.

103. Those who lost their lives while rowing the ocean include: David Johnstone and John Hoare in the boat *Puffin* (1966); Kenneth Kerr in the *Bass Challenger* (1980); Andrew Wilson in the *Nautica* (1980); Eugene Smurgis in *Max-4* (1993); Peter Bird in *Sector Two* (1996); and Nenad Belic in the *LUN* (2001). http://www.oceanrowing.com/statistics/lost_at_sea.htm

104. http://www.oceanrowing.com/statistics

105. Tori Murden McClure, *A Pearl in the Storm: How I Found My Heart in the Middle of the Ocean* (New York: Collins, 2009), 4.

106. Richard S. Westfall, *Never at Rest: A Biography of Isaac Newton* (Cambridge [Eng]: Cambridge University Press, 1983), 274.

107. http://www.aquidneckcustom.com/custom_built_boats/ocean_row_boat-liv.php

108. Cheri Huber and Sara Jenkins, *Buddha Facing the Wall: Interviews with American Zen Monks* (Lake Junaluska, NC: Present Perfect Books, 1999), 69-70.

109. Visit them online today at http://www.monks.org.

110. Bold, underline, and italics my own. Thomas Merton, as quoted in William Harmless, *Mystics* (Oxford: Oxford University Press, 2008), 30.

111. Andrew S. Grove, *Only the Paranoid Survive: How to Exploit the Crisis Points That Challenge Every Company and Career* (New York: Currency Doubleday, 1996), 3.

112. John Shedd, *Salt from My Attic* (Portland, Maine: Mosher Press, 1928) from Fred R. Shapiro, *The Yale Book of Quotations* (New Haven: Yale University Press, 2006), 705.

113. Katie Spotz, "The Day I Stopped Being Lonely," *Reader's Digest* (February 2011), 143-144.

114. Andrew Byatt, Alastair Fothergill, and Martha Holmes, *The Blue Planet: A Natural History of the Oceans* (New York, NY: DK, 2001).

115. Its definition is "impressing the mind with a sense of grandeur . . . inspiring awe, veneration."

116. Amy Tan, "A Uniquely Personal Storyteller," interview by Academy of Achievement, 2008, http://www.achievement.org/autodoc/page/tan0int-5

117. Henry Miller, *Henry Miller on Writing* (New York: New Directions, 1964), 37.

118. http://animals.nationalgeographic.com/animals/invertebrates/portuguese-man-of-war/

119. Kitty Ferguson, *The Music of Pythagoras: How an Ancient Brotherhood Cracked the Code of the Universe and Lit the Path from Antiquity to Outer Space* (New York: Walker, 2008), 6.

120. Peter Pesic, *Music and the Making of Modern Science* (Cambridge, Massachusetts: The MIT Press, 2014), 7.

121. Robert H. Frank, *Luxury Fever: Money and Happiness in an Era of Excess* (Princeton, N.J.: Princeton University Press, 2000), 137.

122. http://thedailyshow.cc.com/videos/pa1013/moment-of-zen---dance-like-nobody-s-watching

123. For more information on his crossing see: http://www.atlanticrow2007.com /index.php/

124. Email from Mary Spotz to Kit Williams, January 5, 2010.

125. Email from Kit Williams to Mary Spotz, January 5, 2010.

126. http://quoteinvestigator.com/2014/04/06/they-feel/

127. C. G. Jung, *Two Essays on Analytical Psychology* (New York: Meridian Books, 1956), 56.

128. Arlynda Lee Boyer, *Buddha on the Backstretch: The Spiritual Wisdom of Driving 200 MPH* (Macon, Ga: Mercer University Press, 2009), 6.

129. Huston Smith, *The World's Religions: Our Great Wisdom Traditions.* (San Francisco: HarperSanFrancisco, 1991), 386.

130. Christopher Maag, "American Will Attempt to Cross an Ocean in a Rowboat," *New York Times*, December 16, 2009. http://www.nytimes.com/2009/12/17/sports/17rowing .html?_r=0

131. Pema Chödrön, *The Wisdom of No Escape: And the Path of Loving-Kindness* (Boston: Shambhala, 2010), 5.

132. http://amma.org/about/how-she-began

133. http://www.nytimes.com/2013/05/26/business/ammas-multifaceted-empire -built-on-hugs.html?smid=pl-share

134. Thomas Merton, *Zen and the Birds of Appetite* (New York: New Directions, 1968), 6.

135. You can listen to the radio interview here: http://www.ideastream.org/applause /entry/29860

136. Bree Loewen, *Pickets and Dead Men: Seasons on Rainier* (Seattle, WA: Mountaineers Books, 2009), 31.

137. Antoine Panaioti, *Nietzsche and Buddhist Philosophy* (Cambridge: Cambridge University Press, 2013), p. 92.

138. Peter H. Hansen, *The Summits of Modern Man: Mountaineering After the Enlightenment* (Cambridge: Harvard University Press, 2013), 4.

139. Katie Spotz to Doo Mullee, 2 August 2006.

140. http://www.livescience.com/528-scientists-finally-figure-bees-fly.html

141. Maurice Isserman, Stewart Angas Weaver, and Dee Molenaar, *Fallen Giants: A History of Himalayan Mountaineering from the Age of Empire to the Age of Extremes*, (New Haven: Yale University Press, 2008), 291.

142. Maya Angelou, "Why We Write," *Thought Economics*, October 14, 2012, http:// thoughteconomics.blogspot.ca/2012/10/why-we-write.html.

143. Thomas Merton, *Mystics and Zen Masters* (New York: Farrar, Strauss and Giroux, 1967), 15.

144. Harold Moody, as found in, William Lowell Randall and Gary M. Kenyon, *Ordinary Wisdom: Biographical Aging and the Journey of Life* (Westport, Conn: Praeger, 2001), 96.

145. "22-Year-Old Makes Rowing History," https://www.youtube.com/watch?x-yt-cl =85114404&v=_2YsSLcGJPw&x-yt-ts=1422579428.

146. "Woman Rows Across Atlantic," https://www.youtube.com/watch?x-yt-ts =1422579428&x-yt-cl=85114404&v=Bk7LvEw7iSg.

147. "The Best Moments of Glamour's 2010 Women of the Year Awards," https://www.youtube.com/watch?v=dXF59fq-4zw.

148. Shaun Assael, "The Adventurer Katie Spotz," *Glamour*, December 2010, p. 240. http://www.glamour.com/inspired/women-of-the-year/2010/katie-spotz.

149. https://www.youtube.com/watch?x-yt-ts=1422579428&x-yt-cl=85114404&v=umw_EAidExk#t=11

150. http://www.rideforyourlives.com/2011/06/almost-like-cycling-with-an-elephant-on-your-shoulders/#sthash.wyFkhFWf.dpuf

151. Paul, Elliot Samuel, and Scott Barry Kaufman, *The Philosophy of Creativity: New Essays* (Oxford: Oxford University Press, 2014), 150.

Acknowledgments

As we said back on Day 14, rowing solo is a team sport. The same applies to writing a book.

Even though there are two author names on the cover, the talent and support of many people made this book possible. To start we would like to thank Elizabeth Armstrong for her expert proof reading and editorial skills. Authors are typically not very good editors, and her eyes and crafty red pencil worked a surgical precision on our manuscript. Any remaining errors are entirely our fault.

A second key member of our team was Amy Freels (see her designs at http://amyfreels.com). She was responsible for the design and layout of our book and her unique abilities make our text come alive. While people say you cannot judge a book by its cover, in reality first impressions matter, and hopefully our content equals Amy's elegant design.

There is a Zen koan that asks: if a tree falls in the forest and there is no one there to hear it, did it make a sound? Likewise if an author writes a book and no one reads it, does it actually exist? We would like to thank Betty Weibel at Yopko Penhallurick (http://yp-pr.com) for managing our publicity campaign. We greatly appreciate her help in building an audience for our work to ensure that the sounds that we make are heard.

Others who contributed to the book in their own special ways include Regina Brett, Aisling Creedon, Frank Kitchen, Peggy Schmidt, Reward Sibanda, Eric Van Lee, and Nick Coughlin.

Finally, there are many costs associated with publishing a book. While we opted to self-publish our work to minimize these expenses, the process to print a physical book, or create a digital one, is expensive. We thank the people at Kickstarter and Go Fund Me for allowing us to generate revenue online. You can visit our Go Fund Me campaign here (http://www.gofundme.com/justkeeprowing). We would like to thank the following people for contributing: Doug and Maria Green, James Field, Dick Klosterman and Kathie Brown, Dave and Nancy Oberrath, Jim and Rachel Ockuly, Marc Cohen, Gary Woeltge, Joan Bowles, Mark and Jeannie Besand, Nikki Wingerson, and Jessica Zangmeister.

On the personal side, Katie would like to thank her parents, siblings Maggie, Danny and Kevin, and all of those people who have shared their advice and support over the years to help make her dreams possible.

Katie would like to sincerely thank the following organizations and individuals for supporting and sponsoring her 2010 row across the Atlantic.

SPIRE Sports Academy, Pentair Water, World Shipping, Kinetico Water Systems, Guardian Technologies. Moen, weatherguy.com, SAT-TRANS USA, Aetomic Web + Print Marketing, Tecmark, Enertia Trail Foods, WaterRower, Clear Choice Custom LASIK Center, H2Row.net, GMN, South African Airlines, SproutPeople, Sailrite, Jetboil, OLM Gifts, Rowing Sport, JL Racing, Mariner Insurance, Tifosi, GreenBoatStuff.com, Aqua Signal, Yakpads, Rite in the Rain, Nuun, H2O Audio, Kakadu Australia, Headsweats, Mentor Harbor Yaching Club, Women Sailing Group of Half Moon Bay Yacht Club, Titan's Gym, Cleveland Rowing Foundation, Ohio Center for Sport Psychology, Performance Health, Yopko Penhallurick, Clif Bar, and Showers Pass.

Mark would like to thank his wife Nancy for love, friendship, and 25 (and counting) wonderful years of marriage.

We have been fortunate to plan an official launch for our book at the Head of the Cuyahoga Regatta. This amazing and yearly event brings over 2,000 rowers from across the nation to Cleveland, Ohio. We thank Kirk Lang, the executive director of the Cleveland Rowing Foundation for making our launch party a success and inviting us to participate in the Regatta.

Katie and Terry Kilbourne on her visit to Tec Inc., an Ohio-based engineering firm and the title sponsor of this book. Terry said, "In keeping with our culture of community involvement and giving back we are proud to support the humanitarian efforts of Katie Spotz as she works to provide clean water to those in need around the world."

About the Authors

Katie Spotz

In 2010, Katie set a world record as the youngest person to row solo across the Atlantic. Along the way she raised more than $150,000 for safe water projects in Haiti, Honduras, Guatemala, Nicaragua, and Kenya.

In 2011, Katie visited water projects and saw the results of the funds raised through her adventures. This journey sparked a campaign to challenge ten schools in the states to help ten schools in Kenya. The schools have raised more than $100,000, or enough to help 10,000 students gain access to safe drinking water. To celebrate, the students gathered and broke the world record for the most people carrying water jugs on their heads!

Katie is currently an ambassador for H2O for Life, a nonprofit organization called that educates, engages and inspires youth to learn, take action and become global citizens. They recently launched a three-year partnership to reach out to 210 schools in 15 major cities across the United States including Minneapolis, Nashville, New York City, Phoenix, and Seattle.

Katie continues to act as a change agent for social causes and is an acclaimed motivational speaker, who has spoken worldwide, including the United Nation's Annual Youth Assembly. She has inspired and captivated schoolchildren and business professionals, and speaks about overcoming adversity and achieving our goals, no matter how steep the odds.

Visit her on Twitter https://twitter.com/KatieSpotz and say hi!

Mark D. Bowles

Mark is professor of history at American Public University System. He earned his Ph.D. in history from Case Western Reserve University and was a Tomash Fellow at the University of Minnesota. He has also earned an M.B.A., an M.A. in history, and a B.A. in psychology.

He is the author of 14 books, including college textbooks on the history of science, United States history, and digital literacy. He has also written several critically acclaimed books about NASA, including *The Apollo of Aeronautics* (2010) and *Science in Flux* (2006). Both won the prestigious American Institute of Aeronautics and Astronautics award for best historical manuscript in their respective publication years.

Mark is committed to promoting social justice projects both locally and globally. At his home in Akron, Ohio, he volunteers his time as the Technology Manager at the Peter Maurin Center, which assists the large numbers of homeless people in the area. He is also involved in *Just*Faith Ministries, which seeks to care for the poor and vulnerable throughout the world.

He has been married to his wife, Nancy since 1990. They are raising their three daughters—Isabelle (b. 2000), and twins Emma and Sarah (b. 2009)—on the edge of the Cuyahoga Valley National Park in Northeast Ohio.

Visit him at ProfessorMDB.com and or email at mdbowles@gmail.com and say hello!

Mark Bowles and Katie Spotz at a fundraiser for Mzomtsha School in South Africa. There is a scale schematic diagram of her 19-foot boat behind them that she used to row across the Atlantic Ocean.

Made in the USA
Lexington, KY
11 January 2016